MAN OF LAW:
A MODEL

MAN OF LAW: A MODEL

MAN OF LAW:
A MODEL

Morris Shumiatcher

Illustrated by Luther Pokrant

Western Producer Prairie Books
Saskatoon, Saskatchewan

Cover design by Warren Clark
Warren Clark Graphic Design Limited
Artwork by Luther Pokrant
Printed and bound in Canada
by Modern Press

Saskatoon, Saskatchewan

Western Producer Prairie Books publications
are produced and manufactured in the middle of
western Canada by a unique publishing venture owned
by a group of prairie farmers who are members of Saskatchewan Wheat Pool. Our first book in 1954 was a reprint
of a serial originally carried in *The Western Producer*, a weekly newspaper serving western Canadian
farmers since 1923. We continue the tradition
of providing enjoyable and informative
reading for all Canadians.

Canadian Cataloguing in Publication Data

Shumiatcher, Morris, 1917-
Man of Law: A Model

Includes index.
ISBN 0-88833-028-6 bd.
ISBN 0-88833-034-0 pa.

1. Lawyers. 2. Legal ethics. I. Title.
K115.S58   340   C79-091131-0

TO ALL MY BROTHERS IN LAW:

Hammer and anvil are we,
striking sparks
creating light
sometimes fire

Contents

Foreword

The author's *Man of Law* is indeed a model, and while I fear that there are few lawyers indeed who are able to combine the learning, industry, personality, courage, and wit which are gathered together in the author's model, he does portray what should be, and often is, strived for.

There is something in this little book for everyone concerned, directly or indirectly, with the legal profession.

The lawyer will find of interest the author's comments on policy-making as a function of the Supreme Court of Canada. The lawyer will be amused by, but concerned with, the author's comments on the draftsmanship of statutes by economists, educators, and political scientists ("that breed of men who are neither politically-oriented nor scientifically trained").

Lawyers from time to time have looked at great edifices, have admired the tangible creations of other professions, and have wondered whether their work was a little fleeting and insignificant, compared to the lasting creations of engineers and architects, and, indeed, men of medicine and science. The author answers such lawyers.

The lawyer, too, will appreciate the author's defense of oral argument in a Trial Court or Court of Appeal, as distinct from written argument.

To my mind, however, it will be the law student or the very young lawyer to whom this book will be of the greatest value. Indeed, the essay on profession, parts of which were contained in an earlier speech which Dr. Shumiatcher lent me, so appealed to me that I (little knowing that its contents would come to be published) plagiarized the author's words in writing a note of advice to first-year law students. To those young men and women who are studying law, and to the young lawyers, I recommend the book.

There is also much for the layman. The working of the adversary system is made clear. At the same time, it becomes plain that the lawyer is not the partner of his businessman-client, nor the accomplice of his client charged criminally. The author explains how there is no such thing as defense counsel "getting a client off." There is down-to-earth advice for the prospective witness. There is humor.

Members of boards, committees, and tribunals may perhaps not like all they read, but they may acquire an awareness of the risk of acting so as to come under the very forceful criticism which the author makes. I particularly appreciated the author's urging that law reform legislation should be piecemeal legislation, directed at correcting a particular fault, without the need for an entire codification, which seems inevitably to give rise to decades of uncertainty.

The book is to be read in pieces. It bears digesting. I found, too, that the dictionary was useful. The writing is colorful; the book is at all times interesting; it is frequently thought-provoking and, by turn, amusing.

William A. McGillivray
Chief Justice of Alberta

CALGARY, DECEMBER 1978

Acknowledgments

When I was very young and played at lawyer, I had notions of the kind of professional I would be. Every child has his heroes, and I was not without a large cast of my own. Some were very real persons I knew; others were people I imagined I knew; many were historic figures.

I remember being told the legend of Pygmalion, the ancient sculptor who carved out of ivory the statue of a beautiful girl. Immediately, he fell in love with his creation. He prayed that Aphrodite might breathe life into his perfect work of art. His prayer was answered, and when his statue quickened and walked and spoke to him, he called her Galatea. Then I discovered a modern version of the story and saw Noel Coward as Bernard Shaw's Pygmalion, masquerading as Professor Higgins. I became convinced that there is no reason why new wine should not be poured into old bottles or new vessels fashioned out of old clay.

Finally, Galatea emerged on the New York stage as Julie Andrews in *My Fair Lady,* and Rex Harrison as Professor Higgins. So illustrious a succession of models caused me to realize that in the arts as in law, what appear to be innovations, in truth spring from long roots that reach back into the subsoil of mankind's ancient inheritance.

My earliest models were those men who practiced law in my home town of Calgary. Lawyers, some of them, qualified as heroes in those days. The profile of the man of law was a distinctive one and he was as highly regarded in the community as the town doctor, the minister, and the teacher. The local newspapers employed several skilled court reporters — men whose career it was to sit through the trials day after day and record as felicitously as a shorthand court reporter prepares a true transcript of the evidence of the witnesses, the addresses of counsel, and the judgments of the court. The career of a lawyer was as closely followed then as the batting record of a baseball star today.

I prayed for the eloquence of Leonard Brockington, K.C. Bent and crippled though he was with arthritis, whenever he was not engaged in the business of being City Solicitor of our cowtown, he was "the premier after-dinner speaker on the continent" and delivered the most eloquent addresses I have ever heard. He left Calgary to become official speech writer for Prime Minister William Lyon Mackenzie King during the war, but he left before it all ended, saying that King was no more sensitive to his well-turned phrases than a billy-goat to an ode of Horace.

I admired and yearned for the poise and self-confidence of Alexander Andrew McGillivray, K.C. (later of the Appellate Division of the Supreme Court of Alberta). He was a legend in his time. Everyone believed it impossible for him ever to be bested in a legal contest in court and I knew a man whom he had freed of an indictment for manslaughter and what it meant to him and his family.

I hoped I might find the wit and waggish ways of Patrick ("Paddy") James Nolan, K.C., Alberta's incomparable court jester. One of the many stories that are told about him appears in the last chapter of this book.

I prayed for the energy and strength of Richard Bedford Bennett, P.C., K.C., whom I sometimes saw walking down Eighth Avenue in Calgary in striped pants embellished with a swallow-tail coat, silk hat and stick, all epitomizing the successful man of law gone public. When he was Prime Minister, and I a grade eight pupil, he presented me with a fifty-dollar scholarship. I sought to respond in kind to his eloquent address, and thereafter we became penpals and corresponded until his lonely death at his lordly residence at Mickleham, Surrey, in 1947.

I wished for the determination and courage of my father, Abraham Isaac Shumiatcher, Q.C. who came to Canada at nineteen with only a kopeck or two in his pocket and as many words of English in his vocabulary. He read *Williams on Real Property*, *Anson on Contracts*, and Odgers' book of *Pleadings*, traveling in railway coaches through Alberta and Saskatchewan as a land inspector for the C.P.R. He served, part-time, as student and articled clerk of George Abram Walker, K.C., then head of the company's law department, until he was called to the bar in 1928.

When I entered law school and came face to face with the life, language, and literature of the law, I wished for the erudition of John A. Weir, K.C., Dean of Faculty at Edmonton; I hoped I might one day share the perspicacity of Dr. Malcolm M. McIntyre, the most perceptive and analytical of all lawyers I ever met, and the most tolerant of men. I longed for the many-sidedness of Lawrence Y. Cairns, Q.C. (later of the District Court of Alberta). I hoped for, though I knew I could never achieve the sense of certainty and the aura of self-confidence of George H. Steer, Q.C., the early bird of the teaching staff of Alberta's Faculty of Law who talked more sound law between eight and nine o'clock each morning before he left for his own law office, than any other man could conjure up in a full week's lectures.

I wished for the human sympathy of Mr. Justice "Billy" A. Macdonald. He was the kindliest lawyer I knew. Because we were both owls who nightly worked in the Calgary Court House library long after the janitor had left, I wanted to be called to the Alberta bar in his court, and he acceded to my request and said that if I continued to burn the midnight oil I might, one day, see the light.

As a graduate student at the University of Toronto, I desired desperately, to acquire the perfection demanded of his students by Jacob Finkelman, Q.C. (later Chairman of the Ontario Labour Relations Board). For him, precise language was the essence of the law and proper punctuation was as significant as principle.

In those same student years at Toronto, I was fortunate to bear witness to the incredible erudition of the Right Honorable Bora Laskin, P.C., now Chief Justice of Canada. I yearned for his breadth of vision and his mastery of the law, and I promised myself that whatever I might do in my reach for knowledge, I would try to walk with his gracious humility.

In later years, when I settled in Saskatchewan, I came to know the Honorable Emmett M. Hall, Q.C. who was to become Chief Justice of the Queen's Bench and Chief Justice of the Court of Appeal of Saskatchewan, and ultimately a judge of the Supreme Court of Canada. In the best judicial tradition, he breathed the breath of life into the *Canadian Bill of Rights* when it had been virtually abandoned and lay moribund in the statute books. I hoped I might emulate the *élan* that marked his long years of great industry on the Bench.

All of these men, and many more, influenced my career at the bar. For what success I have enjoyed, I am indebted to them as models whose qualities I have borne in mind as I sought to play the part of Pygmalion in the process of producing my model *Man of Law.*

There is one great advantage I enjoy that all these eminent lawyers lacked: it is the prescience of my omnipresent mate, Jacqui, a model if ever I recognized one, to whom I address Robert Graves's words of Pygmalion to his Galatea:

> As you are a woman, so be lovely:
> As you are lovely, so be various,
> Merciful as constant, constant as various,
> So be mine, as I am yours forever.

There are many others to whom I am grateful for their assistance in completing this book — modest and inadequate though it be for all of its heroic theme. I especially express my appreciation to the University of Toronto who sponsored the "Symposium on Contemporary Problems and the Law" in 1976, and invited me to present a paper which became the seed of this book; to the Honorable Edward M. Culliton, Chief Justice of Saskatchewan, the very model of a modern Chief of Justices, for his encouragement; to my old friend, the Honorable William A. McGillivray, Chief Justice of Alberta, a man of erudition and empathy, for his delightful contributions to the chapter on humor, for his early reading of the draft, and for his Foreword; to my friend, Luther Pokrant, for his conceptions and drawings that embellish and enrich the book; to John Colombo, that paradigm of proverb, pen, and poetry, for his enthusiasm in the undertaking; to Dorothy Sherick and Carlotta Lemieux for reading the manuscript and making many helpful suggestions to improve it; to my law associates, Donald G. Findlay, Eric J. Neufeld, John E. Friesen, Q.C., Robert E. Bamford, Robert J. Gebhard, and Aaron A. Fox, who accommodated me in our offices from day to day; and last but by no means least, to Ulla Thunberg and Merren Fleming for their preparation, typing, and retyping of the manuscript.

COLONY SURF, HONOLULU
FEBRUARY 1979

Morris Shumiatcher

Why a Model?

A sergeant of the lawe, war and wys,
That often hadde been at the Parvys,
Ther was also, ful riche of excellence.
Discreet he was, and of great reverence —
He semed swich, his wordes weren so wise.
Justice he was ful often in assise,
By patente and by pleyn commissioun.
For his science and for his heigh renoun,
Of fees and robes hadde he many oon.

Nowher so bisy a man as he ther nas,
And yet he semed bisier than he was.
GEOFFREY CHAUCER'S *MAN OF LAWE*,
IN HIS "PROLOGUE" TO *THE CANTERBURY TALES*, 1387

Voltaire said he was financially ruined but twice in his life: once when he lost a lawsuit and once when he won. A century earlier Oliver Cromwell, as revolutionary, remarked that the law, as it stood, served only to maintain the lawyers and to encourage the rich to oppress the poor. In every age, cynics and rebels have inveighed against the law, and inevitably their attacks have lapsed into invective against those participating in its administration. *Argumentum ad hominem* is always the last refuge of the desperate adversary. The ultimate, of course, was Shakespeare's Dick in *Henry VI*: ". . . first thing we do, let's kill all the lawyers!"[1]

And so the ancient proverb, "A good lawyer must be a great liar," dates back to the fifteenth century. "A clever lawyer, an evil neighbor" is an ancient French saying — a less perceptive assessment than the English adage that "lawyers' houses are built on the heads of fools and lawyers' gowns are lined with the willfulness of their clients."

Even Dr. Johnson, that paradigm of propriety, could say to the barristorial Boswell, while dining at the Cheddar Cheese in Fleet Street, that although he did not wish to speak ill of any man behind his back, he thought that the stranger at the table opposite was an attorney. In the seventeenth century the Levellers went to extremes,

1

advocating that all men of law — judges, lawyers, and clerks — should be liquidated. Like the French revolutionaries a hundred years later, and like the egalitarians of our own day, they preached that if only the ordinary, simple men and women were to settle their disputes according to basic moral principles, justice would be done, contentment would prevail throughout the land, and lawyers would no longer make fortunes by pressing the poor and plundering the rich.

Such critics overlook the fact that a lawyer's role is the very antithesis of oppression or plunder. His is a duty to protect and preserve persons and property. It is a function that becomes necessary wherever there exist differences of opinion and whenever there arise conflicts among human beings. The freer the society, the more multiplicitous are the ideas, interests, and opinions, and it is inevitable there should follow differences and conflicts among those who hold them. That may be why lawyers serve more prominently in democratic societies than in authoritarian states.

The great interest of man on earth is justice. It has been called the ligament that holds civilized beings and civilized nations together.[2] If that be so, then the lawyer whose chosen duty it is to espouse the cause of justice for the citizen, performs the most honorable of all services for man. Whether in the sheltered quiet of his private chambers he advises his client of his rights and duties, or in the open courtroom (that greatest of all human arenas) he advocates his client's cause, the man of law serves as the custodian of society's security, the explorer of its liberty, an arch-critic of its philosophy, and a principal engineer of its improvement.

In every age and in every society trouble has been man's stubborn neighbor, stalking him in unexpected places, menacing his life, demanding his property, and assaulting his peace of mind. When trouble enters, it is an unusual person who will not search for an ear to listen to his problem, a mind to analyze the facts, a tongue to advise, and a whole person to dedicate his strength and energy to avert disaster. In his ultimate search for a defender, the man in trouble turns — albeit as apprehensively as the victim of a toothache turns to his dentist — to a member of the venerable company of barristers and solicitors, seeking an anodyne for his woes. The process in each case often involves a certain amount of pain. A client may feel resentment when he has to relate unsavory facts that show him to have been a knave or a fool. He may be deeply pained when he must submit to deep probings into his affairs, or long

2

cross-examination in public at a time that he faces the perils of fine and imprisonment or the loss of his property or his good name. It is understandable that a client should feel unhappy when, after all that can be said and done for him has been well said and wholly done, he must nevertheless pay the high costs of litigation — win, lose, or draw.

While it may be perfectly unreasonable, it is not unnatural that if he succeeds in the contest, a client should ask his lawyer why he should expect to be paid for defending an innocent and blameless man. And if the client fails and goes to prison or is mulct in heavy money damages and costs, it is also not surprising that such an unfortunate person should ask why his lawyer should claim a fee for presiding over so disastrous a denouement. Whether the lawyer's efforts have resulted in success or failure, a finding of innocence or guilt, his client may well wonder whether his services were really necessary. Could he not have done as well himself?

He will find small comfort if reminded of the time-tested truism that he who acts as his own lawyer has a fool for a client and a fool for a lawyer.

Egalitarians would have us believe that he could act as his own counsel, but they overlook several essential facts. There is virtually no one who can view his own case objectively. Clearly, the strongest bias is self-bias. The average person is not equipped to conduct his own case. It is not simply that he lacks a knowledge of the intricacies of the law. He may also be limited by intellect or ability. Historians Will and Ariel Durant put it succinctly when they wrote: "We are all born unfree and unequal."[3] The man of law recognizes the importance of equality, its needs and possibilities, but only in two areas: equality in the legal administration of justice, and equality in the opportunity to acquire knowledge and education. Certainly the ignorant should be educated, the foolish enlightened, the weak strengthened; and all of this will undoubtedly change and possibly improve the human condition. But it will not make equal what is unequal. We are all subject to an heredity we cannot control. We are differently endowed in health and strength, in mental capacity and temperament.

The fact is,

Nature loves difference as the necessary material of selection and evolution; identical twins differ in a hundred ways and no two peas are alike.[4]

3

From the tips of our toes to our finger prints, we are, each of us, unique.

The social reformer may postulate a future for mankind in which all will be equal, and all will be free. The concept is a chimera, the dream a deceit. Of this, Will and Ariel Durant say that "nature smiles at the union of freedom and equality in our utopias. For freedom and equality are sworn and everlasting enemies, and when one prevails the other dies."[5]

Since nature establishes orders and degrees among men, those who, by their special learning and ability come to master a discipline, have always been a small company and singled out for a special destiny. By virtue of the skills they have mastered theirs is a responsibility heavier than others. It is they who erect for themselves a model of excellence to which they aspire. It is a model that serves to move them to a high standard of performance. According to this model, the professional in every field must dedicate his ability and fashion his life. Save for rare miraculous flashes, he will never achieve his heart's desire. But the model can become the prototype for the ideal marriage of work and wit that the freely-expressed impulses of our age may engender, and the organization of human governments must allow.

Lawyers are among that relatively small company of men and women who seek excellence on a grand scale. They are specialists, but in no narrow sense of that term. It is true that an increasing number now confine their work to limited areas of the law — some to tax law or labor law, to criminal law or to counsel work at the bar. All are specialists in the sense that they have taken law, equity, and justice to be the province of their life's work. Because they have undertaken as a career the task of mastering a branch of human knowledge that is interfaced with more intimate human interests and more universal concerns than any other discipline evolved by man, they are at once specialists in the law and generalists in human affairs.

In an age that worships at the multi-idoled altar of the expert, the man of law remains the unique generalist. His usefulness and influence in society have grown out of the necessity to reject the parochial and embrace the ecumenical, discard the pedantic and adopt the pragmatic, simply because he serves men and women of all classes and callings. And those whom he serves, while generally more deeply concerned with material results than with legal theories, are nevertheless capable of moving mountains when provoked by a sense of injustice.

4

Lawyers have maintained their role and a strategic place in society with virtually no plan and with little introspection into the reasons why the entrancing warp and woof of their profession should have become the very fabric of society itself. They have not considered why, for centuries, the rules of law and the principles of equity should have served as the most powerful and persistent civilizing forces among nations. Only occasionally have lawyers related these principles to their venerable source of morality. Self-analysis is always deferred, especially by lawyers whom Chaucer recognized so long ago as being busy, albeit never quite so busy as they seem.

Lawyers are far busier today than Chaucer's "sergeant of the lawe" ever dreamed of being. It is because of our occupations as lawyers and laymen, and our preoccupation with the proliferating brambles of the law, that I invite members of the legal profession and those who are bound to be affected by that profession (and this includes virtually everyone who is a legal person or an individual, the very old and the very young, the dying and those waiting to be born) to consider a model of that man of law — to observe his functions and the qualities they demand; his gifts and the benefits they bestow; his duties and the burdens they entail. A model is the personal conceit of the artist who perceives it and translates it from stone or bronze or wood or silver, into an artifact or ornament useful to civilized human beings. I propose to create my model from words. If reality can create art, as assuredly it does, then art in turn may affect the real world around us like the presence of some unseen but gently reigning Karma.

I am encouraged to sketch such a model by the recent work of my friend Dr. Humphry Osmond, that brilliant psychiatrist who, with Miriam Siegler developed "the medical model." Of that model, Siegler and Osmond said:

When it is functioning properly [it] appears to be almost invisible because it lies outside awareness and, in spite of its great age, has been an object of scientific scrutiny for a relatively short time. It is only when it does not function properly that attention is drawn to it.[6]

Some have pointed an accusatory finger at the lawyer and have compared him with the professional prostitute or the organized criminal. He is said to be in league with all lawbreakers because the fee that is paid him is said to give him a special interest in the ill-gotten gains of his client.

It is not a new allegation, but it has less impact than might be expected in an age in which almost every established institution has been under attack by populist fronts that often display more energy than erudition and more venom than valor. To criticize the lawyer who represents a client charged with crime is as unreasonable as to condemn the physician who treats a drug addict for his needles or a lover for his syphilis or a terminal patient for the lung cancer his smoking has induced.

The power to influence human behavior by generalizations and forecasts has been exercised, even if not fully understood, for centuries. Such statements become self-fulfilling prophecies when they are made often enough, authoritatively enough, and convincingly enough.[7] So if a political leader tells citizens that economic conditions are so desperate that the government must take over and manage their affairs for them, or that free choice and the free market are dead, people will believe what they hear and the country will have gone a long way toward the general acceptance of an authoritarian state.

Since the formation of opinions about the character of individuals and groups of people or institutions will affect their behavior, it is of importance that lawyers as individuals and as members of an ancient, learned profession should maintain insights into their own reality which others believe they perceive and are all too quick to interpret, and on occasion, to misinterpret. Should people ever become convinced that lawyers are rogues or fools or cowards, and not dedicated men with intelligence and courage, their interactions with lawyers would be quite different. Similarly, the behavior of lawyers may well depend upon the popular concept of their role in society, and this, in turn, is likely to affect their ability to act out their roles with dignity, wisdom, and understanding. Most important of all is the insight the lawyer has into his own nature, the awareness he possesses of his own strengths and weaknesses, and the conscious assessment he makes of his special role in the place where he lives and plays his part as a professional.

How then does the lawyer see himself as an individual in the context of a society that claims the right to be ruled neither by whim nor superstition, but by the law? And how do citizens whose lives today are more closely regulated and directed by law than ever before, regard the men and women who labor to be learned in the law and who seek safely to steer their clients' vessels between the Scylla of free will and the Charybdis of despotism?

Few lawyers hold a clear or consistent view of the complex, puzzling, and ever-changing relationship that exists between themselves and the world. And little wonder! The universe in which we live is an ever-expanding one, and in its explosive atmosphere it is not easy for man to construct a cohesive, rational, integrated model of himself that may be fairly examined and evaluated and that may serve as a compass to hold him steadfast to the lodestone of virtue that some have described as natural law.

The man of law has seldom concerned himself with fashioning a model to emulate. He generally contents himself with a consciousness that in his profession he is confronted with an individual who seeks his advice and his help because a client has been accused of killing a friend or relation, or is locked up and deprived of his liberty, or he stands to be evicted from his house, or his marriage has broken down, or his children have been taken from him, or his property has been expropriated, or his job has ended, or he faces deportation from the country, or he has lost his right to do business, or he is sued for breaking promises, or he has made too much money and paid too few taxes, or he has lost too much money and is bankrupt. The man of law gives counsel and succor — and in doing so, he sallies forth as a champion to battle the dragons that threaten his client or that seek to filch from him what his client believes to be justly his.

What, then, are the elements of the model man of law? What are his components? How are they to be analyzed and described?

The model of the man of medicine is a relatively simple one that is readily recognized and accepted by members of the medical profession and by most people everywhere. Simply stated, its components are *first*, to diagnose disease; *secondly*, to cure the patient suffering from that disease; and *thirdly*, to ensure that no one is blamed for the disease. In medicine everyone is on the same side fighting the common enemies of sickness, pain, and death.

But the lawyer who seeks to defend his client against an indictment of crime stands alone and does battle, not against germs and viruses, but against another lawyer who, with the same high purpose, the same knowledge and skills, and the same sense of propriety, seeks to deprive the client of his property, his freedom, or

7

his life. The lawyer who espouses the cause of a tenant who may be dispossessed of his house is opposed by another lawyer, with ideals just as high as his own, who asserts the right of the landlord to repossess the property with vigor and competence just as great as his own. The lawyer who represents the widow who has lost her husband in a vehicle collision, and with him, the source of her support, finds himself at odds with a lawyer who represents the driver of another vehicle who stoutly maintains that it was a third party and not his client who was responsible for the death, and it is the third party who should accordingly pay.

Is it any wonder that the public, seeing members of the same profession espousing opposite sides of the same case, should conclude that neither could be sincere in pressing his client's cause? That both lawyers could not possibly be right? That the honest and decent thing for the lawyers to do would be to settle their clients' differences quietly without making a public spectacle of their sophistry?

It may not have occurred to them until they are themselves litigants or accused persons, that there are always at least two sides to every question and that in espousing and arguing one or the other, the lawyer is neither insincere nor dishonest. The lawyer does not conjure up differences or concoct conflicts. It is because individuals are prone to adopt different views of the same facts or see them or remember them differently, that they grow disputatious and litigious. Differences must be defined, argued, and resolved in order that men may be free to express their views, but at the same time, they are obliged to assert them peacefully. To achieve these ends, the legal profession came into being. It is designed as a vehicle to achieve just decisions that will lay contention to rest and bring tranquillity to the land. It is not the lawyer who creates dissension; it is the dissenter who produces lawyers.

Because there can be no ordered society where laws do not play a dominant role, the lawyer or priest or shaman with knowledge of the rules and a sensitivity to the individual's yearning for justice, is an important person in every civilized community. He exercises great authority. His is a visible presence publicly displayed.

I refer to my model as a *man* of law, mindful of the fact that in recent years women have entered a profession which for centuries was as strictly reserved to the members of my sex as the traditional priesthood. Only Shakespeare dared to challenge the convention, but even he could bring Portia into court only by a stratagem.

Naturally, I perceive the model man of law through the senses and experiences of a male, but I would like to think that the model lady lawyer will feel it necessary to seek alterations to my ideal man of law only cosmetically, if at all. I have avoided the phrases "law person" or "person of law" for two reasons. First, they are awkward phrases, as clumsy as "chairperson," "foreperson," or "lumberperson," and, in my view, they are simply unaesthetic and tasteless. Secondly, assuming "sexism" to be a quality that English nouns are capable of possessing, and assuming that "man" describes only the human male, the word "son," whether standing alone or coupled with the prefix "per" must equally partake of "sexism" — to be condemned no less than "man" if the time for his extirpation has arrived. If "man" must go, whatever will happen to woman's humanity — or indeed, to "woman" herself? Is she hereafter to be referred to as a simple "wo"? Assuredly it must be just as chauvinist to call her "woman" as to refer to her as female.

In his novel, *Eyeless in Gaza*, Aldous Huxley has one of his characters ask another why he plays so much with words. The other replies, "Because words express thoughts — and thoughts determine actions. If you call a man a bug, it means that you propose to treat him as a bug!"[8]

Justice Cardozo expressed the same idea in a way that is vaguely familiar to us all. "The search is for the just word, the happy phrase, that will give expression to the thought, but somehow the thought itself is transfigured by the phrase when found."[9]

The early female fervor of Lady Lib is all but spent. The abrasiveness of the early activists has polished away the roughness of staff and distaff alike. Male lawyers are now able to settle down on good terms with the women who are their colleagues, accepting them as peers within a profession that is without peer. The lawyer inevitably devotes his most trenchant attentions to his proverbially jealous mistress, the law. Yet, in his moments of relaxation and freedom he may still lustily and lovingly embrace the lady to whom he is wed. Therefore, when I write of "man" or the "man of the law," I also have in mind that other gender which the man of law yearns to embrace as amicably and steadfastly as the paramour he first wooed at law school.[10]

It has been said that Her Majesty may create a Queen's Counsel or a judge, but she can never create a lawyer. The qualities and skills of the model man of law cannot be conferred, even by a queen, for they are the product of continuous exploration of our heritage of knowledge and the continuous cultivation of those gifts of nature that, bounteously or frugally, have been bestowed upon each individual. It is not possible to catalogue all the ingredients that go to make up the "complete man" of any calling or profession. At the risk of omitting some qualities that may be more significant, I have chosen ten human attributes that I consider to be the hallmarks — indeed, the *sine qua non* — of the model lawyer. They are qualities shared by all men and women in some measure, but nowhere are they more conspicuously displayed than in the professional life of the many-sided man of law. Let us then consider his —

I	Sapience	VI	Artistry
II	Profession	VII	Charisma
III	Omnitude	VIII	Obligation
IV	Ambivalence	IX	Judgment
V	Expedition	X	Humor

I

SAPIENCE

Est enim sine dubo domus iuris consulti, totius
oraculum civitatis — For the house of a great lawyer is
assuredly the oracular seat of the whole community.

CICERO, *DE ORATORE*, I, 45

Pursue the study of the law, rather than the
gain of it; pursue the gain of it enough to keep out
the briers, but give your main attention to
the study of it. The next is, not to marry early; for an
early marriage will obstruct your improvement;
and in the next place, it will involve you in expense.
Another thing is, not to keep much company, for the
application of a man who aims to be a lawyer must be
incessant; his attention to his books must be
constant, which is inconsistent with
keeping much company.

JEREMIAH GRIDLEY, ADVICE GIVEN TO JOHN ADAMS IN 1758,
WORKS OF JOHN ADAMS, 46

By sapience or sapiential authority I mean the lawyer's knowledge and skill. It is because the lawyer is able to guide people through the labyrinthine intricacies of the law that the citizen seeks him out. Without a special knowledge of the law, a keen appreciation of human behavior, and an acute awareness of public affairs, the lawyer has virtually no *raison d'etre*. If the public did not believe the man of law to be possessed of these gifts, his chambers would be as desolate as the pyramids.

Knowledge is come by in many ways, but in the legal profession there is none more effective than a study of the English law reports that go back more than nine hundred years, and of the gargantuan body of reports of cases decided in every country whose institutions are founded on the common law of England. That knowledge is augmented by reading the great and growing body of text books and commentaries that would be the admiration of Tyndall, Blackstone, and Halsbury, and the journals that almost every law school now publishes and which every lawyer and every law student should not only read, but aspire to enrich with his own contribution.

But the lawyer's sapience must encompass more than the law itself. Because the lawyer's competence depends upon a sense of continuing curiosity, the scope of his reading will be reflected in the breadth of his understanding. No one has described more beautifully the virtues of reading, than Francis Bacon, Lord Chancellor of England.

> Some books are to be tasted, others to be swallowed, and some few to be chewed and digested; that is, some books are to be read only in parts; others to be read, but not curiously; and some few to be read wholly, and with diligence and attention . . .

> Reading maketh a full man; conference a ready man; and writing an exact man. And therefore, if a man write little, he had need have a great memory; if he confer little, he need have a present wit; and if he read little, he had need have much cunning, to seem to know, that he doth not. Histories make men wise; poets witty; the mathematics subtle; natural philosophy deep; moral grave; logic and rhetoric able to contend . . . There is no . . . impediment in the wit, but may be wrought out by fit studies.[1]

No less important for success at the bar than knowledge, is a command of the language — English without question, and French if one is far-sighted. Indeed, every language that can be mastered is an arm and a leg to the man of law. While it is now considered that the ancient languages, particularly Latin, require more effort in the learning than they are worth, a knowledge of the classics will always distinguish the lawyer who has mastered them. How else can knowledge be attained except through language? Knowledge of events long since past; an awareness of the thoughts of men and women dead a thousand years and more; a familiarity with distant places and unfamiliar creatures and esoteric sciences and the vast treasure house of the arts. Except for the present and the immediate — what one sees, hears, smells, tastes, and touches — there is really no way to knowledge except through language.

The tools of the law are language. And the most precise tool is the English language. Not only is its vocabulary greater than any other language in the world; it is more versatile, more exact, more varied. Its capital now exceeds a million words — many times the vocabulary of the richest of all other languages. George Santayana, the Spanish-American philosopher and poet, said: "English is remarkable for the intensity and variety of the colours of its words. No language, I believe, has so many words specifically poetic."[2] Those who know and intelligently use the English language are the happy beneficiaries of one of the greatest — *the* greatest — of literatures ever known to mankind.

In my view; there are no poets more lyrical than Spenser and Keats and Shelley; no playwrights of deeper insight than Shakespeare and Marlowe; no satirists so engaging as Swift and Shaw; no essayists so learned as Bacon and Addison and Lamb and Mencken; no writings more stimulating than those of Milton and Bunyan and Dryden and Pope; no novels more enduring than those of Dickens and Hardy and Galsworthy and H. G. Wells. These are some of the masters — writers of the English language who shine forth as authorities on the human state, and their words are as binding in their field as the judgments of the chief justices and lord chancellors are in theirs. A knowledge of our literature and a facility with the language of those who created it are tools that the man of law will acquire and keep in good repair with as much diligence and affectionate care as he will bring to his task of compiling and augmenting his legal precedents and his authorities on the law. If anything, language to the lawyer is more important than law itself because, as George Santayana put it, "The structure of language ... becomes a mirror of the structure of the world as presented to the intelligence."[3]

How can a man's thoughts be more profound than the sum and total of his vocabulary? By vocabulary I am thinking of his command of words and figures and symbols, linguistic, mathematical, musical: the stuff and fabric of which a civilized culture is made. How tragic is the spectacle of the semi-literate graduate of our high schools and universities, struggling to express the simplest of ideas. "You know what I mean, you know ... " he begins. "It's like, I mean yuh gotta dig it, man ... like bein' cool — man real cool — you've gotta put it all together, yuh know. Like that's where it's at. Yuh see, it's like I say, yuh know, you've gotta groove it, see? You've gotta let it all hang out man — like. Like what I mean yuh know ... yuh know, huh? ... " The unhappy truth is that you do not know what he means; and I do not know what he means; and I suggest that he does not really know what he means either. Without words how can anyone have ideas? Without *some* faculty of intellectual human expression, how can the intellect develop beyond the level of the Neanderthal?

The lawyer knows that many facts may be communicated by pictures and model structures and sounds. But in the end the facts must be expressed in literary form; the concepts of the law and their application must be described, and can be understood only through language. Without words, there can exist neither man nor law, and the stature of each is enhanced by the fullness and felicity of the other.

In Scott's *Guy Mannering*, the novelist portrays an engaging man of law, Counsellor Pleydell. He shows Colonel Mannering his Chambers in High Street in Edinburgh and points to his books which, he says, are "the best editions of the best authors" — a fine collection of the classics. Then he says: "These are the tools of trade. A lawyer without history or literature is a mechanic, a mere working mason; if he possesses some knowledge of these he may venture to call himself an architect."

That is why I shall not forget Professor Desmond Morton,[4] who, with his infinite generosity and inimitable humor once described me to an audience at the University of Toronto as a "poet lawyerate."

There is not a culture nor a nation that has thrived without a vigorous sensitivity for language that has broken forth into strong branches and burst its buds with verdant leaves.

An ancient Chinese sage was once asked what he would do first if he had power to manage the affairs of his country and he answered: "I should see to it that language is used correctly."

"But surely," his interrogators protested, "language is a small matter! Why do you regard it as so important?"

The wise man replied: "If language is not used correctly, then what is said is not meant; if what is said is not meant, what ought to be done remains undone; if this remains undone, morals and art will be corrupted; if morals and art are corrupted, justice will go astray and the people will be left in helpless confusion."

The language of ancient laws is often exciting. Consider the French language that came to England at the time of the Norman Conquest. Old French forms and phrases were much used in the courts of England until the time of Cromwell. French legalese was revived to some extent after the Restoration and there are examples in the law reports which are highly entertaining to lawyer and layman alike, even if they are not apparently relevant today. I think of the famous sentence, so dearly beloved by the legal profession, that describes the reaction of a judge to a prisoner who: "ject un Brickbat a le dit Justice que narrowly mist, & pur ceo immediately fuit Indictment draw per Noy envers le prisoner, & sone dexter manus ampute & fix al Gibbet sur que luy mesme immediatement hange in presence de Court."[5]

The English language has been immensely enriched by French, just as the French language (notwithstanding the disapprobation of the French Academy) has been enlivened by English. The beauties and subtleties of the French language are now becoming familiar to Canadians. To be sure, France has never produced a Shakespeare, but it had a Racine, a Corneille, and a Molière. And French-speaking Canada also has a rich literature, superior to that of English Canada, according to some critics. Whatever language the man of law adopts is less important than his mastery of it. I would defend the right of every lawyer to say that he will, provided he says it well. Certainly, in or out of court, he must be more than "a sophisticated rhetorician, inebriated with the exuberance of his own verbosity"; more than a man "gifted with an egotistical imagination that can at all times command an interminable and inconsistent series of arguments to malign his opponents and glorify himself."[6]

Lest he grow cynical as his successes and his years multiply, even though he may see more on the surface than is seen by the eyes of most people, the man of law will not content himself with examining only the skin of life. He will devote some of his time to diving below the surf and tides of human nature. Neither will he be content if, for all his verbal virtuosity, he grows cynical and, with Oscar Wilde, says that "... to truth itself I gave what is false no less than what is true ..., and showed that the false and the true are merely forms of intellectual existence ... I summed up all systems in a phrase, and all existence in an epigram."[7]

Sapience is more than a mastery of language. A lawyer possesses sapiential authority because he knows, or appears to know more about the problems of law and the riddles of life than those who consult him. He is, of course, only able to advise, to persuade, to argue. He possesses no statutory authority over clients or over any other body and he cannot order anyone to do anything. His influence depends upon his knowledge, his personality, and his energy. His is a rare role in an age when status bestowed by the state is fast becoming the exclusive test of authority and when official seals and certificates confer more power than the fullest complement of wisdom, judgment, and competence.

Today it is popularly believed that the ability of the large legal firm to serve the public is greater than the individual practitioner's capacity. There is some merit in the view that the present proliferation of laws and regulations makes specialization inevitable; that a combination of specialists in a single firm eases the burden of each lawyer and is therefore likely to assure the acquisition of more accurate knowledge of the law by the solicitor and hence the presentation of sounder advice to the client. This may be perfectly possible. It may have been plausible before the big bulge we now witness in all offices and business and industry — with its sluggish effects upon knowledge and efficiency and productivity. The more people who engage in doing a particular piece of work, the less any one of them will know about that work; the more people there are, the longer it takes to discover what is happening, what has happened, and what should be made to happen. At a time when governments are as eager to create "jobs" as rabbits to multiply, I offer a simple "law of work" as I have discovered it in legal offices, whether private, governmental, or industrial:

The quality of work alters inversely with the number of jobs created to perform it.[8]

The big law factory has brought with it disenchantments. Highly skilled and eminent lawyers unquestionably make up the most significant part of the membership of the large firm. Nevertheless it is not the size of the law firm but the stature of lawyers in the firm that determines the quality of work that is performed there. You can get more water and better water from one deep well than from ten shallow ones. The computers that are now coming of age in the world of the law may be made to perform the useful work of scouts and tabulators. But the law is still a place where individualism counts and where the human brain remains the best and most reliable computer of them all.

While sapience is the *sine qua non* of the man of law, it is only the first mark of the model.

As early as 1669, there was published a book on how to succeed in the law. *The Compleat Solicitor* has a contemporary ring from which lawyers may profit even today. This is a list of "the qualities wherewith a solicitor ought to be endued to make him Compleat":

First, he ought to have a good natural wit.

Secondly, that wit must be refined by education.

Thirdly, that education must be perfected by learning and experience.

Fourthly, lest learning should too much elate him, it must be balanced by disgression.

Fifthly, to manifest all these former parts, it is requisite that he have a voluble and free tongue to utter and declare his conceits.

A more recent type of book, "The Common Place Book," better known to men of law two generations ago than now, was once the practicing laywer's best friend. It was a black notebook that the young attorney bought on entering practice. In this book he made notes of cases of interest as they came to his notice in reading the law reports or attending personally in court. Of course there always existed the printed law reports that contained important decisions going back to the days of the Norman Conquest, but these reports were no substitute for the lawyer's own "Common Place Book." That book was a very personal cyclopedia, much relied on before *Halsbury's Laws of England* were published or the gentle Hedley Auld created the *Canadian Abridgment* or Kent Power worked over the *Canadian Encyclopaedic Digest* and his slender book on *Practice*.[9]

The finest "Common Place Books" I ever saw were those of my dear friend and neighbor, Percy Gordon — a great counsel who graced the Bench of the Saskatchewan Court of Appeal for more than a quarter of a century. He had lost his right arm in a hunting accident at fourteen, and his left-handed penmanship was poor. But the typewriter was his instrument and with one hand he played its keyboard like a virtuoso, all *allegro vivace!* His "Common Place Books" were of loose-leaf design and lent themselves to expansion and amendment. They contributed, but only in small part, to his phenomenal knowledge and memory. I have known no man so steeped in the classics, nor anyone whose legal learning was so gracefully embellished by his poetic recollections. In short, there was none so sapient. For an hour and more, he would recite poetry without pause, much of it written by authors who lived during the early part of the century and who were so obscure that their words were totally unfamiliar. On such occasions I would tell Judge Gordon that I really did not believe he was reciting from memory at all but that he was making it all up as he went along. He was capable of doing precisely that, so great was his knowledge of the language and so abiding his affection for it.

However, books and authorities can never serve as the lawyer's sole source of sapience. Law without facts is like a mouth without a jaw. The facts of real life as they relate to a client's cause are the bones and blood and flesh out of which the man of law must design the body that will determine the nature and quality of his case. Without a client, a lawyer is without facts or fees. Without facts the study of law could quickly shrink into a metaphysical exercise. Without fees the lawyer will be no better equipped to serve his client than his client to serve himself. Musings and speculative exercises may offer an appeal to the academic who is content to direct his mind to things theoretical; but the model man of law I envisage has never been satisfied with panning the agitated mountain streams for nuggets to be hoarded up in indexed cabinets for display on celebrated occasions. There is not a member of the practicing bar who does not owe a debt of deep gratitude to the professors of law who have stimulated his appetitite for knowledge, or to the academic community grazing in green pastures that serve to assuage it. On rare occasions the outstanding man of law who has made academe his mistress will outgrow his gown and hood. Carrying his

19

notebooks with him he will change his pace and take his place on the bench. Mervyn Woods of Saskatchewan and Jean Beetz of Quebec are numbered among the academics who have achieved eminence there. Like Bora Laskin, the academic may become Chief Justice of Canada. Or he may decide to change the law itself and, like John Diefenbaker or Pierre Trudeau, become Prime Minister of Canada. Man is a mercurial creature, and there is none more lustful for action than the man of law. His are not the cloistered virtues. His need is to sally forth to test his armor in mental combat with his peers, the fiercer the better.

The model man of law, however much he loves the reported judgments of the courts, can never divorce himself from the realities that produced the problems and the paradoxes that made a judgment of a court of law necessary. He can never cease to wonder what the intention of the man charged with murder really was when he took hold of the knife — if he took hold of the knife — that was found deep in the victim's chest.

The story of the growth of English law is written in reports of the quarrels among men and women, great and small — princes and potentates, societies and governments, bishops and boards, and burglars, and bankrupts. Each law report describes the troubles of a litigant. It records the facts, the decisions, and the reasons for each decision. In writing a judgment, the man of law who sits on the bench may ornament the body of the law, refining it, expanding it, or restricting its application. The absorbing process has gone on for nine centuries.

The Common Law has grown like a great coral reef composed of the minutest of sentient bodies that live and die, the spiny skeletons of which — billions of them — go to make up the body of a great shoal. There is no master plan. There is no "coral king" that directs the birth and death of these tiny oganisms whose lives are destined, in the aggregate, to become a thing very different from what they seemed originally to be. The Common Law is like that. It grows from minuscule events into a mighty structure. The result of countless decisions made by thousands of judges and by unnumbered, unrelated juries over many centuries and in many corners of the earth, is a superb body of laws and principles that now govern the lives of free men.

Judges have to make decisions in hard and difficult real-life cases. It is the court that resolves disputes peacefully and assures domestic tranquillity. A court does not deal with theoretical questions. The facts may seem simple and picayune, and they usually appear to have no universal application or relevancy. A decision is made, and reasons for that specific decision are given. But out of that judgment may emerge a principle that will be applied to other future cases. The principle may vary with altered facts and circumstances. Ultimately, there will be defined a clearcut rule within a relatively narrow ambit. It is that principle in respect of a given set of circumstances that becomes a part of the Common Law.

As I believe in the ultimate worth of each individual human being as constituting the best measure of the good society, so in reaching decisions at law, I entertain a greater respect for a judgment that is made in a particular case by a learned and thoughtful judge, than I have for statutes that propound general rules with only limited regard for the particular, and that too often are drawn in haste to achieve a fixed political result in a current crusade or debate. Too often, Parliament hastens to devise, for expediency's sake, a set of rules that are at odds with the seasoned experience and the settled behavior of human beings. Legislation is not the best, nor ought it to be made the normal means of attempting to affect human behavior.

Legislation cannot alter the human body by a single centimeter — except to destroy it. It cannot improve the human brain — except to inhibit it. It cannot affect human compassion — except to institutionalize and emasculate it.

The lawyer may be steeped in the constitution and may know and admire the ingenious manner in which scores of judges have succeeded for more than a hundred years in dovetailing the forty-six heads of sections 91 and 92 of the *British North America Act* into a viable, workable relationship among the hydra-headed federal and provincial governments of Canada. But he can never grow into the model man of law until he has immersed himself as deeply in the realities of his country as in the black letters of the law. He must know something — the more the better — about the producers of the wealth of his country; its farmers, ranchers, miners, drillers, fishermen, tailors, carpenters, plumbers, steelworkers, truck drivers, engineers, seamen, chemists, pilots, cooks, teachers, roadbuilders, writers, painters, musicians, and postmen. He must know how wealth is created and wealth is invested; how projects, great and small, are financed; how wages are bargained and payrolls are paid; how money is borrowed and interest is earned or charged, received or invested; how profits are made and losses sustained; how credit flows through the nation like a great river nourishing its growth as it moves evenly across the land; and how its waters, when swollen, devour everything before it; how its currents run rampant, overflowing its banks, crushing and carrying houses and barns and whole factories downstream to the sea in ruin and total destruction. He must understand the market — not just the law of primogeniture or the law against perpetuities — but the law of supply and demand that overrides all of the laws that Parliament may pass, just as the ocean tides overrule the commands of the King Canutes of every generation in history. The model man of law must know not only the *Bills of Exchange Act* and the *Bank Act,* but *Gresham's Law* — "Bad money drives good money out of the marketplace" — just as robbers and muggers and junkies drive honest men off city streets at night. He must understand why inflationary policies more cruelly destroy contractual rights, the labor, and saving of a lifetime, and all of the great human expectations than an earthquake or a tidal wave. The disasters of inflation are calculated and man-made. Courage, invention, and honest work can overcome them. They need never be endured stoically as if they were acts of God.

The sapient man of law must understand that laws are designed to settle contention and not to foment it; to affirm the accepted ways and habits of citizens and not to agitate and disturb or alarm them; to assert peace in every neighborhood and not to engender envy or animosity or strife; and to recognize the value of the inestimable right to be let alone — so that every man may find his salvation and make his own way in the world, the state neither directing his thoughts nor restraining his words, neither supporting his idleness nor commanding that he work, neither taking his lands nor plundering his substance by oppressive imposts. Man should be free to move where he wishes and associate with whomsoever he chooses, so that in truth and the veriest of realities, "They shall sit every man under his vine and his fig tree. And none shall make him afraid."[10]

All of this requires a deep understanding of human beings and a profound knowledge of their history. Since the man of law must begin somewhere, the writer of contemporary history can offer him the surest guidance. Every newspaper reporter learns the lesson as a cub. Rudyard Kipling gave it to the newsroom years ago when he wrote a quatrain of his *modus operandi* in India:

22

> I had six honest serving men —
> They taught me all I knew:
> Their names were Where and What and When
> And Why and How and Who.

These are the factual questions the lawyer must ask his client, his witnesses, his investigators, his experts — and himself as well — when he embarks upon the adventure of a new case.

Facts win law suits. A single witness is likely to be worth more than a whole barrelful of barristers' arguments. Principles of law are of great importance because they will tell you what facts it is necessary to prove. But principles and theories and statistics can, at best, only raise probabilities. In court, the certainty of truth can only be established by evidence through documents or through the mouths of witnesses who, of their own knowledge, can testify to the facts. Edmund Burke recognized the importance of facts in all public affairs:

> [They] are to the mind what food is to the body. On the due digestion of the former depend the strength and wisdom of the one, just as vigour and health depend on the other. The wisest in council, the ablest in debate, and the most agreeable companion in the commerce of human life, is that man who has assimilated to his understanding the greatest number of facts.[11]

The indefatigable Samuel Johnson went even further. When he instructed James Boswell (the young Scottish lawyer who chose to become the great man's biographer rather than the poor man's barrister) upon the study of law, Johnson observed that the knowledge that a man was to be hanged in a fortnight "concentrates his mind wondrously."[12] But, happily, he also said that prayer has a like effect. This was Johnson's "Prayer Before the Study of Law":

> Almighty God, the giver of wisdom, without whose help resolutions are vain, without whose blessing study is ineffectual; enable me, if it be thy will, to attain such knowledge as may qualify me to direct the doubtful, and instruct the ignorant; to prevent wrongs and terminate

contentions; and grant that I may use that knowledge which I shall attain to thy glory and my own salvation . . . Amen.[13]

The model man of law, energetically, endlessly (*in saecula saeculorum*) will seek to acquire the knowledge that Johnson prayed for.

II
PROFESSION

Attornies at the Common Law, men verrie honest
and learned, yea, and also very necessarie for the civil
businesses; insomuch that by no means their labour
and services may want. And yet such is the unthankfulness
of this age that even their own clyents (of whom
they are best deserved) when they have served their
turns so that they see no present occasion to
use them any longer, for the fault of some few will not
afford the best of them one good word for many
good deeds. Nay, which is worse, they will generally slander
and condemn them all as covetous persons and
disturbers of the common peace and quietnesse of
all men by unnecessary suits. Where, in verie
truth, the most part of the said attornies being verie
peaceable do oftentymes dissuade their clients
from the same so much as they can, by means whereof they
greatly offend their minds insomuch they will for
that only cause, suspect them of affection towards the
adverse parties and threaten earnestly that if they
will not intermeddle therewith, others will.

WEST'S *SYMBOLEOGRAPHY*, 1590

Profession, in the sense that it is an integral part of the model man of law, is the lawyer's dedication of his gifts in the service of the law. His is a devotion to the idea of the law's supremacy in the conduct of human affairs. It is a concept as essential to his probity as theism is to the priest or beauty to the artist. The man of law brings more than principle to his work. His role generates a sense of vocation — the consciousness of being called to a service that fulfills his own inner need to enhance the lives of others. It is a willingness totally to dedicate his time, his talent, and his vitality to his work that distinguishes the man who practices a profession from the man who merely transacts business. This sense of profession nourishes the roots of the lawyer's virtue. Without it, the lawyer is unlikely to withstand the temptation to abandon the rigors and strictures of the practice of law and to enter the Antaean arena of government or the Midas-like milieu of finance or the Elysian Fields of teaching.

Daily, the lawyer is pressed by his client to achieve for him a result. It may seem that he spends half his time getting his clients out of situations and institutions they don't like, and the other half in getting them into situations and institutions they do! Without a client and his cause, the lawyer may feel he is a mere fiddler without a single tune to play. It is, therefore, not surprising that the lawyer's will to prevail and to succeed is among the strongest of his motivations. Just as the ethic of the corporate executive is to win out in the competitive struggle for profits and markets and stock values; just as the ethic of the politician is to get power and hold it; so, for the lawyer, to win his case and earn his fee and establish a reputation that will enable him to win a more important case and gain a yet higher fee next time, motivates him and recharges his energies. To the client, "the bottom line is what counts."

My old friend Percy Gordon died in his ninety-fourth year. The day before he died, I talked to him about some of the great achievements of his life — of his eminence as counsel, his well-reasoned judgments on the bench of the Court of Appeal, his years of dedication as Chancellor of the Anglican Church, as national president of the Red Cross, and of his triumphs as a horticulturalist. (He had produced many new varieties of lilies.) "Of all things," I asked, "what have you enjoyed most in your life?" To which he at once unabashedly replied: "I like to win!"

To the man of law, the result matters a great deal. But it is not the only thing, or indeed the most important thing, he counts among his achievements.

The lawyer must temper his zest to win, his zeal to prevail, with the principle that although "the bottom line" is important, the components that go into its computation are of even greater significance. For the end can never justify the means. It is obvious that to resort to illegal means to achieve a result, however desireable or however moral it may seem to be, is itself to act illegally and immorally. It is a fact of life that the means employed to attain an end inevitably shape the ends that are achieved: indeed, the means we use determine the kind of character each of us forms and the kind of person each of us ultimately becomes. With Ulysses we can all confess, "I am part of all that I have met."[1]

The ambitious, energetic young barrister, hoping to establish a clientele quickly and gain financial independence, may dash into court unbriefed and ill-prepared for a score of clients in a single week. He will promise himself that when he becomes better established and financially independent, he will devote more time to reading law and more care to briefing his cases for trial. But today, he must succeed by hook or by crook. The means he employs to reach that perfect but elusive success will so fix his habits and affect his early ideals that in ten years he will have joined a very different *genre* of men, unrecognizable from that model which he so admired when he began. His swivel standards will mirror his habits, and his compromises with excellence will have reduced him to a hack. There are irreconcilable conflicts enough in the practice of law to convince the lawyer that the better course is to eschew all compromises with his own high standards of craftsmanship and to treat every case he accepts as the most important in his whole career. The effort spent by the model man of law in the preparation of his brief for a client from whom he has received a very modest fee (or none at all) must be precisely the effort expended to advance the interests of the client who has paid a normal or a very generous fee. I have observed that many counsel will work harder for the client who pays nothing for his services in order that it may never be said or thought of him that he measured out his effort or the standards of his performance in court by the weight of the coinage he received for them.

The junior barrister's gown of stuff and cotton retains an ancient vestige that serves no present purpose, but is a reminder that in early days a barrister depended upon his client's generosity for his fee.

The oval cut of cloth that hangs from the shoulder of the gown was once a bag. Into it, a client, sitting behind counsel, intently listening to his argument, might drop a sovereign if he felt a felicitous phrase or a well-directed shaft had been loosed from his quiver, shattering or shaking his opponent's case. Or a disgruntled client might cast threepence into the bag to express his displeasure. Having undertaken to prosecute a cause or to defend it, the model man of law performs his duty according to his fullest capacity whatever his remuneration may be.

Out of his declaration of faith in the supremacy of law which legitimizes the role of counsel, there arises a dichotomy in the demands which the legal profession makes of every lawyer. On the one hand, he has the duty to help his client — to do for him what the client would do for himself had he the lawyer's training, knowledge, and skill.

On the other hand, in assisting his client, however worthy the cause, the lawyer may not break the law. Neither may he resort to means that are dishonorable, however much his client might urge him to do so. His posture is much like the hockey player's: his career depends upon his ability to win. Like Schultz's Charlie Brown, he knows that "winning isn't everything, but losing is nothing." But like the hockey player, the man of law can win only if he adheres strictly to the rules of the game. In court, as on the ice, watchful referees are ever present, and in both places, to break the rules is to lose the match.

The idea of simple fairness runs like the recurring theme of a fugue through every volume of the common law. Impartiality, equity, justice: these are only variations upon a theme that has its origin in the idea that fair play is a quality that distinguishes the civilized man from the barbarian, the man of culture from the brute, the gentleman from the slob. These concepts that have grown out of the common law may well owe their vitality to the felicitous marriage of Judeo-Christian ethics with the gamesmanship of the cricketer on the playing fields of England. Heavy duties are laid on Israel in the Decalogue and they are encapsulated in the Christian catechism as "My duty towards God and my duty towards my neighbor."

Whether or not Wellington really said that the Battle of Waterloo was won on the playing fields of Eton, I am convinced that the common law could never have come to command so preeminent a place among people of the civilized world had England's men of law been less dedicated to the games they played and to the spirit of the play that influenced their standards of conduct. Although I have not played cricket, as a boy I could never help but be excited by Newbolt's poem:

> There's a breathless hush in the Close to-night —
> Ten to make and the match to win —
> A bumping pitch and a blinding light,
> An hour to play and the last man in.
> And it's not for the sake of a ribboned coat,
> Or the selfish hope of a season's fame,
> But his Captain's hand on his shoulder smote —
> 'Play up! play up! and play the game!'[2]

What is all of this but an ode to duty and an eulogy to the spirit of fidelity and fairness?

Counsel's duty is to play the game. It is not to judge his client's cause but to present it as effectively as he can within the limits prescribed by personal and professional honor. Some lawyers choose to act only in cases that appear to offer them certain success. That is why I suspect the lawyer of whom it is said that "he never loses a case." I have never known or heard of any lawyer whose trial record was one of unbroken wins, and I am quite certain that anyone making such a claim could have appeared only in a small handful of trifling trials. If a lawyer is to accept only cases or clients that please him, men and women will be deprived of the legal advice and service to which they are entitled. If the lawyer accepts only cases in which he personally believes, he may do a great injustice to those whom he refuses. Possibly, he will do an even greater injustice to those whom he represents in a cause to which he is personally committed, because there then exists a great temptation to use his client's misfortune to advance his own personal views. These, the man of law must repress lest they distort his motives and color his judgment. A client who employs a particular lawyer in a cause simply because his views (business, political, or religious) coincide with his own is like a stutterer who engages another stutterer for speech therapy. There is no virtue in compounding weakness.

The lawyer's role, I think, is best expressed in the maxim of the patron of all lawyers, St. Ives: *Pro Deo te adjuvabo* — for the sake of

God, I will help you. *Semper et ubique, semper paratus, semper fidelis* —
always and everywhere, always ready, always faithful.[3]

Lawyers may not fully appreciate the importance of St. Ives's
simple declaration to a person accused of crime. When a man finds
himself suspected of wrongdoing or charged with a criminal offense,
he suddenly feels that the hand of everyone is raised against him and
that his country is determined to prove him guilty and destroy him.
There are terrifying overtones to an indictment that charges crime
and declares that Her Majesty the Queen has marshalled all of the
limitless forces of the law against one of her most insignificant
subjects — most abject and most alone. The more heinous or
revolting the crime alleged, the more terrified the person accused
will be. To whom can a man accused turn for protection and
counsel? Whom can he trust to advise him and whom to defend him?
Who will assume the unpopular role of advocate for those whom
society condemns? And what advocate will endure the contumely of
the ignorant, believing that a lawyer is the prisoner's accomplice
after-the-fact?

It is not by accident that the most compassionate role in which
the founder of Christianity is cast in the Common Prayer Book
should be that of mediator and advocate before the throne of
heaven. The lawyer adopts precisely this role when he undertakes
the defense of a man accused of crime. It is he who stands between
the accused and the whole world when there is virtually no other to
defend him. It is an awesome responsibility. It invests the man of law
with a measure of the high and solemn calling of the ecclesiastical
condition. It is analogous to the dedication of the priest to his
parishioner who knows no loyalty save his loyalty to God whom he
would serve, and to his fellow man whom he would help.

Since counsel must be a man not simply for all seasons but for all
persons, the obligation he owes his client and the court is to refrain
from using his position to express those views or principles or
prejudices that he personally may embrace. Instead, he must
advance the arguments that are most likely to be accepted by a jury
as being plausible and in harmony with the experience of ordinary
men and women who sit as judges of the facts and, again and again,
are instructed by the court to use their reason and their common
sense in reaching their verdicts. Often, I have told a jury that while
they must render a verdict based only upon the evidence they have
heard and seen in court and put out of their minds anything they
have read in the newspapers or heard on radio or seen on television

or picked up as local gossip concerning the case, they have not left their reason or their common sense at home. These they have brought into the court room with them, to be used to decide what evidence to accept and what to reject, what to regard as important and what to consider trifling. It is then for counsel to direct the jury's attention to those facts that most perfectly support the theory of his case and that are most likely to advance his client's cause.

Similarly, counsel must present to the judge those arguments that are consistent with the facts in evidence, and that the law, both statutory and judicial, supports. There are perimeters within which counsel may argue. If, in his eloquence, he strays too far beyond these bounds, his case will take on a sense of unreality and all of his forensic pains, however zealously pursued will prove an exercise in futility. "Your argument is most ingenious, Mr. Thompson," he will be told, "but the law you are arguing should be presented in a case with different facts." For counsel to make an address or an argument that pleases only himself is to depart from his duty and abandon his employment. The lawyer receives his fee to exercise a well-stocked brain, not a bleeding heart. He is not paid to feel but to think; not to sympathize but to synthesize. He is thanked not for whining but for winning. He is a professional. As such, he performs better when he is objective in his quests than when his emotions are made captive of his client's cause. In pursuit of objectivity, he will not make impassioned personal appeals; he will make submissions. He is not his client's mouthpiece or heartpiece, his property or his tool. He may reflect his client's interests, but he will be no chameleon. He will retain his own identity. He is most effective and best speaks for his client, most intimately entering his mind and heart, when, like Marc Antony, he can say:

I show you sweet Caesar's wounds . . . and bid *them* speak for me.

Although the emotional appeal has its place before a jury, emotional influences are most effective when they are carefully measured out and dispensed as subtly as Shakespeare's Antony expressed them over Caesar's corpse.

Within the authorities and precedents that bind him, counsel is free to advocate a result for Mr. Jones on Wednesday that is quite opposite to the result he urged upon the same court for Mr. Smith in a different cause on Monday. *Stare decisis* — the need to follow precedent — does not restrain the advocate in the same way that it binds the court.

"Yesterday, Mr. Moss, you argued that the municipality had no right to expropriate your client's land," said the judge. "Today, representing a city council, you argue that its expropriation is lawful. How do you explain that?" To which learned counsel, unabashed, is reported to have replied: "Yesterday, my Lord, I was only of the opinion that the municipality was wrong. Today, I am quite sure that the council is right."

Since counsel is able (and, indeed, often is obliged) to take opposite positions upon issues that concern different clients at different times, and since there are bound to be different views entertained and expressed by various counsel appearing in the same cause, there can never be unanimity among members of the bar.

That is why a consensus among laywers is so rare. Lawyers' associations, such as the Canadian Bar Association, often encounter this obvious fact of life when framing their resolutions. But it is no weakness of the profession. On the contrary, in this phenomenon lies its greatest strength. Were all lawyers to hold the same view at the same time on important issues, the legitimate or imagined rights of some people might never see the light of day or be heard for lack of an advocate to espouse and express them. It is precisely because unanimity is the hallmark of the dictatorship, that the legal profession can never flourish in the unfree countries of the world. Lawyers are never so much needed as when the rule of law gives way to tyranny. Invariably, the lawless society is also the lawyerless society. Although lawyers are a beleaguered class where freedom is repressed, they continue to recognize and respect the fifteenth-century dictum of Sir John Fortescue that "freedom is a thing with which the nature of man has been endowed by God. For this reason if it be taken away from man it strives of its own energy always to return." The tradition of the man of law impels him instinctively to achieve the ends of freedom and he is, therefore, the most venerable of freedom fighters.

While the lawyer knows only his client and wholly dedicates himself to his cause, he also owes an allegiance to his profession and to its code of ethics. Not only is he a debtor to his profession in the sense that it has opened for him the doors to new perceptions and new activities, but by his oath he has chosen to abide by a code of conduct from which he may not depart save by abandoning his profession. Like the novitiate, he pledges himself to uphold the supremacy of the law, well-knowing that should he transgress the rules, he would not only disqualify himself as a member of the profession, but by his deviant conduct he would diminish his effectiveness in serving his client and he would thereby erode the law's influence upon society.

Let me illustrate. Consider the model of William Kunstler, "civil rights lawyer" in the United States who paid a visit to the University of Toronto several years ago for the purpose of regaling those who came to hear him with a demonstration of his confrontation tactics in court. (It ended when Kunstler was himself confronted by a phalanx of sophomoric law students who dampened his ardor and swamped his charisma with a few buckets of cold water.) Kunstler specialized in unpopular causes. For a brief period he was much in demand in many parts of the United States and he acquired fleeting fame for his defense of terrorists and dissenters who had been charged with crimes ranging from homicide, robbery, and violence to unlawful sit-ins, assemblies, and demonstrations. His principal defense was that these acts, unlawful though they might be, were necessary to effect much-needed social and economic changes — that they were political in nature and not justiciable in the courts. His principal means of advancing this defense was to cause disorder in the court room, to disrupt the proceedings, to terrify the court officials, and in every way possible, to discredit the forum of the trial and the institutions of justice. In the face of the greatest provocation, the judges who presided at these trials where the script of a kind of Theater of Conspiracy was acted out, preserved the dignity of the court and the public's respect for the judicial process. It was successfully argued that the acts complained of were crimes in themselves and, if committed for political purposes, they were steps in a calculated programme of sedition designed to promote the overthrow of the government of the United States by force.[4]

A new vocabulary developed out of these events and their counterparts in many parts of the world. *Newspeak* is what George Orwell in his novel, *1984*, predicted would be the language of the future "designed to meet the ideological needs of Ingsoc or English Socialism. Its 'B vocabulary' would consist of words which had been deliberately constructed for political purposes; words, that is to say, which not only had in every case a political implication, but were intended to impose a desirable mental attitude upon the person using them."[5] In the result, murders perpetrated by organized terrorists are now called "executions"; assaults are "acts of war"; robbery is an act of "liberation" — a form of taxing the rich to finance the poor in their struggle against oppression. "Violence" can mean anything the "new Left" regards "unacceptable" to it. This was Father Raymond Schroth's absurd description in 1968:

> Violence is any offence to human dignity, or political destruction of one's humanity as much as his body. . . . Hunger, bad housing, rats in the cellar, low wages, unemployment, religious prejudice; all these are violence. The hypocrisy of political and religious leaders who cry for "law and order" and a return to fundamental values but who fail to speak out on poverty and racism is violence. Fear is violence. Authoritariansim is violence . . .[6]

In normal parlance, as well as in law, the word "violence" primarily means "the use or threat of immediate force." But such a meaning would not satisfy the objectives of *Newspeak*, which so debases the language and inverts the meaning of words that the *status quo* must come to mean a continuous state of seige, and violence and murder on the streets must mean self-defense and justifiable homicide. Similarly, *Newspeak* demands that when the phrase "law and order" is uttered, it denotes "an attack by the establishment upon a minority." This debasement of language, the currency of our thought, was not brought about by any decree of government, socialist or otherwise. It is a calculated distortion of fact by revolutionaries and their dupes, brought about by means of manipulating words in order that emotions may be aroused, issues obscured, and the rational resolution of differences rendered impossible. The theory that criminals may enjoy immunity from punishment was developed from the fiction that an individual's private declaration of war against a society that he elects to condemn as "unjust," creates a special sovereignty that shields the wrongdoer acting upon that declaration from the sanctions of all domestic laws. Thus, there has emerged the practice of terrorists and hijackers and murderers proudly to proclaim responsibility for crimes that only the most desperate people would perpetrate and only the most barbarous of regimes would embrace or tolerate. An unrealistic vocabulary shields the rebel from condemnation, just as it obscures the essential quality of his crimes.

Kunstler entered upon his defenses with all the zeal and personal animus of the activists he represented. He regarded himself as a partisan in the people's war against a decadent establishment. It was his very ardor in this role that moved such defendants as Abbie Hoffman and the Chicago Seven to enlist him in their cause and retain him at their trials. In representing them, Kunstler did not adopt the normal model of counsel. He invaded the courtroom like a guerrilla. His language, his tactics, and his hostile demeanor were scarcely distinguishable from his clients'. Zealousness in a cause may be commendable in counsel, but it is an explosive element when its excesses move counsel so to identify with his client that he adopts the client's questioned conduct as his own.

The result of acting as the *alter ego* of a client is to do injustice to counsel and client alike. If a lawyer permits his client so to influence his conduct, he may ultimately discover that he must defend not one accused, but two. What Kunstler's clients needed was a skilled and able lawyer knowledgeable in the law, understanding of human nature, and expert in advocacy. In the result, they were served by an accomplice who grew so enmeshed in their own affairs that he was himself dragged through the treacherous slough of contempt proceedings.

The lawyer who fancies himself a social activist in the courtroom departs from his obligations as advocate. No longer does he plead his client's cause, but his own. Or possibly it is the advancement of some organization's social, economic, or political ambitions he espouses. It is here that the lawyer abandons his traditional role. If he enters the arena, not to advance his client's objectives within the bounds of the law, but to exert pressures to achieve political or economic results by intimidation or threats or violence or terror, he runs the risk of losing his client's case and his own credibility and honor. The revolutionary who appears as counsel is the fifth columnist who comes into court not to fulfill the law but to destroy it. And, in the process, possibly his client as well.

I am aware that, historically, great trials have sometimes served to do more than settle the immediate disputes that bedevil people and bring them as litigants into court. Occasionally, such a trial has been the rallying point for a nation to change the law and even to change society itself. John Hampden, opposing the payment of "ship money" — a tax that King Charles I levied without the authority of

Parliament — and going to prison for his pains, was the precursor of the revolution in which the English lost their freedom and Charles his head, the first temporarily, the second irrevocably. The Roncarelli[7] case began with the refusal to issue a liquor license to a restaurateur, but it so discredited Quebec's Premier Duplessis that, as a result of Frank Scott's advocacy in court, the Union Nationale was driven from office, and corruption in the high places of the Quebec government ceased to flourish, the first irrevocably, the second, only temporarily.

Clarence Darrow, in his defense to save Leopold and Loeb of Chicago from Cook County's electric chair in 1923, brought about legislative changes which sparked the abolition of capital punishment in most of the jurisdictions in the United States. These were resounding achievements of lawyers who, battling their clients' causes in the courtrooms of their time, raised voices that reverberated throughout the land and changed the lives and destinies of generations who were to know nothing of the judges and lawyers whose adjudication and advocacy in the trial of but a single man, changed the watersheds of history.

Nevertheless, to the lawyer who fights such cases, the political consequences of the trial ought to be of secondary importance lest his client be reduced to the status of a mere instrument to be manipulated for another's gain. It is the client's interest that must be the lawyer's paramount consideration. It is the client's interest that the lawyer is duty-bound to advance, not his own; it is the client's future that the lawyer holds most precious, not society's. For society's greatest achievement lies in the fashioning of the complete, ideal individual.

What of the client who is bent upon self-destruction? What if his purpose be martyrdom and his object to seek a verdict that will destroy him in order that he may claim to be the victim of injustice? What if his motive be to discredit the court that tries him or to undermine the society that has established the court, by making of himself a sacrificial offering? Ought counsel to aid him in his purpose?

Louis Riel might have been such a man. He was charged with sedition upon overwhelming and unequivocal evidence that he had waged war against the settlers of the North West Territories and committed treason against the state. He was defended by Canada's most eminent counsel of the day — Charles Fitzpatrick, who later became Chief Justice of Canada, and F. X. Lemieux. The only defense they could advance with any hope of success was their client's insanity, a plea that Riel, his eyes fanatically fixed on martyrdom, rejected out of hand. Nevertheless, this defense was argued in three courts — all the way to the Privy Council in England.[8] It failed. If Riel were tried today, having regard to the great advances of medical and psychiatric science in the intervening decades, a plea of insanity would probably succeed. Riel would end his days in a mental hospital. Had such a verdict been given at his trial in Regina, Riel's image could never have been so metamorphosed as to convert him for public purposes from a pretentious paranoid into a cosmetic Canadian folk hero. All of which is a very sound argument for the abolition of capital punishment, since it is easier to idolize the criminal condemned to die by judge and jury, than the demented consigned for treatment by psychiatrists and nurses.

Riel, of course, was not so bent on martyrdom as to renounce life and embrace the gallows. At his trial he said, "I am sure that my mother country will not kill me more than my mother did." And to Nicholas Flood Davin who interviewed Riel on the eve of his execution, he expressed the hope that at the last moment his sentence would be commuted and his life spared.[9]

Like the Encyclopoedia of the Soviet Union, each new edition of which revises the ranks of all of the revolutionary personalities in the Marx-Leninist panthenon, and consigns to ignominy and oblivion those who have fallen out of favor, George Orwell's *Newspeak* attempts to rewrite our own history.[10] It is the fashion (a transient one to be sure) that the heroes of the past be denigrated and the villains raised to high esteem. Perhaps it is simply a manifestation of the cynicism of the times that the anti-hero should be enthroned as hero, just as at Mardigras, fool is crowned king, or on Madison Avenue, Uncola is declared greater than Coke. Apparently, the governments of Manitoba and Saskatchewan are as susceptible to *Newspeak* as the teeners on the street. Why else would they erect monuments in prominent places within the spacious gardens of their legislative buildings to the memory of Louis Riel, the condemned felon, but none to the men who served Canada in uniform during the North West Rebellion of 1885? They came from many places, these men — some from Ontario, others from Prince Albert, North Battleford, Qu'Appelle, and Winnipeg — and they gave their lives to defend the peaceful settlers of the Territories whose only sin it was that they were the pioneers of our country.

The deeds of these brave men are recorded only in a monument in Queen's Park as though they were strangers to the history of the West. Sporadic campaigns have sought to press the Canadian government to grant a full, free pardon for Riel in order that the unprovoked bloodshed he caused might somehow be made to appear justified. Riel's "rehabilitation" is sought not by those who genuinely are striving to advance the position and prosperity of Canada's native people, but by a militant minority that seeks to legitimize revolution and rebellion as instruments to change society, not in Riel's time so much as in our own.

Responsible Indian, Inuit, and Metis leaders today have found better ways than Riel ever knew to improve their economic position in Canada. They learned and remembered better than anyone else, that the violence and hatred engendered by Riel won nothing for their people but years of poverty, degradation, and frustration during which their lives deteriorated on their reserves and their presence produced suspicion and fear outside.

Much of that has changed in the past two decades. Instead of going on the war path, native leaders discovered the law. Bloody battle became obsolete. Instead of buying or stealing rifles and ammunition as Riel had done, they began studying their Treaties with Queen Victoria. Instead of organizing their strongest chiefs to fight, they sought out the best lawyers to represent them. Instead of bringing out their feathers and war paint, they issued statements of claim and writs of summons out of the courts of judicial centers across the country. By invoking the Canadian constitution, the Canadian Bill of Rights, and the common law (remedies available to everyone, great and small alike) native people succeeded in taking giant steps to bridge the millennia-wide gap that separated them from the culture and technology of the civilized world. The old chiefs were wise enough to recognize and to call it "the white man's ways and cunning," and when the Treaties were negotiated, they prayed that soon they might be taught these skills.

In the euphoric years that followed the signing of the Treaties, it was believed that "education" like some magic wand, would instantly change the native, his life, and his status. But "education" is never enough. (Even Erasmus called the medieval lawyers of his day "a learned class of very ignorant men.") Riel was the beneficiary of more education than any of his Metis brethren; yet, all of his learning, could produce in him neither stability of mind nor soundness of judgment. To his people, he brought nothing but a century of misery. Had he regarded the law as an instrument capable of recognizing the merits of his cause, sufficiently powerful to expand the opportunities he wished for his people, Riel might, indeed, have raised their spirits and their status high. But he spurned the law and earned the gibbet and now it remains for another generation to learn from his mistakes and to achieve by peaceful means, what he failed to gain in war.

Even in the unlikely situation when a client, such as Louis Riel, is bent on self-destruction, the lawyer's constant, never-ending duty is to preserve both his client and the law — just as it has been the duty of the physician since the age of Hippocrates, to preserve the life of his patient, and the means by which he can best be served. Socrates provided the exquisite example of achieving immortality for himself and for the law. He drank the hemlock because the law of Athens required that he do so, and he insisted that the law must be served. Xenophon's report of the trial reveals that Socrates was aware of the injustice of his conviction and of its significance to Athens. It was this that saved his reputation and immortalized him:

> Apollodorus being present, one who loved Socrates extremely, said to him: But it grieveth me, my Socrates, to have you die so unjustly!
> Socrates, with much tenderness, laying his hand upon his head, answered smiling: And what, my much loved Apollodorus! Wouldst thou rather they had condemned me *justly?*[11]

Unlike Socrates, the average person who is acquitted after a trial that has revealed an excess of zeal on the part of his prosecutors (an all-too-common failing of this class of public servants) is incensed at the injustice of the accusations brought against him. Often he is bent on suing his accusers for malicious prosecution in order to recover exemplary damages for the expense of his defense and for the agony of his trial. Such actions are rare — as rare as a charge of perjury brought against an accused who testifies in his own behalf, but whom the court disbelieves. Although such lawsuits may well be justified, it is generally wise to discourage them, since almost invariably they serve only to perpetuate bitterness and the sense of injustice for which no money award can serve adequately to compensate. They debilitate a man's energies and consume his years. The remedy the law accords is money, and as the ancient Chinese have sagely observed, "an inch of gold will never buy an inch of time." It is better, by far, to move on and feed in fresh green pastures, than to remain mired in a slough of despond to regurgitate stale fodder. Confronted with such a client, the man of law may usefully ponder the case of Socrates. For his client, he may then paraphrase the wise words spoken to Apollodorus. Then the client may one day come to regard the losses brought on by his dreadful experience, as having been what Justice Oliver Wendell Holmes called "the fleece I have left upon the brambles of the law."

As a professional, therefore, the man of law should hold the welfare of his client first and foremost in his heart and mind. He should ponder his client's position with the wisdom of the dolphin, prepare his case with the industry of the ant, pursue his remedies with the swiftness of the dove, enter the courtroom with the strength of a lion, approach witnesses with the caution of a fawn, speak as sweetly as the nightingale and, like the bee, inject the sting, but only when all hope to win with honey has been spent.

That is profession!

III

OMNITUDE

Our Lady of the Common Law — I say it with the
humility that is due from an old and faithful servant —
our Lady in these days is no longer an easy
one to please. She has become insatiate in her demands.
Not law alone, but almost every branch of human
knowledge, has been brought within her ken, and so within
the range of sacrifice exacted of her votaries.
Those who would earn her best rewards must make their
knowledge as deep as the science and as broad
and universal as the culture of their day. She will
not be satisfied with less.

BENJAMIN N. CARDOZO,
COMMENCEMENT ADDRESS TO FIRST GRADUATING CLASS,
1928, 13 ST. JOHN'S L.R. 231, 232 (1939)

OMNITUDE

The man of law is a man for every season. His is a sense of wholeness within the sphere of his profession, and considerably beyond it, so that his intellectual interests and accomplishments extend into many fields and his concerns lie in every area of the community of which he is a part. Like the dentist who recognizes people by their inlays, and the barber who sees mankind as a hirsute kaleidoscope of changing fashion, so the lawyer's world mirrors the law that surrounds us all and affects the life of "every child that's born alive" — and those unborn as well. Like the tinker, the tailor, the candlestick maker whose concerns are with pots and pans, needle and thread, wax and tallow, the lawyer must come to know something (and always all he can) concerning every trade and a great deal more besides. People working at trades (and those who are not at work but at play) are every moment of the day and night bound by laws and rules and practices — and frequently they spawn disputes and quarrels and suffer hurts and inflict or sustain injury. If a lawyer is to be of any value to the person in grief, he cannot rest content with a knowledge of the law that is material to the legal issues alone. He must also become an expert in all of the physical processes (and some psychical as well) that have a bearing upon his client's business. Happily, he need not be an expert in all things (though this would be as highly beneficial as it would be impractical); but he must have the faculty, speedily and accurately, to comprehend the elements that combine to produce an effective tinker or tool-maker, tailor or television actor, candlestick maker or hydro-electrical and atomical engineer. While there is equality under the law — equality of general rules and conduct upon which our liberty depends — there have developed innumerable, very special laws that govern every conceivable trade and business, every profession and occupation; every kind of building, roadway, structure; every mode of movement or travel; every type of teaching and learning, cutting and trimming, sowing and reaping, hunting and fishing, breeding and killing, buying and selling, walking and riding, driving and flying, producing and reproducing, and living and dying.

The model man of law must first be totally committed to the principle that liberty demands that governments treat all persons equally. People are, in fact, different and unequal. Laws relating to various businesses and occupations are bound to vary. The lawyer should have the facility to learn something of them all and to apply to all of them the principles he has learned. Curiosity may be a fatal feline disease, but for the lawyer I believe it to be the indispensible elixir on which he best thrives. Curiosity is his very life blood. This trait he shares with all humans, along with our equally pronounced characteristic of laziness. It is the combination of inquisitiveness and sloth that has been most responsible for mankind's survival. His physical qualities would have condemned him to early extinction in a predatory world were it not for his curiosity. It is this that came to his rescue and prodded his brain to ask questions and to seek answers, to invent, to adapt, and to create. His natural indolence and love for play spurred him to harness his inventions to work and so free himself of necessity's yoke — all to augment his comforts and satisfy his appetites.

By virtue of the demands that are made upon him, the man of law is perpetually restless, always curious, inquisitive. The odds and ends of knowledge he picks up here and there will invariably serve to find a place somewhere in his bric-a-brac brain. One can never know when a bit of random knowledge will fit into a vital place at trial, or how it may make all of the difference between success and failure, guilt or innocence. I shall not forget how a casual conversation with my optometrist on perception led me to demonstrate to a jury that red was an unreliable color for big game hunters to wear in the fall, and that yellow or blue (colors unheard of for that purpose at the time) were safer. This stray piece of information led to an acquittal of my client, who had been charged with criminal negligence in a shooting incident; it resulted in legislative changes in dress that now affect hunters in many parts of the country.[1]

Sir Norman Birkett felicitously expressed the omnitude of the true man of law when he said: "Great advocacy . . . is in the last and supreme analysis, the product of what the man is who produces it. . . . [T]he lawyer when devoting his life to the law, indeed consecrating his life to the law, should enlarge the sweep of his mental vision so that nothing that is human, or that affects humanity, should be to him common or unclean."[2]

The lawyer is the last of the great generalists, and there can be no higher praise than that he is a contemporary edition of the renaissance man: a man for every season, who is "by season seasoned."[3] Specialization has diminished the art of almost every profession and calling — the physician, the surgeon, the architect, the dressmaker, the restaurateur, the tailor, the cobbler, the carpenter, the mason. It has tended to reduce such people to the status of mere technicians. It may be a fact that the great proliferation of knowledge in this century demands that the world be partitioned and every task segmented, so that each worker knows more and more about less and less. Specialists, it is said, are as necessary among humankind as among bees or ants. But I reject the popular saw that it is inevitable that members of the learned professions are necessarily condemned to a fate so dismal as would bring them ultimately to know virtually everything about absolutely nothing. The lawyer can — and indeed must — continue to draw upon the rich repositories of knowledge of every profession and every trade; he must be at home in the animal, mineral, and vegetable worlds; he must be familiar with the wonders of the land, the mysteries of the deep, and the marvels of the air as they relate to the astonishing situations he considers in his practice. His province, then, must be all of knowledge in order that he may understand the facts — and the theories that bear upon those facts — for it is upon these that the exercise of his skills depends. As it was immodestly said of Sherlock Holmes, so it may be facetiously said of the model barrister — that all other men are specialists, but his specialism is omniscience.

The man of law must be multifarious, for in his profession he is not only an adviser, trustee, and advocate. In a sense he is also a lawmaker.

As lawmaker he plays two vital roles. Consider first his place in litigation. As I have already described, the great edifice of the common law was built, molecule by molecule, in the courtrooms of judges as they decided the cases that came before them and pronounced judgments that affected not only the specific parties in court, but ultimately all future litigants and those who will never face a court of law but, conforming to the law, are affected by those judgments.

Where did these principles originate? One of the early theories was that, searching deep into their breasts, judges discovered the principles of natural law. As Sir William Blackstone wrote two centuries ago, they existed in "time whereof the memory of man runneth not to the contrary" as a divine gift to mankind. To these principles judges applied reason. They created no new laws. They simply gave expression to the law nascent that awaited only man's discovery. The judges who created this concept and applied it, were possessed of the kind of courage that inspired a remarkable confidence in the law, and it established stability in society. Centuries passed before the positive, creative role of judges was acknowledged. Yet even today expression is seldom given to that important role.

The principle of *stare decisis* is a sound one: every citizen is entitled to know how a court is likely to treat his case when it comes to trial. Predictability in legal matters is a highly desirable objective. That it is an ideal that can never fully be realized in no way detracts from its importance and usefulness. It is from this idea that the phrase *stare decisis* — to stand on decisions — emerged. Every court is expected to stand by the principles of law enunciated by the judges of that court; they are bound to follow the decisions of the judges of higher courts. The principles so enunciated have all the force of law and are binding upon litigants and judges alike. The principle of standing by what has been decided and not disturbing what has been settled, is a wise policy, because in most matters it is of the greatest importance that people know what they may expect the courts to decide in matters that may concern them. The law must be something more than the whimsy of the caliph sitting at the city gates "doing justice" to his subjects as he pleases. Because it is unjust for anyone to be taken by surprise, it is of prime importance that the law be settled so far as it is possible to settle it and that citizens may know in advance what the consequences of their acts are likely to be, and so, assume obligations and govern their affairs in the knowledge that the laws will not suddenly change and set their plans at naught.

The United States Supreme Court does not regard the rule of *stare decisis* as inflexible in constitutional matters. As Mr. Justice Brandeis said: "*Stare decisis* is not, like the rule of *res judicata*, a universal and inexorable command. Whether [an earlier decision of the court] be followed or departed from is a question entirely within the discretion of the court, which is again called upon to consider a question once decided."[4]

Before appeals to the Privy Council in England were abolished, the Supreme Court of Canada was strictly bound by the decisions of that body. But the Privy Council, unlike the House of Lords which has always been the court of final appeal for the United Kingdom, never regarded itself as bound by its own decisions.[5] The Privy Council also said that "on constitutional questions it must be seldom, indeed, that the Board will depart from a previous decision which it may be assumed will have been acted upon by both governments and subjects."[6] In 1951, Bora Laskin, then a professor of law at the University of Toronto, in a learned article published in the *Canadian Bar Review*[7] canvassed the various approaches that the Supreme Court of Canada might take once its decisions could no longer be reviewed by a higher court. It was his view then, that "law must pay tribute to life; and that in constitutional litigation especially, *stare decisis* cannot be accepted as an inflexible rule of conduct." He indicated then, the approach that he is now taking as Chief Justice of Canada in adjudicating constitutional issues. "What is required," he wrote "is the same free range of inquiry which animated the court in the early days of its existence, especially in constitutional cases where it took its inspiration from Canadian sources. Empiricism not dogmatism, imagination rather than literalness, are the qualities through which the judges can give their court the stamp of personality."[8]

It can be expected, therefore, that policy-making may become a function of Canada's Supreme Court, just as it has been a consideration of the judges of the Supreme Court of the United States in constitutional matters. The traditional model of the man of law, as judge, may gradually change.

In theory, the House of Lords, for centuries, paid lip service to the concept of *stare decisis*. But when a principle became unworkable or appeared unreasonable, the Law Lords were sufficiently practical and innovative to draw factual distinctions between cases, to refine principles in the interpretation of statutes and to probe the intent of the authors of earlier judgments. There are no better illustrations of judicial statecraft at work than the reasoning of such eminent judges as Lord Hobhouse, Viscount Haldane, and Lord Sankey that brought about the expansion or contraction of the legislative powers of the Parliament of Canada and of the provinces under the provisions of the *British North America Act*, as economic and political realities made necessary. Finally, in 1966, Lord Gardener, speaking for himself as Lord Chancellor and for the other Lords of Appeal, declared that while the use of precedent remains "an indispensible foundation upon which to decide what is the law and its application to individual cases", nevertheless, "too rigid an adherence to precedence may lead to injustice ... and unduly restrict the proper development of the law." Thus, the House of Lords also decided to modify its practice and "to depart from a previous decision when it appears right to do so."[9]

Recognized even less than the judge's innovative role is the part the lawyer plays in the judicial growth of the law. Counsel at the bar, no less than the judge on the bench, is a discoverer and innovator. Into the offices of the man of law, clients each day bring the rawest of human materials: A man's complaint against his neighbor's broken fence through which his cattle strayed; a girl's sickness after drinking a bottle of ginger beer with a snail inside it; a young man's sudden death in a dentist's chair while having ten teeth extracted under anesthesia; a wife's discovery that the property she believed was partly hers is now all claimed by her estranged husband. The lawyer never receives a neatly packaged statement of the facts. Neither is he given a documented brief of the law or a bundle of logically marshalled arguments to support his client's complaint against loss and injustice. What is handed to him, or more often spewed out in expletives, or scattered over his desk like flack, is an amorphous sprinkling of disoriented bits of fact and pieces of fiction, seemingly irrelevant complaints and rumors, scraps of paper, names of people, and a few uncertain dates — all bound tightly together with the elastic of high emotion, deep-seated anxiety, and ill-concealed self-justification. These, he must sort out and classify, inquire into and weigh. With care and diligence he must bring a semblance of order into the apparently unconnected fragments. As he proceeds, he must apply his experience and imagination to the development of a theory that may support his client's claim, if he can find one. As this labor proceeds — possibly for weeks or months — it may be that a case, civil or criminal, emerges into the light of day. Claims are drafted, potential witnesses are interviewed, examinations are held, documents of the adversaries are produced and examined. When the suit ultimately reaches the trial court, its reception or rejection will depend in large measure upon the skill and imagination that counsel has brought to the task of transforming his client's suspicions and uneasiness and his persistent sense of injustice into a cause for legal action for which he believes the law has a ready remedy, or for which the court will feel that justice demands it find one.

In this intricate formulative process, the role of the man of law is a uniquely creative one. The lawyer cannot manufacture facts out of thin air. Facts must have an independent existence. But the manner in which facts are assembled, their relationship one to the other, the view which is taken of them and the inferences that can be drawn from them, all contribute to the creative process of conceiving, planning, and painstakingly building a case. The lawyer who has spent many days in court is bound to be impressed not so much by the variations in the testimony of witnesses as by the multi-faceted nature of truth itself. The creative lawyer who wrote the lyrics for *H.M.S. Pinafore* knew what he was speaking about for it is indeed true that

> Things are seldom what they seem,
> Skim milk masquerades as cream.[10]

The man of law may leave the courtroom and carry his role of creative lawyer a step further by becoming a legislator. Parliament is an ancient place in which the man of law has been as much at home as in his seat at the bar. His prominence in Parliament has raised the perennial criticism that there are more successful politicians who are lawyers than the members of any other profession or calling. It is said that wherever there is an odium of politicians there follows, close by, an eloquence of lawyers. Yet they are not so bad a lot when compared with the consternations of social workers or the confusions of economists that warm and wear the leather of the seats of every legislative chamber. The fact of life remains that the lawyer's metier is the law; he is schooled in the law, and were he less active in the law-making process, he would rightly be criticized for shirking the responsibilities that his skill and training render him fit to assume. It is no more surprising that lawyers should be prominent in the law-making councils of the country than that welders should have a high profile on building sites or that surgeons should dominate the operating rooms of our hospitals. Lawyers are to the legislative process what hens are to the miracle of hatching eggs.

There is but one instance in the history of England where criticism levelled at lawyers resulted in the king refusing to allow any members of the profession to sit in Parliament. Henry IV at Coventry in 1404 summoned knights, burgesses, and citizens to a Parliament from which all lawyers were excluded. It sat. But, significantly, that Parliament became known as the *Parliament of Dunces*. Some called it the Lawless and the Unlearned Parliament.[11] There has never been another to which members of the legal profession were not called or elected to sit as members.

Although it is a fact that for many years, more members of the House of Commons and the Senate of Canada have been members of the legal profession than of any other profession or calling, they have generally failed to bring into the legislative forum the expertise and experience in the law that one might reasonably expect of them. Their legal knowledge, skilfully applied, would add luster to our laws. The separation of the powers of government — legislative, judicial, and executive — is an integral part of the American constitution. It is therefore understandable that lawyers who gain political prominence in the United States as Senators and Congressmen should shed their legal feathers on entering the legislative sanctuary and unabashedly behave as politicians and not as men of law. This was Richard Nixon's tragedy at Watergate, that the consummate politician within him, overwhelmed his sense of propriety as a lawyer. But no theory such as the separation of powers is found in the more flexible Canadian constitution. The role of the Member of Parliament, learned in the law, is no less that of advocate and lawyer in the House of Commons than in the ordinary courts across the land. As a Member of Parliament he has no clients, and must have none, save his own conscience. In the private practice of law, it is the client who often produces the great counsel; so in political life, it is his conscience that will create the great public figure.

With some sadness I must observe that even a cursory examination of contemporary legislation does the lawyer *qua* politician small credit. For this, there may be two reasons. First, it is a notorious fact that fewer statutes and regulations are written by lawyers than in times past, and lawyers in Parliament appear unable to stop the practice and seem unwilling to assume personal responsibility for these duties. Economists (those prophets of the gloomy science) and political scientists (that breed of men who are neither politically oriented nor scientifically trained) and educators (the wrecking crew whose "new reading" and "new math" have succeeded in extending illiteracy into places it had never reached before) have taken to writing an increasing number of statutes themselves. These are often couched in vague and amorphous vocabularies that have never been tested or applied by the courts. The meaning of many phrases they use is not settled, and as a consequence they become a source of misunderstanding, suspicion, and dispute. Such laws become wretched quagmires. Their application breeds litigation and is costly to the country and its citizens because of a failure to employ known standards and tested words and well-established procedures. People who would never think of building a motor car or an aircraft "from scratch," without the guidance of older models or the benefit of technicians and engineers and other professionals, think nothing of drawing and passing new laws as casually as they pass water; of condemning precedents because they are "inhibiting," and lawyers because they are conservationists of the old, and courts because they are the repositories of the tried and the tested — and *all* because obviously they are venerable persons, and that is sufficient reason, they say, to ignore or retire them.

The influence of the economist and the accountant (but not the lawyer) is clearly visible in Canada's "tax reform" legislation of the 1970s. These are not lawyers' statutes. They are the acts of state bureaucrats and their accountants and economic claques, and the language is George Orwell's language of *Newspeak*. The *Income Tax Act* is only one example of a statute that has become a nightmare incomprehensible to the citizen, a source of contention and uncertainty in the offices of industry and government, and a burden to the economy so shifty and changeable, so menacing and unrestrained, that it inhibits normal productivity and growth, and infects creative citizens with sloth and decay, and the country itself with national paralysis.

The second reason why the man of law in his role as legislator may perform less satisfactorily than in his office or in the courtroom, may be attributed to the fact that it is one thing to act as counsel to an individual on a specific case; it is a very different matter to appear as the voice of a whole constituency that has elected him to public office. When the man of law essays that task, he becomes, in effect, advocate in his own cause, for, however much he may consult with the constituents, he alone must judge the wisdom of the policy he advocates, and in the end, he alone instructs himself and takes responsibility for what he says and does. He no longer makes "submissions" on behalf of others. He now makes pronouncements and, in effect, gives evidence of fact and opinion by which he is bound.

Since Parliament has come to dominate so much of the nation's life and to consume so large a part of its members' time, the man who decided to dedicate only a part of his life to politics soon finds he has had to make a full-time career of his membership in the House of Commons. Thus, politics becomes his profession. His absence from home removes him ever more distantly from the people whom he is pledged to represent and from the profession that provided his sustenance and guaranteed his independence. Politics having become his new profession and his sessional allowances and expenses his principal, if not his only, source of income, with every passing year it becomes more important that he be elected and reelected. The model undergoes subtle changes as the man of law becomes a man of state.

When he sits as a member of a political body and not as its adviser, the man of law departs his traditional role. His barrister's gown remains folded in his bag; his law reports stand neglected on the shelves of his library gathering dust. His advocacy, once at the command of the most obscure citizen whose small but agonizing problem consumed all of his devotion as though his very life depended upon it, now is diverted to national concerns. To him, the powers of the state come to rank high and the importance of the individual's defenses against them correspondingly diminishes. His principal client becomes his career. It is then that he runs the risk of making self-service his greatest service. Of Sir Richard Stafford Cripps, one of England's greatest counsel-turned-statesmen, Winston Churchill said:

> The trouble is, his chest is a cage in which two squirrels are
> at war, his conscience and his career.[12]

Unquestionably, the well-trained lawyer is better able to draft a statute and to read, understand, and apply it than any other member of Parliament. Were the legal model to prevail over the political, and were the lawyer sitting in the Commons to consider the business coming before the House as he treated the affairs of the client who consulted him in his professional practice, what a metamorphosis would overtake the nation's business! The lawyer-politician's advice would be altruistic; it would be expressed clearly, succinctly, and in practical terms; it would be designed to advance the well-being of that very significant client, the nation. Any politician who misstated or misrepresented the facts would do so at his peril. Lies and exaggerations, bombast and humbug, would give rise to actions for damages brought against him personally by gulled and jaded citizens. Budgetary overspending would be treated as larceny and fraud, and the same principles of responsibility would apply to ministers and their deputies, members of Parliament and public servants, as apply to ordinary citizens. Simply stated, they are encompassed in the cryptic couplet:

> The guy who spends what isn't his'n
> Is sure one day to go to pris'n.

The auditor general's report would no longer be seen as titillating cocktail-hour trivia prompting a mild tongue-clucking response from press gallery and public. The budget, public accounts, and the auditor-general's reports would serve as the meat for a clubhouse indictment against the illegal spenders in the government's permanent service. The unauthorized or the self-aggrandizing spending of public funds would be seen for what it is and condemned as criminal conversion of money or as a breach of trust. Elected representatives, like the publicly employed, are the trustees not only of the funds and property they control, but of the public lands and the whole of the public domain. This includes not only public property of Her Majesty, but lands held in trust for native people. In a sense, it also includes privately-owned lands that comprise the whole of the territories and of the provinces that go to make up our country and which Parliament has a duty to protect against foreign aggression and preserve against secession. These may be neither alienated nor extorted, neglected, purloined, pilfered, or plundered, save at the peril of appropriate criminal prosecution or civil suits, brought by interested citizens, for conversion, breach of trust, negligence, and damages.

The lawyer in Parliament would serve his country well were he to impress upon his person, as an honorable member of the House, the marks and signatures of the man of law — chief among them being the principle of personal responsibility. Assuredly, it may be a risky business, but if risk there be, who, if not the trustees of the public purse and public domain, should bear it? It might deter the pusillanimous from pursuing a political career. More likely, it would serve as a challenge to those who choose to serve a country committed to high principles in public affairs. The heavy responsibility would probably move politicians to limit their careers in office to four or five years — a sufficiently substantial part of one's life to devote to the commonweal, yet, a part sufficiently small to preserve the lawyer's ties with his career in the real world of farms and fisheries and factories, of families and fences and flying boats and fancy clothes and fun times at the fair.

Whether politician or practitioner, the man of law is nature's first ecumenicist. In a world of narrowing loyalties and expanding nationalism, he marches to the beat of many different drummers. He is capable of playing roles without number, and the lines he speaks may be the echoes of the learned and the skilled in other professions and trades and callings, a measure of whose expertise he acquires. He is also a collector: a collector of miscellany, old and new, of facts and forms and fancies, of philosophies and photographs and films. He is a repository of clocks and carpentry and cardiacs; of beds and bees and bigamy and beer; of death and dying, drugs and devils; of diplomats and dissidents and dogs; of gastrology, pathology, biology, cosmology, ethnology, histology, and every ideology.

If he rejects a field of inquiry, he does so at his peril; if he eschews a source of knowledge, he will come to rue it. He is a collector of the extraordinary in all things that are within the province of mankind, cognoscente of what is trite and mean and cruel, a connoisseur of what is goodly, true, and elegant. His interests — which span the seen and unseen, known and unknown, experienced and only half-sensed, real and unreal, perceived and imagined, envisioned and dreamt — are cosmic. He is an eclectic, and the diameter of his circle moves far beyond the earth's circumference.

Better than any, the man of law knows that whatever he learns and remembers, whatever he picks up and carries with him in his head, all become the valuable inventory that goes to make up his capital. This he packs forever — weightless, invisible, yet accessible at a split-second's notice. Exempt from the tax collector, free of the customs officer, secure against the burglar, sequestered against all of the devouring elements save time, that eventually must bring his active days to a close, he knows that these attributes are the only commodities that lose nothing of their worth through inflation and economic chaos, revolution and war. They only grow in value with every vibrant day of his professional life. And though in the end he may lay aside his gown and his bag of books and leave his active practice at the bar, he will never cease to be what always he has strived to become — a Francis Bacon who dared to tell his friend, Lord Burleigh, at the beginning of his writing career: "I have taken all knowledge to be my province."[13]

IV
AMBIVALENCE

Law looks not with eyes but with the mind
And therefore is sage justice painted blind.

SHAKESPEARE, ADAPTED FROM
A MIDSUMMER NIGHT'S DREAM, I, 1, 234-5

If the advocate refuses to defend from what *he
may think* of the charge or the defence, he assumes
the character of the judge; nay, he assumes it
before the hour of judgment; and in proportion to
his rank and reputation, puts the heavy
influence of perhaps a mistaken opinion into the
scales against the accused

THOMAS ERSKINE, *TRIAL OF THOMAS PAINE*
(1792) 22 HOWE'S STATE TRIALS 358, p. 412 ·

He that wrestles with us
strengthens our nerves and sharpens our skill.
Our antagonist is our helper.

EDMUND BURKE,
REFLECTIONS ON THE REVOLUTION IN FRANCE, 1790

"There was a society of men among us," wrote Jonathan Swift, when Gulliver traveled to the land of the Houyhnhnms, "bred up from their youth in the art of proving, by words multiplied for the purpose, that white is black and black is white, according as they are paid."[1] They were, of course, barristers representing their clients in litigation. For Swift, the ambivalence of the lawyer's role was incomprehensible. As a churchman he might well have been reminded that there existed the equally ancient, honorable, and useful ecclesiastical office of devil's advocate.

The adversary system of arriving at a true and just result in a trial at law has often been regarded by those who have never participated in debate to be as archaic as the medieval trial-by-combat of which it is, in fact, the direct descendant. For all its imperfections, no more effective method has been devised to test the soundness of a principle or the truth of an allegation. The process depends upon the ability of men of law to champion the cause of the disputants and to urge, each for his client, the soundness of his position and the justness of his cause.

That lawyers should be willing to support a position in which their sole interest is said to be the fee they earn, has been regarded by some people as betraying flaws of insincerity and cynicism in the character of the man of law. The detractors of the role played by counsel in the adversary system never appear to have considered that the lawyer's great concern is to perform his work honorably and as perfectly and impeccably as his knowledge and skills permit. Whatever his fee, it is the model barrister's professional pride — his vanity, if you will — that moves him to spare neither himself nor his purse in preparing and presenting his client's case. It is a practice that still persists, even in the shadows of the vast contemporary structures that legal aid has erected. The "dock brief" that has traditionally been accepted by counsel without fee when handed to him by a judge when an accused without a lawyer is arraigned in court, becomes as great a challenge and is as seriously served by the model man of law as the brief that brings him a generous return.

The lawyer need make no apology for urging now one side of an issue, now another. Nor need he apologize for the fee he receives for his service. In taking his fee, he frankly declares that his loyalty is to his client's interest and his purpose is to advance it, whatever his personal feelings may be and however slim his client's hope of winning may seem.

The story is told of a young man who consulted his solicitor concerning a serious claim and asked that an action be launched at once. The lawyer listened carefully to the young man's story and dutifully drew the pleadings and began the suit in the Court of Queen's Bench. In due course a defense was filed, examinations for discovery were held, the matter was set down for trial, the witnesses appeared and gave their testimony to which the judge carefully listened, counsel presented argument, and the court took time to consider. Finally, judgment was delivered. The young man's action was dismissed with costs.

Receiving the bad news with good grace, the young man asked his lawyer, "Where do we go from here?" The lawyer told him it was possible to bring an appeal to the Court of Appeal. "But, this," he said, "would be a slow and expensive procedure." He suggested the young man consider his position before undertaking further expense. Without a moment's hesitation, the young man said, "I don't care what it costs. Appeal it!"

The lawyer dutifully prepared the Notice of Appeal and had the lengthy appeal books printed. He drew the factum and all of these books he filed for the consideration of the learned Justices of Appeal. Upon an appointed day, a full year after the trial had ended, counsel appeared with his client before the five judges of the court. They carefully heard the argument of both counsel; they asked appropriate questions and reserved their judgment. They, too, took time to consider. After some six months, judgment was delivered. By the unanimous decision of the five judges, the appeal was dismissed with costs.

In due course, the young man again appeared in his lawyer's office to receive the bad news. After the full impact of the loss was explained to him, he turned to his lawyer and said, "Well, where do we go from here?"

The lawyer explained to him that with two courts holding against him, a reversal would be unlikely in a higher court. "However," he said, "you can appeal to the Supreme Court of Canada. But again, I must warn you that your chances for success are small and your expenses will be large. I suggest you consider such a course carefully before embarking upon further litigation."

"Appeal it!" the young man said without a moment's hesitation.

Again, a Notice of Appeal was prepared and filed, fresh appeal books were printed and a new factum prepared. After two years, the appeal was heard by the Supreme Court. Nine learned judges sat. The appeal occupied two full days and counsel on both sides were closely questioned by the court. At the end of the hearing, the Chief Justice advised counsel that the court would consider the matter and deliver judgment in due course. Months passed. Finally, the written judgment appeared. The appeal was dismissed.

Again, the young man attended at his lawyer's offices; again he was advised of the failure of the appeal; again the lawyer expressed regret that his client had been put to such trouble and expense and that all had been in vain.

"It's true," said the client, "that I have lost in three courts and that a total of fifteen judges have found against me. But that doesn't trouble me because I believe they are wrong and I am right. Tell me, where do we go from here?"

The wise lawyer eyed his client admiringly. "Young man," he said, "are you married; have you a wife?"

"Why yes, I do have a wife; why do you ask?"

"Well," said the lawyer, "I suggest that you go home at once and find your wife. As soon as you can, I suggest that you take her in your arms. And then, waste no time. Procreate! Procreate! Procreate! The legal profession needs people like you!"

It is not usual for an unsuccessful litigant to speak pleasantly of his experience in court. Horatio William Bottomley was an exception. He spent years as a litigant and an accused in the courts of England in the early part of this century. Addressing the Business League of London in 1912, he said, "I'm Bottomley . . . I hold the unique distinction of having gone through every court in the country except one . . . the Divorce Court. . . . Although I'm nominally a bankrupt, I *never* had a better time in my *life*." After all his litigation was over, a friend found him stitching mail bags in prison. He said, "Ah, Bottomley, sewing?" Bottomley replied: "No, reaping."[2]

The man of law is totally committed to his client's cause. But he pursues it in accordance with the practices of his profession and the ethics that it prescribes. And in pressing his client's interests, he is mindful that he is no partner to the businessman whose right to property he is upholding; neither is he an accomplice to the man he defends against a criminal indictment. He is no more the mouthpiece of his client than the member of Parliament is (or at least ought to be) the mere mouthpiece of his constituents. He is a representative;

he is not his client's *man*, and while his skills are for sale, his conscience is not.

The conflict of loyalties apparent in the lawyer's role as representative of a client's cause, even though it may have originated in crime, and his role as a member of a society that condemns such conduct, is more apparent than real. Consider the lawyer who acts for an individual charged with theft. Society will uphold the inviolability of private property. In defending a person who has broken the rules of private property, the lawyer does not attack society for he does not condone theft or any other willful breach of the law. On the contrary, if he does his job, he will insist that the law be applied according to its true intent and purpose. But he will also insist that all of the principles of the common law and statute law designed to facilitate the proof of the offense charged, all devised to assure a fair trial for his client, be applied evenly and justly. A lawyer does not connive at law-breaking. On the contrary, his professional commitment requires that he insist that the law be obeyed, recognizing that the sword of justice has two cutting edges, one to carry out the work of society as a whole, the other to preserve the rights of an accused. Defense counsel will, therefore, be indefatigable in his insistence that his client be accorded the fullest protection of the rule that presumes him innocent however heinous the offense alleged against him. He will be watchful that no improper or irrelevant or prejudicial evidence (hearsay or gossip or rumor) will be presented at trial. He will ensure that every essential ingredient of the offense charged be proved beyond reasonable doubt. And in the end, he will warn both judge and jury that if the prosecutor has failed to produce and firmly fasten every link of a chain that firmly, and beyond all reasonable doubt, binds and locks the accused to the crime with which he is charged, the prisoner must go free. If, in the mind of a single member of the jury there remains any reasonable doubt as to the existence of a single fact required to be proved by the prosecution to fasten guilt on the accused, that doubt must be resolved in favor of his client. If there be any doubt in the mind of the judge concerning the meaning or effect of any point of law raised by the defense, that doubt must likewise be resolved in favor of the accused. In these areas defense counsel can have no conflict of duty or interest or conscience.

It is sometimes forgotten that in vigorously defending an accused against even the most heinous and revolting criminal charge, counsel is not merely protecting the interests of his client. He is also protecting the most precious values of society. How else may anyone be assured that he will not be arrested on the street at the caprice of the police? Held incommunicado for days or weeks? Charged at the whim of the people's protectorate? Tortured to confess? Tried in a barracksroom at the midnight hour? Carried off to prison or exile in stealth, or shot at dawn in a public square?

Roy McMurtry, Q.C., Attorney-General for Ontario has reminded us that the "use of the power of the state against an isolated individual can only be justified if established legal procedures are strictly adhered to. Only the unquestionable availability of able defense counsel provides an independent guarantee to society that the state's power is being wielded fairly and accurately. It is that guarantee which promotes public support for the rule of law."[3]

Charles Phillips, an English barrister, in 1840, was defending one Courvoisier, a Swiss valet, charged with murdering his employer, Lord William Russell. Phillips had been instructed by the accused who professed his innocence.[4]

Chief Justice Tindal presided at the trial, and with him, as junior judge, not trying the case, sat Baron Parke. On the second day of the trial, the accused, standing in the prisoner's dock, beckoned to his counsel. "I called you here to tell you that in fact, I did kill Lord Russell. Now go on with the trial and see how well you can defend me!"

Shaken by this new intelligence, Phillips asked for an adjournment to consider his position. Could he continue to defend a person under these circumstances? He had accepted the brief on the assurance given him that his client was not guilty as charged. Now that he had learned otherwise, where did his duty to his client lie? Where lay his duty to the court? How could he square the defense given the accused with his own conscience? Should he continue with the trial? Should he withdraw now that he knew the truth? If he withdrew, should he give reasons to the court for withdrawing? And if he gave reasons, would he not be condemning his client and breaching, as well, the confidentiality of their relationship? Phillips was faced with a very real dilemma. He and his colleague decided that they should consult with Baron Parke and hear his view as to the duty of counsel under such circumstances. They attended upon Baron Parke privately in his chambers. After hearing what they had to say, Baron Parke asked whether Courvoisier still wished Phillips to represent him. When he was informed that Courvoisier insisted

63

that he do so, the judge advised Phillips that he was duty-bound to continue the trial and see it through to an end.

His duty was to defend his client just as vigorously as he had done before receiving the unusual and disturbing information. As counsel, he had the right, indeed the duty, to use all fair arguments arising out of the evidence that might assist his client in securing an acquittal. Thus, his duty still was to test the credibility of every witness, and thereafter, to point to the errors, deficiencies, and conflicts that emerged from their testimony in addressing the jury. He had the right and the duty to ask that his client be acquitted on the evidence adduced on oath in court. Nothing else was relevant. The only restraint that the strange information placed upon him as counsel, was that he must refrain from casting guilt upon any other person. To do so would be improperly and unjustly to implicate the innocent in a crime in which counsel now knew, only his client had played a part.

Phillips honorably discharged his obligations to his client. In the end, the accused was convicted. But he could never complain of the defense he received. Neither could he claim that he was denied the judgment of the court which the law guarantees.

Mark M. Orkin, Q.C., the brilliant expositor of legal ethics and the most engaging satirist of Canadianese, has observed "no advocate has the right, still less [the] duty to set himself up as judge and determine whether [his client] is guilty or not guilty. To do so would be to usurp the function of both judge and jury, without even hearing all of the evidence."[5]

Lord Bramwell spoke in like terms of counsel's duty and his client's rights in clear, unequivocal terms:

A man's rights are to be determined by the court, not by his advocate or counsel. It is for want of remembering this that foolish people object to lawyers that they will advocate a case against their own opinions. A client is entitled to say to his counsel, *I want your advocacy, not your judgment: I prefer that of the court.*[6]

The young lawyer encountering this dilemma can find guidance in the words of old Samuel Johnson who was asked by Boswell whether, as a moralist, he did not think the practice of law hurt "the nice feeling of honesty" that everyone is expected to experience. To this, the great lexicographer said: "Why no, sir, if you act properly, you are not to deceive your client with false representations of your opinion: you are not to tell lies to a judge."[7]

Boswell persisted and asked Johnson what he thought of supporting "a cause which you know to be bad". Johnson replied:

Sir, you do not know it to be good or bad until the judge determines it. I have said that you are to state facts fairly; so that your thinking, or what you call knowing, a cause to be bad, must be from reasoning, must be from supposing your argument is to be weak and inconclusive. But Sir, that is not enough. An argument which does not convince yourself may convince the judge to whom you urge it: and if it does convince him, why, then, Sir, you are wrong, and he is right. It is his business to judge; and you are not to be confident in your own opinion that a cause is bad, but to say all you can for your client, and then hear the judge's opinion.

Continuing to press him, Boswell finally asked his mentor:

Does not effecting a warmth when you have no warmth, and appearing to be clearly of one opinion when you are in reality of another opinion, does not such dissimulation impair one's honesty? Is there not some danger that a lawyer may put on the same mask in common life, in the intercourse with his friends?

To this, Johnson, said:

Why no, Sir. Everybody knows you are paid for affecting warmth to your client; and it is therefore properly no dissimulation; the moment you come from the bar you resume your usual behaviour. Sir, a man will no more carry the artifice of the bar into the common intercourse of society than the man who is paid for tumbling upon his hands will continue to tumble upon his hands when he should walk on his feet.

This last of Johnson's comparisons has been criticized by some who claim that there ought to be no "artifice of the bar" and that a lawyer should be as sincere in all he says to the court as he is in his personal conversations with his friends.

But Johnson was using the term, not as a clever trick or stratagem, but rather in the sense that the barrister is indeed an artificer. He is one who is as skilled and inventive in his field as any able craftsman, but his skills and conventions are reserved for the courtroom just as the arts of the surgeon are applied in the operating theatre. One can no more criticize the lawyer for not carrying his craft of advocacy into the drawing room than one would think of carping against the surgeon for not cutting up his friends at his club.

Finally, Sir William Forbes said he thought an honest lawyer should never undertake a cause he was satisfied was not a just one.

Dr. Johnson said:

Sir, a lawyer has no business with the justice or injustice of the cause which he undertakes, unless his client asks his opinion and then he is bound to give it honestly. The justice or injustice of the cause is to be decided by the judge. Consider, Sir, what is the purpose of courts of justice? It is, that every man may have his cause fairly tried by men appointed to try causes. A lawyer is not to tell what he knows to be a lie: he is not to produce what he knows to be a false deed; but he is not to usurp the province of the jury and of the judge, and determine what shall be the effect of evidence — what shall be the result of legal argument. As it rarely happens that a man is fit to plead his own cause, lawyers are a class of the community, who, by study and experience, have acquired the art and power of arranging evidence, and of applying to the points at issue what the law has settled. A lawyer is to do for his client all that his client might fairly do for himself, if he could. If, by superiority of attention, of knowledge, of skill, and a better method of communication, he has the advantage of his adversary it is an advantage to which he is entitled. There must always be some advantage, on one side or other; and it is better that advantage should be had by talents than by chance. If lawyers were to undertake no causes till they were sure they were just, a man might be precluded altogether from a trial of his claim, though, were it judicially examined, it might be found a very just claim."[8]

Shakespeare, in his greatness of heart recognized that ambivalence, of necessity, must be a part of every advocate's career. The strife of the courtroom, where contention is the very life blood of the judicial process, must not be so bitter as to render reconciliation impossible. Conflict must at least give way to camaraderie and companionship among colleagues. All who are true counsel are dedicated to learning and to genuine love for the law, and so when the battle is ended and the litigants go home, like classic warriors who recognize and genuinely admire the strengths and capabilities of their adversaries, the men of law bind each other's wounds, recount their experiences, and learn from the errors of the day: their own, their colleagues', and the judges'. Then

> [They] do as adversaries do in law,
> Strive mightily, but eat and drink as friends.[9]

It has been said, deprecatingly, that lawyers opposing each other at trial are like the two parts of a pair of shears: they cut what comes between them but not each other. If shears are what the situation requires to cut an irksome marriage knot or to put an end to any other kind of intolerable partnership, how can their purpose be better served than by cutting what needs to be severed and by preserving the tools that will be needed on some other day?

In my salad days of practice, like most young lawyers I sought above everything else, the esteem of my clients. Clients are of first-ranking importance to the beginner. They are the straw without which bricks cannot begin to be built. Nothing can then be more important than to attract a client and preserve him as your own. But time passes, and battles fought for a client who "struts and frets his hour upon the stage and then is heard no more," ultimately end. Each client will depart in victory or defeat, and oftentimes with a mixture of success and failure. At law, the winner does not necessarily take all.

In due course, counsel who are adversaries leave the arena too. They go "the way to dusty death." Only a few of the hardy old gladiators I have faced now remain, and it is at such times that I find myself more concerned to have earned and held the esteem of my colleagues than the praise and purse of my clients. A client brings bread to the lawyer's table and without it none of us could survive, but a lawyer's colleagues put spirit into his heart, without which no man of law can live and thrive.

Mr. Justice Crampton, in 1844, laid down the forensic duty of the advocate in words that bear repeating because they have never been excelled:

> This Court in which we sit is a temple of justice; and the Advocate at the Bar, as well as the Judge upon the Bench, are equally ministers in that temple.

> The object of all equally should be the attainment of justice; now justice is only to be reached through the ascertainment of the truth, and the instrument which our law presents to us for the ascertainment of the truth or falsehood of a criminous charge is the trial by Jury; the trial is the process by which we endeavour to find out the truth.

> Slow and laborious, and perplexed and doubtful in its issue, that pursuit often proves; but we are all — Judges, Jurors, Advocates and Attorneys — together concerned in this search for truth: the pursuit is a noble one, and those are honoured who are the instruments engaged in it.

> The infirmity of human nature, and the strength of human passion, may lead us to take false views, and sometimes to embarrass and retard rather than to assist in attaining the great object; the temperament, the imagination and the feelings may all mislead us in the chase — but let us never forget our high vocation as ministers of justice and inter-preters of the law; let us never forget that the advancement of justice and the ascertainment of truth are higher objects and nobler results than any which in this place we can propose to ourselves.

> Let us never forget the Christian maxim, "That we should not do evil that good may come of it".

> I would say to the Advocate upon this subject — let your zeal be as warm as your heart's blood, but let it be tempered with discretion and with self-respect; let your independence be firm, uncompromising, but let it be chastened by personal humility; let your love of liberty amount to a passion, but let it not appear to be a cloak for maliciousness.

The Judge then turned to the suggested doctrine that counsel was the mere mouthpiece of his client, and said 'Such, I do conceive, is not the office of an Advocate. His office is a higher one. To consider him in that light is to degrade him. I would say of him as I would say of a member of the House of Commons — he is a representative, but not a delegate. He gives to his client the benefit of his learning, his talents and his judgment; but all through he never forgets what he owes to himself and to others.

He will not knowingly misstate the law — he will not wilfully misstate the facts, though it be to gain the cause for his client.

He will ever bear in mind that if he be the Advocate of an individual, and retained and remunerated (often inadequately) for his valuable services, yet he has a prior and perpetual retainer on behalf of truth and justice; and there is no Crown or other license which in any case, or for any party or purpose, can discharge him from that primary and paramount retainer.[10]

What is truly just and right at any specific time and in any specific place for any client or for any case, can never be expressed by a general principle. Such a judgment requires the utmost exactitude and certainty. No one can put his finger on the ends of justice and say, "It is this" or "It is there." Justice is like the Kingdom of God. It is not outside us or a thing apart. It is neither an act nor a fact. Rather, it exists within us as a great, unsatisfied yearning which the man of law aspires to understand and hopes to harmonize with the actions and motives of his client, with the brief he holds, and with the law as it has existed and as it grows from generation to generation.

V

EXPEDITION

Lawyers know life practically. A bookish
man should always have them to converse with;
they have what he wants.

BOSWELL, *LIFE OF JOHNSON*, 1778

Society cannot exist without law
and order, and cannot advance except through
vigorous innovators.

BERTRAND RUSSELL

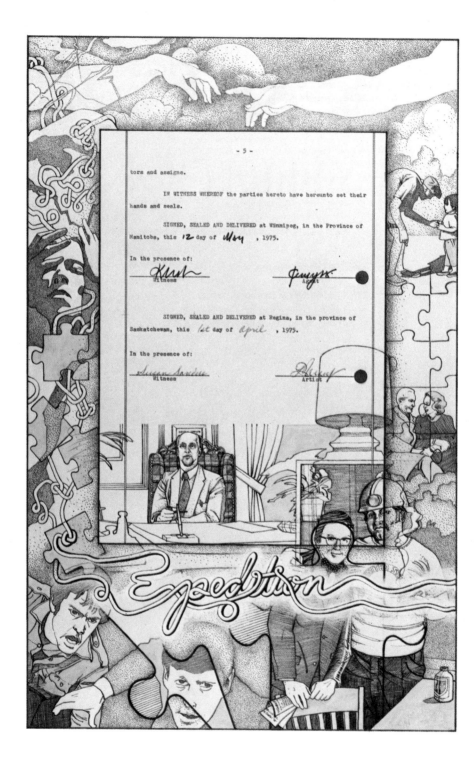

- 5 -

tors and assigns.

    IN WITNESS WHEREOF the parties hereto have hereunto set their
hands and seals.

    SIGNED, SEALED AND DELIVERED at Winnipeg, in the Province of
Manitoba, this 12 day of May , 1975.

In the presence of:

_____   _____
    Witness   Agent

    SIGNED, SEALED AND DELIVERED at Regina, in the province of
Saskatchewan, this 1st day of April , 1975.

In the presence of:

_____   _____
    Witness   Artist

Expedition

He is the very miracle of a lawyer, one that persuades men to peace, and compounds quarrels among his neighbours without going to law."[1] So John Webster expressed astonishment over the practice of a seventeenth-century lawyer who appeared strangely out of step with the legal stereotype of his time. It is not surprising that the man of law, working as peacemaker, should be misunderstood in his community, although that is one of the first facets of his role as expediter. Only those who have consulted him privately, perhaps surreptitiously, can know the intimate facts that are disclosed to the lawyer: only those who were privy to the problem the lawyer considered and solved may ever understand the part he played in quieting the angry, moving the uncompromising, persuading the unreasonable, settling the insoluble, and, withal, avoiding public expense and scandal. The lawyer's clients generally keep his advice to themselves, as it is the better part of wisdom and their perfectly natural right to do.

As for the man of law, sealed lips have always been as much his special hallmark as the physician's and the priest's. Entrusted as he must be with the secrets of his clients' personal affairs, he may never disclose to the world the quiet settlement of a family squabble or the resolution of a personal scandal or the compromise of an outrageous demand. Neither, of course, may he disclose facts communicated to him in confidence by a client who consults him concerning a crime with which he is charged. The privilege of confidentiality is the client's. The principle that the public may repose full confidence in its legal advisers is so important to the administration of justice that the law guarantees that nothing a client tells his lawyer may be disclosed to anyone by the lawyer, and no court may compel the lawyer to give evidence on the subject. The purpose of this rule is to protect the client, not the lawyer. If he chooses, the client may release the lawyer of his obligation to remain silent. The only exception to this strict rule arises where the lawyer has become *particeps criminis* — an accomplice in a crime of the person he has advised.

A recurring nightmare to the lawyer is a wild-eyed stranger who rushes into his private office when he is alone with his thoughts. The stranger says, "I am in deep trouble and I need your services. I just killed a man. I pumped three bullets into him. Here is the gun!"

With that, he throws on the lawyer's desk a .38 revolver that still has the smell of burnt powder upon it.

What is the lawyer's duty in such circumstances? Should he call the police and turn the man in? This would violate the very fundamental principle that communications between a solicitor and his client are privileged. The privilege is that of the client and to pass on to the police what the lawyer has heard, would be an obvious breach of the client's right to retain and have confidence in the lawyer of his choice.

Should he return the gun to the client and tell him to take it away and destroy it or hide it? This would be improper since it would counsel the destruction of evidence that would unquestionably be relevant at trial.

Should he take the gun from the client, place it in his desk or in his filing cabinet and say nothing about it? Would that render the lawyer an accomplice after the fact?

Should he tell the intruder whose actions have virtually rendered him a captive-counsel on his behalf, that he ought to consult another lawyer and be more discreet about displaying his weapon? It might well be the better part of wisdom. If that advice were followed, would the lawyer so unwittingly made a possible witness, be subject to subpoena at the trial of the accused?

These are some questions to which no final answers exist so far as I know. David Humphrey, a distinguished counsel in Ontario, was bedevilled by a similar problem that was settled in a manner that was accepted by everyone, but which truly satisfied no one. It is one of many illustrations of the hard fact that every problem does not necessarily have a solution. The man of law learns that to every question he puts, there does not necessarily exist an answer.

Much of the lawyer's work as expediter is not widely publicized. To be sure, the actual law courts are very public places, and a lawyer who performs outstandingly may gain adulation for his brilliance or his wit. But for every burning star in the legal firmament there are a thousand steadily glowing candles that illuminate the treacherous places and provide light and safety where there would otherwise be uncertainty, fear, and peril. This modest illumination of the unknown, which men of law continue to provide year after year in their role as counsellors to all who approach them, offers guidance and inspires confidence in those who carry on the tasks of the nation's business. It was men of law who carved the cuneiform and hieroglyphics of the Persians and Egyptians, perpetuating the ownership and uses of property five thousand years ago and more. It was men of law who inscribed the words of indentures on parchments that safely passed the titles to lands of ancient families from generation to generation in comity and peace. It was they who drew up the complex contracts among traders and business folk and bankers and brokers; they who devised rules and refined and so applied them that peace in the marketplace was assured and prosperity in commerce became a reality.

The warranty of continuity is the hallmark of the expeditious man of law; good faith and integrity are his credentials. To artists and writers he can offer the protection that the copyright laws allow; to inventors, the benefits of profit from their innovations; to investors, the confidence that mortgages and debentures and bonds — all legal innovations — will inspire for the promotion of enterprise and the employment of human brains and human brawn. Without the written phrases of the law, civil life would be unknown and civilization itself would have yet to be born.

The words and phrases of the law that the untutored condemn as archaic, serve as the links that bind the past to the present and provide a continuity in mankind's affairs. To the man of law falls the obligation of preserving these historic bonds with our past, for they are a record of human experience and they serve as familiar guides to every succeeding generation that recognizes and heeds them. Mindful of the past, the perceptive man of law may bring to those who consult him an awareness of the precedents (which, in common parlance, are simply the "track record" that others have made) and a wariness of novelty (which is nothing more than the law of probabilities in the rolling of dice).

These are qualities of an indeterminable dimension that the man of law invokes into the equation of the affairs of every active, thinking person in society. The word for this eclectic element in the lawyer's arsenal is "expedition." Although it is an esoteric quality, difficult to describe, its application is a homey one, down to earth, and embedded in grass roots.

An old definition of a lawyer's function, often quoted by Lord Green, still rings true today. His duty is "to protect his clients from being persuaded by persons whom they don't know to enter into contracts they don't understand to purchase goods they don't need with money they haven't got."[2]

When Geoffrey Chaucer made of the Man of Lawe a pilgrim on his way to Canterbury, he had in mind the lawyer's role not only as counsel but as expediter, "discreet . . . of great reverence [and] wordes wise." No man was so busy, said Chaucer. But there was annoyance with the law's delays even in the England of the fourteenth century, and hence Chaucer added testily that the lawyer always "semed bisier than he was." For much more than five hundred years the lawyer has been a busy man, and very much a man of business — not of his own so much as of his clients'. As expediter, the man of law is still a man of action. He conducts, negotiates, and transacts the business of strangers and is the representative and agent, deputy and surrogate, of those who trust him with their silver, their secrets, and their sins. The day when the father confessor was the central figure of the village may have passed, the heyday of the Freudian psychotherapist may be over, but the search for a solicitor who is able to provide kindly counsel and commonsense advice has in no way abated. Laws have grown awesome and bureaucrats burdensome. The man who can explain the inscrutable and expedite the ineffable becomes a jewel of rare worth to his community. His neighbors seek him out. Whether over the back fence or by telephone, early in the day, and often in the middle of the night when small worries grow fearsome, he is called to answer a gnawing question on the law or even to settle a dispute. Of Sir Mathew Hale, the great English judge of the seventeenth century, it was said that when he was a practitioner, differences were often referred to him which he settled; but he would accept no reward for his pains, though offered by both parties together, after the agreement was made. He said in those cases, he was made a judge, and a judge ought to take no money. If they told him he had lost much of his own time in considering their business, and so ought to be paid for it, his answer was, "Can I spend my time better than to make people friends? Must I have no time allowed me to do good in?"[3]

As legislator, the lawyer may write the words designed to clothe the human will (though often, in retrospect, they seem an ill-fitted suit). As judge, the lawyer is the tailor measuring and adjusting an imperfect garment to fit the human frame, of which no two are alike. As lawyer, he moves in the boisterous bazaars where tailors, fitters, basters, cutters, button-hole makers, pattern-designers, sewers, pressers, and a score of others all work and hang and sell and trade and bargain and are the producers of the nation's wealth. It is the man of law who expedites the business of that whole pantechnicon and makes of it the freest and the safest place for people to make their choice, pay their pounds and pence, buy their baggage, sell their stock, say their say, and live their lives, untidy though they all may seem, in the chaos of that great marketplace. And all is preserved from utter anarchy by nature's law of supply and demand and the genius of the ancient law merchant, the common law, and a relatively few spare but sensible statutes.

In these roles, the man of law eschews the character of theorist. He is no idle spectator mourning the passing of good manners among men. Legislation has so often changed and even abolished whole heirarchies of customs which were once comfortable, that the lawyer has learned to accommodate his clients and himself, a hundred times over, to the new signs and symbols of the times.

Changes in the structure of the courts have become commonplace. The traditional Court of Chancery, which was custodian of the "King's Conscience" and applied reason and fairness to mitigate against the rigors of the common law, was merged into the superior courts that have administered both law and equity for more than a hundred years. Special new family courts are assuming authority over all disputes that touch the lives of wives and husbands, their children, and lovers. How any judge will retain a measure of sanity and sense of balance presiding over a court to which will be served up a diet exclusively drawn from domestic strife, is difficult to imagine! The many-faceted mind, neither insular nor specialized, can best adjudicate upon human affairs: witness the judgment of Solomon and the child he directed to be cut in two! The trend condemned so vigorously in Lord Hewart's *New Despotism* more than half a century ago, continues to disarm judges, dismay lawyers, and disappoint litigants. Administrative tribunals, many of them the illegitimate progeny of bureaucratic burglars, coupling with political prostitutes, now masquerade as the sole solicitous champions of the meek and the poor. Currently, they are claiming the right to inherit the earth. (If they have their way, the estate will hardly be worth litigating!) But the man of law adapts himself to their ways as best he can, that he may expedite his clients' business. The passage through these judicial and administrative mazes may not be speedy, easy, or inexpensive. While accommodating the tribunal, the lawyer still applies his knowledge of the law and his sense of fairness to its procedures. Notwithstanding the resistance he generally encounters, he can and does succeed in influencing administrative bodies to reflect the principles of natural justice in their procedures and to demonstrate a concern, not for the state alone, but for the individual, in their decisions. And when he fails to achieve this end, he may move his arsenal and deploy his troops in another forum and seek the redress to which his client may be entitled in the superior courts. Happily, they continue to exercise a benign supervisory control over most administrative tribunals.

The philosophy of the law is present to the expediter's mind, but not as the *summum bonum* of his calling. The lawyer as expediter naturally examines each section of a statute carefully for its capacity to serve his client. He will use each phrase of every enactment as an instrument to advance the objectives of his client and do for him what, for lack of skill, knowledge, or experience, he cannot do for himself.

To the lawyer as expediter, the law is the greatest of all public utilities. From it he draws light and power to move men and mechanics, corporations and governments, to serve useful and desirable ends. Energy is the stuff and substance of which his secret formula consists. Not the energy that emerges from the bowels of the earth, but the energy that is generated from an active human brain in control of a healthy human body. That is the source of all power. No one need fear the depletion of the world's resources of oil, gas, or coal who himself is possessed of that energy, for in good time man's genius will continue to discover new sources of power and his ingenuity will harness it to useful ends. There can be no real energy crisis so long as the individual is not denied his strength nor drained of the incentive to use it. So long as he is not dragooned in his search for knowledge or diverted from his curiosity to explore "the untravell'd world whose margin fades forever and forever," our nights will not be darkened nor our hearths grow cold.[4]

As expediter, the task of the man of law is as practical and pedestrian as the physician's and many of the qualities that go to create the effective healer are also capable of producing the successful lawyer. Each adopts a pragmatic approach. Seldom does a client come to his solicitor asking his views upon theoretical or esoteric questions. The lawyer is expected to consider a slice of the real world, and he is prepared to talk about the world as it really is.

What the public sees in the courtrooms of our country is but the tip of the human iceberg. The beastly bulk of conflict, dissent, frustration, and hate that are the solicitor's daily fare seldom are revealed to the public gaze. The nine-tenths of the ominous, amorphous iceberg that is submerged must be discovered by the lawyer if he is to do his work, and it must be probed, chipped at, sampled, and ultimately exposed, analyzed, understood, and *used*. This is the stuff out of which the role of the man of law as arbitrator, mediator, compromiser, and expediter is made.

One of his most common, yet difficult, tasks is to achieve settlements out of court between a client and his adversary, a process that lacks glamour but most often produces the deepest satisfaction. The antagonisms of husbands and wives, the complaints of buyers and sellers, the measures of architects and owners, the interests of borrowers and lenders, the demands of insurers and claimants, the conflicts among children of the dead, the mystery of teachers and students, the envies of professionals, and the xenophobia of cheek-to-jowl neighbors whose fields share a common fence or whose lands share a common planet: all of these lie within the province of the man of law to mediate, arbitrate, and, with a little luck, to settle.

The law expanded the world into a neighborhood long before Marshall McLuhan ever wrote of the global village. The negligent manufacturer of a drug in west Berlin learns that a pregnant woman in Johannesburg, unknown to him, takes thalidomide as a sedative on *bona fide* advice and in good faith. As a result, her child is born with abnormally shortened limbs. The manufacturer suddenly learns that he has acquired a new neighbor — unborn at the time the drug was taken — who suddenly looms out of the void as a formidable plaintiff, and the law tells him that he owes a duty to that child.

Where such circumstances generate a sense of injustice or the need for help, it is to the man of law that the threatened instinctively turn. They may seek redress or they may demand retribution. It is a wise solicitor who distinguishes between the two, and who succeeds in converting a vengeful hunt for reprisals into a positive quest for restitution and accord.

It has been my experience that self-interest is the astringent that most effectively restrains a client from an excess of zeal. Often I have been told: "Sue the bastard! No holds barred! I want to teach him a lesson once and for all! It's a matter of principle with me and I care not what it costs!"

To me those familiar words of bravado turn on a dozen flashing red lights all signalling danger. I respect the man who, in forthright terms, claims money or advantage and insists that these are justly due him. He enlists my aid to achieve that end. Self-interest is a normal instinct, and if fairly pursued, it produces healthy, honest, self-reliant people and, generally, a relatively simple and a just result. But I am wary of the man who claims that his purpose in pursuing another is to teach him a lesson in principle. It is then that I grow uneasy. Instinctively, I feel that such a man's real motive is not to instruct but to injure. It ill-becomes the lawyer's role to do an injury to the adversary of his client, to humble or degrade him, in order to gratify a client's sense of outrage or to serve as his instrument for retribution. There are occasions when counsel may feel he must reject such a course of action. To buttress my view, I have sometimes told a client that to be soft may be better than to be hard, especially if he is elderly or suffers from a heart condition. For those who are yielding last longer than those who are rigid and unbending. That is why our gums remain with us long after we have lost our teeth.

Nevertheless, the advice that the solicitor can give his client is only as good as the facts that he is able to assemble concerning his client's problem. Its quality and worth depend upon the disclosure of all of the minutiae, of every detail concerning the affair in hand. I have found that usually there exist three sets of facts — the client's, his adversary's, and God's. It is in the nature of the human condition that each of us observes the world through his own senses. We see what we expect to see; we hear what we want to hear. I had one client who insisted that he knew precisely what the court must do in his case. "It is," he said, "what God would have done if he only had all of the facts."

Given the facts, the lawyer's capacity to counsel his client wisely depends upon many factors, not the least of which is the limited reservoir of his own experience. Hence the old French adage — "Choose a young doctor but an old lawyer." It is a sound principle, provided old lawyers keep abreast of new law and retain their vigor.

It is as important to the man of law that his body be as fit as his mind. The Romans understood this perfectly: *"mens sana in corpore sana,"* they said. The lawyer who neglects his personal health neglects the affairs of his client. If he be weary and listless when he meets his client, his advice is hardly likely to be wise or helpful. Regular exercise and rest are as necessary to his effective performance as the diligent study of his brief and his books. Frequent, short vacations refresh the mind, and though they may cause anxiety to the client who likes to feel his counsel is at his elbow or at least at the end of the telephone line (his affairs are always urgent) it is not inappropriate for a lawyer to remind him that his retainer is of the whole man, and that a lawyer's body and brain, like the parts of a contract, are generally not severable.

A lawyer must be able to work at full capacity, for, to expedite the favorable resolution of a dispute, he must acquire a knowledge concerning the case that is no less thorough than his client's. In a matter of a few hours or a few days, he must compress all of the years of his client's relevant experience and assimilate it as his own.

When the wheels of the law do not turn quickly (and they seldom can) a client may complain. Not all are able to do so as gracefully as the plaintiff who wrote this good-natured soliloquy to his counsel:

> While my legal affairs go unsolved
> And I wither and die on the vine,
> Can it be that my lawyer's involved
> With cases still older than mine?

As expediter, the man of law is forever a man of affairs. His consultations are more often upon non-legal matters than upon the law itself. The young lawyer who, when approached by a client upon how to go about asking his boss for a raise, impatiently tells him, "That's no affair of mine — go see a psychologist!" betrays more ignorance than his client. The question may not fall within any well-defined subject of the law, but the obvious answer is to be found in a lawyer's ordinary common sense and good manners — two commodities of which there appears to be a dwindling supply. He who holds himself out as counsellor without common sense or manners is as likely to succeed in his profession as a color-blind painter or a vertiginous window washer.

There is an ancient Persian proverb that Robert Kohaly, a wise Saskatchewan lawyer, long recognized and often applied: "A pound of learning requires ten pounds of common sense to apply it." And Malcom McIntyre, one of my early law teachers told his class: "If you haven't grace, the Lord can give it to you. If you haven't learning, I'll help you get it. But if you haven't common sense, neither I nor the good Lord can give it to you."

What is the law if not a compendium of the good manners of mankind? What are the rules of the road by which all motorists are bound if not simply a statement of etiquette that any lady or gentleman using the highway can be expected to accord to others who must also occupy and use the same space? Such rules ought not to be regarded as a means of promoting one's own survival (though that is a fairly good reason to obey them)! Compliance simply demonstrates that each of us has been sufficiently civilized and educated to act in a mannerly fashion because we are men and not beasts.

Similarly, why should a contract be enforced? Simply because it is an ill-bred man who gives his word and then retracts it. Why should the law require that if you damage my property wilfully or recklessly you must restore it to me? Simply because it is boorish and a bullish thing to wreck a china shop. Why should shoplifters be punished for stealing? Some claim it is the shopkeepers, the corporate demons who are to blame for thieving because their wares are so attractively displayed, no one can resist pocketing them. Consequently, *they* and not the thieves should be punished. But the simple fact is that stealing is for slobs. It is ill-mannered; and bad manners make poor morals. So long as law continues to be rooted in morality, there is a good likelihood that when your manners are bad you are offending your neighbor, and when you hurt your neighbor you are probably breaking a fairly simple and a very old law.

Were jailers to instruct prisoners in good manners and common etiquette, the recidivist would cease to return to the scene of his crimes or the place of his punishment. But then, if parents taught, and children learned good manners, what need would there be for prisons?

"Manners," said Edmund Burke, "are of more importance than laws. Upon them, in great measure, the laws depend. The law can touch us here and there, now and then. Manners are what vex or soothe, corrupt or purify, exalt or debase, barbarize or re- fine . . . They give the whole form and colour to our lives. According to their quality, they aid morals, they support them, or they totally destroy them."

Thus, the man of law can be expeditious when he remembers that, just as manners maketh a man, so law was created for man, not man for the law, and that to use the law to ease a man's burdens and raise his stature is to fulfill the law. It is a principle that is understood by almost everyone—except tyrants—and least of all by the pettiest.

In his role as expediter the man of law seeks to accomplish promptly what his client alone has probably sought to do for weeks or months or even years without success. The lawyer is impatient of impediments that clog a speedy resolution of a soluble problem. He is intolerant of unnecessary procrastination — that conspicuous curse of incompetence. His function as expediter often brings him in confrontation with officials who may consider it their duty to apply some cryptic concept of public policy designed to "do good" to all mankind rather than do justice to the individuals who seek a hearing and claim a remedy in law.

The utility and disutility boards; the natural and unnatural resource agencies; the transport commissions railed and derailed, airborne and grounded, mobile and immobile; the marketing boards, long, hard, and thick — those experts trained in the legerdemain of converting natural productivity into bureaucratized problemization — the labor boards and the lazy boards, the workers' boards and the welchers' boards; the taxers and spenders, the graspers and gifters; the agencies of culture, non-culture, sub-culture, anti-culture, and outright slobbery; all confer power and status and an overflowing cornucopia of somnambulent security upon the newborn barons of bumbledom.

Many people have come to believe that government despotism is the creature of the law and that its control lies within the power of lawyers. The reasoning is sound, but it is the truth and tragedy of our time that many public agencies are no longer required to conform to the law and would gladly hang all lawyers if a regulation could be passed quietly enough to authorize it. Statutes creating some agencies, such as workmen's compensation boards, place them beyond the law. Such boards *are* the law. Their members may exercise a discretion without regard to principle, precedent, or precept. Their findings of fact are not subject to appeal. Privative clauses sanctify their jurisdiction, the exercise of which may not be reviewed by the courts. Like every despotism, the despot's justification is the overriding claim of the "national interest" (and historically, a declaration of "public interest" is usually sufficient to discourage and silence all but the most intrepid).

The unique and certainly the most effective force capable of challenging the bureaucratic despotisms of the state lies within the small, unprepossessing body of the man of law who carries his client's papers home with him at night and in the quiet of his library considers how he may pull the teeth of the predators, preserve the

83

freedom of people who have the strength to speak out and the will to make themselves heard, and so prepares reasons that he will present in the morning to a court of law, showing why the zeal of governments must be blunted, and how that arch-demon of despots may be controlled.

There are some who believe that in dealing with the bureaucracy, fast footwork rather than forensic faculty will serve the lawyer best; that in meeting with government representatives the lawyer can be an instrument for good only if he abandons his role as man of law. "After all," they say, "in the jungle there is no law." Oliver Cromwell, the great grandfather of British bureaucracy, would and, indeed, did agree, coining the classical cretinism that "necessity knoweth no law." John Milton confronted him and the censors of his time. Taking aim at the bureaucrat's long grasp for power, he scorched Cromwell:

> So spake the Fiend, and with necessity
> The tyrant's plea, excus'd his devilish needs.[5]

Encountering the tyranny of big government presents problems that are no different from the hazards encountered by the lawyer in dealing with others, save that it is patent that no debtor is more unscrupulous than the government, no creditor more cruel, no plaintiff more ruthless, and no defendant more evasive. It has been said with some justification that the commandment "Thou shalt not steal" does not apply to Parliament. And that when Parliament sits, no man's life or property is safe.

By endowing the administrative agencies of the state with power to ignore the principles of the law and to make their own rules and endow ministers with power to change statutes, Parliament and the legislatures have fostered among public servants a sense of conscious lawlessness. They have distorted judgment. They have spawned in those, whose bounden duty it is to serve the law, the Neitzchean myth that there is a race of supermen whose superior abilities raise them above the restraining power of all laws. Happily, these extravagant views have not discouraged the hardier members of the legal profession from challenging administrative lawlessness. In the result, the new baronetcy of public bureaucrats has unwittingly come to serve as a spur to the man of law, causing him to inquire, to probe, to prod, and to question — all with the object of reducing administrative impediments to the citizen's natural impulse to conduct his lawful business without undue interference from the state.

To expedite the business of the ordinary citizen is to reduce the number of laws and not to multiply them, to simplify regulations and not compound them, to expand freedom of action and not to inhibit it, to reward success and not penalize it, and to control the controllers and not the citizen. If men of law do not succeed in curbing the rate of lawmaking, very shortly we shall become a nation of centipedes and as much preoccupied as that fabled insect in deciding which leg should be moved first, second, twentieth, and thirtieth. That wretched centipede was reduced to a state of nervous paralysis. We are following close behind.

The model man of law is not obsequious to governments that threaten his independence of thought or expression. The more restrictive the bureaucracy, the stronger will be his response. To enshrine the role of expediter, the man of law, consciously or by chance, has appropriately borrowed for his escutcheon the words inscribed upon the head of the woodsman's axe: "Either I will find a way or I will make one!"

Members of the public today generally recognize that the modern man of law does not impede the speedy conclusion of his business; he expedites it, often under trying and adverse circumstances, which in some cases may be of his client's making. Litigation itself may be human folly, but it is to be preferred to war, piracy, hijacking, kidnapping, or robbery as a means of having one's way. Churchill said of democracy that it was the worst form of government that ever existed in the world; the trouble is that it is better than any other. So with the judicial system — it is probably the worst way of settling disputes — the slowest, the most costly, the most uncertain, the most exasperating — but there exists none that is better or, in the long run, more expeditious.

VI

ARTISTRY

Artistic growth is, more than it is anything else,
a refining of the sense of truthfulness. The
stupid believe that to be truthful is easy;
only the artist, the great artist, knows how
difficult it is.

WILLA S. CATHER, *O PIONEERS!* (1913),
PT.II, CHAP. 4

Accuracy and diligence are much more
necessary to a lawyer than great comprehension of mind
or brilliancy of talent. His business is to refine,
define, split hairs, look into authorities and compare
cases. A man can never gallop over the fields of
law on Pegasus, nor fly across them on the wings of oratory.
If he would stand on *terra firma*, he must descend.
If he would be a great lawyer, he must first consent
to become a great drudge.

DANIEL WEBSTER

I have always envied the artist: the potter who transforms inanimate clay into a utensil of beauty; the sculptor who releases from a shapeless piece of inert stone the spirit of a new being that has a life and personality of its own; the painter who, with pigment brushed upon a two-dimensional immobile canvas, can engender life in all its dimensions — its action and passion, its motions and emotions — creating a multi-dimensioned experience; the musician who animates the atmosphere with sound, conjuring out of air a realm of fantasy, a host of dazzling denizens and demi-gods that populate the heavens. When I see these men and women in their workshops and studios, I am elated by the processes of their creation.

Whenever I visit my friend Joe Fafard at his house in the tiny village of Pense, Saskatchewan, I am enchanted by the seeming simplicity of his skill in gathering a few handfuls of dry, gray clay and with his magic fingers molding it into a small human form so realistic that I am persuaded he is a spiritual surrogate of the Creator, who from the dust of the earth fashioned the first man.

My friend Ted Godwin is a painter of that rare and happy company whose genius filches the forms and colors of living things and with the authority of nature so felicitously fastens them upon his canvas that, within the compass of a few square feet, he paints a portrait of the world in miniature that so insinuates itself into the viewer, it grows more acceptable to the heart than reality itself.

I lusted for the gift of Minuetta, my sister, who, when only a child, created melodies that found their way into the songs and piano works, concerti and suites, toccatas and fugues she wrote describing the places and people we both knew well, and which neither of us can ever forget. Often I hear myself whistling or singing them as I run through the park in the early morning.

Without the skill to draw or sculpt or paint convincingly or to carve, mold, etch, or even whittle, I long felt deprived of one of the richest gifts with which nature endows those whom she favors most. It is genius to see the world outside the human eye, and far beyond its range, and so to gather from the infinitely varied strands of light and shadow a few bare threads sufficient for the artist to fashion images more compelling and profound than the outside world that has moved him. The hunter emerged from the sculptor's stone; the flower revealed through the painter's pigment; vitality made manifest in the composer's music. These are the ultimate realities. When the bells of my inner being are set ringing, it is the artistic work that becomes the reality, and I, that dwindle into a dream. It is then that they seem more myself (my *id*) than I. They do not then reflect real life: they of themselves *are* new life made manifest. They are the *other* world that Plato inferred as being not a mere shadow, but the veriest of realities, when he said: "We see only our own shadows or the shadows of one another. Shadows that the fire throws on the opposite side of the cave," which is the world we all inhabit.

It dawned on me one evening, as I sat in my office drafting an agreement between two men to provide for a partnership between them, that as a lawyer perhaps I was, in fact, no less creative than the artist. On the plain white sheet of paper before me, I wrote not a series of telephone numbers nor the purchases I proposed in a shopping list but an agreement or indenture that ultimately bound two men as partners. Under its terms they would pool their assets and combine their abilities and pledge their fortunes to found and carry on a business they hoped would be profitable to themselves and beneficial to others. That is what would make their relationship successful and all worthwhile. The sentences I wrote at once converted a nondescript foolscap of white bond, with no more significance than butcher's wrapping paper, into a document that would come to animate two men to action and would continue to guide and govern their conduct for years to come. It was an act of creation, as significant as Joe Fafard's conversion of dry, gray clay into a unique human form or Ted Godwin's metamorphosis of flat, stretched canvas into light.

There is history in the word "indenture." When agreements were written by clerks with sharpened quills on parchment, lawyers went to great trouble to prevent forgeries and to assure their clients that their intentions would be perfectly respected and carried out. The words of the agreement were laboriously written twice in order that each party might have and carry away with him, the contract. There existed then no carbon paper with which to make copies, nor any photomachine. The large sheep's parchment, employed for its durability, was divided in two equal parts. On each part the clerk wrote the whole of the contract — once upside down — so that the first words of each, "THIS INDENTURE WITNESSETH" began in the center. When his work was done, each party attended with his witnesses at the solicitor's chambers and the parchment was signed by all present. The red sealing wax was melted and applied, and the seals pressed on the hot wax. Then the solicitor brought out his shears and cut the parchment in two, making indentations as he cut. These indents between the words "THIS INDENTURE WITNES-SETH" as they appeared, top to bottom, across the middle of the parchment, remained forever on the two parts of the parchment. Then the solicitor formally delivered to each, his half of the document containing the whole agreement, seals and all. If a dispute arose upon the agreement and the parties found themselves in litigation, the two pieces of parchment were brought before the court and placed side by side. The indentations were then matched like a jig-saw puzzle. If they fitted, the documents were known to be genuine. The court would then proceed to interpret the contract which came to be known as an Indenture (the name by which it is described to this day).

Many times each day a clean immaculate sheet of white paper lies on my desk. It contains within its four corners all of the possibilities that the written word is capable of producing. With a pen, that sheet of paper may be transformed into a vehicle carrying directions that will guide the lives and fortunes of men who consulted me and their associates — and their friends and families as well — for a hundred years or more.

The will that I drew up this morning on a few sheets of short bond paper for the young man and his fiancee about to be married might change their lives and the future of their children, yet unborn, in ways that neither they nor I can ever know. In the statement of claim that I wrote on clean lined paper today, I launched a lawsuit in the Court of Queen's Bench, claiming damages for fraud and breach of trust. I gathered all of the fragments of my client's life that he thrust upon me. He had heaped papers without number upon my desk, and I raked through them as he sat in my office describing his complaint. He left a rubble of facts, conjectures, rumors, and grievances expressing all of the fears and misgivings, the rage and the hopes his grievance spawned within his agitated brain.

Separating fact from fiction, reality from fantasy, the relevant from the extraneous, and the significant from the picayune, the lawyer enters upon the creative task of fashioning portraits of his clients and their adversaries in a setting that will reflect the environment in which they live so that he can felicitously recount the events when they come before the court. The man of law as artist must capture all the realism of life. He must draw the contours accurately, warts and all, and convey the facts as they emerge from the evidence with all the emotional impact of the original events: the plaintiff who is crippled for life — victim of the negligence of an incompetent bus driver; the widow whose husband was electrocuted as he worked on an improperly assembled transformer; the physician who was slandered by the over-zealous and misinformed political candidate; the long-suffering wife of the alcoholic seeking divorce; the overly conscientious teacher dismissed for strapping a student who had sued her and her school board for assault. These facts can, and should be phrased in words as graphic as counsel can command. The statement of claim is the first information of the case the judge will have. There is no reason why a lawyer should not couch this important document, in something more than mere legalese. There is such a thing as legal literature. While the precedents always serve, they can be improved by sentences that ring the changes of a client's cause in words that are not only accurate, but memorable, by sentences that not only satisfy the requirements of the law, but are eloquent and convincing. The task of advocacy begins with the firing of the first gun — and there can be artistry in every salvo of the advocate's artillery fire.

There is no lawsuit that does not portray a true-life drama more poignant than a television soap opera, whose characters are no less unique, and whose problems are as tangled and insoluble. They are the stuff out of which the fabric of the law is woven. Being true, they are stranger than the writer's conceits, more exotic than the painter's imagination, more eccentric than the musician's harmonies — or dissonances. Many of them may seem inconsequential to the stranger, but none of them is unimportant to a client who confronts his lawyer with the evidence. A tiny pebble lying on the beach is of no consequence in a world of vast deserts and high mountains, but that tiny pebble in your shoe generates more personal hurt than all the sand of the Sahara and all the rubble on Fujiama.

Relatively few legal scenarios will ever attract the journalist; fewer still will claim a headline in the daily press. Yet, prosaic though trials may seem, they are likely to mirror the content and conflicts of people's lives with greater exactitude than all the statistical data it has grown fashionable to collect for the purpose of conjuring up a theory or (by gallup nose-counting) of creating popular public policies. Never have I known a statistic (or a whole battalion of statistics) to describe the anguish of a mother fruitlessly seeking compensation for the injury suffered by her child or the joy of a man accused of a homicide whom a jury has acquitted — or the impact of these experiences upon the patterns of human behavior.

The success that attends the lawyer's task in assembling his words and marshalling his thoughts depends as much on his artistry as upon his wit. Like the painter, he selects the subjects that are likely to attract the brightest light, the deepest shadow, the sharpest contrast, and, if successful, the clearest judgment. But, just as there is no canvas capable of containing every element of the vista that becomes a landscape painting, so there is neither trial nor hearing that can encompass within its limited scope every person whose presence produced the legal scene, colored its constituents, or influenced its subjects.

The artist is a gleaner of the most precious kernels to be found in a vast field which others have harvested and left, believing it to be barren. Like the artist, the lawyer also gleans where others have many times passed. His diligent search for the facts will sometimes yield surprises and will often produce happy results, but it will never wholly satisfy the lawyer's need to be assured that nothing, however small, has been overlooked, nothing, however obscure, has been forgotten, and nothing, however onerous, has been spared.

Law is not a science but an art. It is the art of discovery and arrangement and design. Its possibilities and facets are as varied as the people whom it affects, and richer than the situations that give it birth. In its practice, the lawyer adopts the role of artist whose task it is to paint a picture that reproduces so felicitously the result he seeks to attain, that all who see it are moved to accept it and adopt it because it is fit and apt and serves its purpose, and seems wholly right.

The computer has come to the aid of the modern man of law. Libraries are developing large storage banks of legal precedents and these are available to speed research and provide counsel with some assurance that nothing has been overlooked in the preparation of his client's case. I have used the computer to analyze financial statements and accounts. It can assemble significant data upon a grand, macrocosmic scale that appear impressive, indeed, overwhelming. But the computer cannot *think* for anyone, and will not win a single case in court. If one does not ask it to provide opinions or deliver judgments, it will be an indefatigable and faithful servant. If we ever ask it to do more, we shall be made its prisoners and its abject slaves.

I know of no case that has ever been presented perfectly. After the trial is over, however successful the result, there is always the gnawing recognition that an argument might have been better stated, a cutting comment to opposing counsel might better have been left unsaid, a question from the Bench might have been better answered. When I walk down the steps of the court house I seldom fail to think of a fresh argument that eluded me or what I believe to be a witty phrase that escaped me when I was before the court. While *l'esprit d'escalier* arrives too late to be shared, it is cheering to know that its fruit can be banked and drawn upon, for another battle on another day.

All of the minutiae bearing upon a client's case are of concern to a lawyer; even though some must be rejected, all should be considered. When young Boswell told Samuel Johnson that he was afraid to put in his journal too many little incidents of his subject's life, the great man said: "There is nothing, sir, too little for so little a creature as man. It is by studying little things that we attain the great art of having as little misery and as much happiness as possible." Every reader of detective stories will know by studying and remembering little things, the villain will be found out and the innocent will emerge triumphant.

The effective management of counsel's case at trial is his artistic masterpiece. It is a unique kind of play composed of fragments collected over the centuries from medieval jousting and from the morality and miracle plays, arranged and rearranged to suit the times and meet the needs of people of all classes in every society that has experienced the traditions of English law for a thousand years.

In the trial-by-combat of medieval times, each disputant might choose his champion to do battle for him in the lists before the king or the feudal lord who presided over the contest in which God would determine who should emerge victorious. The process was meant to invoke heaven's signal. From the result of battle the king perceived and declared the divine will. To the "client" of the victorious champion went the success of the day and all the fruits of victory. In theory, the purpose of the battle was not to decide who was the most competent or artful adversary in the saddle, but rather to invoke divine intervention on the side of the litigant whom God and justice favored. Of course the reputation of the successful champion grew with his successes, and clients were prone to choose their champions then as they choose their counsel now. While God was known to decide the issue, a mighty arm was acknowledged to strengthen the will of the Divine.

As the decades passed, the arts of battle became more refined and sophisticated. Champions polished their armor and sharpened their lances and so sought their fortunes in these earliest of forensic forays. The duration of trial-by-combat was short-lived; it ended after less than a century. But divine intercession in the search for truth and justice were still to be invoked. In the hearts of many judges and lawyers that entreaty has never been silent, even though the clash of arms has been stilled over the years, and maturity has come to substitute more subtle and suitable means to ascertain the facts, to combine established principles of law with reason and to apply compassion to the issues in contention.

Today a trial may be an intellectual debate between counsel; it is a matching of witnesses, a contest of facts, a weighing of evidence, a balancing of principles of law to determine which rules are the most cogent and which should govern. And yet the role of the contemporary man of law still savors of its early combative origins:

> All arm'd I ride, whate'er betide
> Until I find the holy Grail.[1]

The sculptor's notion that justice is a blindfold woman holding a set of scales wherein the facts are weighed is a romantic representation of the impotant principle that all are equal before the law — rich and poor, black and white and yellow, Christian and Jew and Moslem and agnostic and atheist: men and women and even little children. That monument of a strong but compassionate woman, became mankind's first and most revered Charter of Human Rights. Its message has reverberated among the thousands of such statutes and from the countless judicial decisions made within the court houses before which this ideal concept of justice was translated into stone.

Because a trial concerns itself with the life and liberty of individuals and the right of each of them to express himself without fear, to move where he wishes, to use his knowledge and skills to enrich his life, to acquire and use property as he chooses, and so to join with other like-minded persons in doing all of these things, there is bound to be conflict and contention in the world. The purpose of the man of law is to confine that conflict to the courtroom where it can be impartially examined and ultimately extirpated.

The modern court house may seem as far removed from the jousting field of the fourteenth century as the ballistic missile is from the lance and shield of the medieval warrior, but the contest and the smoke of battle are ever-present in the adversary relationship that exists among human beings by virtue of their very nature. A trial is an encapsulated sampling of the animated human state — a state which, by definition, postulates an adversary relationship. Yet a trial is a highly sophisticated and civilized confrontation since it is played out in a forum to which citizens may resort for the ultimate judgment when all other means of settling their differences have failed. It is a peaceful means by which pugnacious creatures may resolve "insoluble" problems without destroying each other. The process can never be devoid of passion. And rightly so. Passion may itself be a purgative. The *animus* generated in the trial can be a therapeutic device by which the contesting parties (and their champions too) can express their hostilities and purge their animosities. In the end, they may emerge from the ordeal (winner or loser) conscious of the irrebuttable fact that the court has ruled and delivered its decision in the cause and that (subject to the possibility of an appeal) the time has come to lay all contention to rest. The dispute is dead. Its obituary is the court's judgment. Conciliation and reconciliation among feuding individuals is an ideal method of settling differences. When this fails, there is no civilized substitute for the court's *fiat.*

When the martial trappings of the medieval trial slowly disappeared, in their stead emerged the art of oral examination and personal confrontation. The champions assembled not their lethal weapons but their witnesses. Each came forward and, invoking the Deity to attest to his veracity, he related what he knew and how he learned what he knew concerning the dispute between the parties. Then followed the testing of the story of the witness with jousting of words and parrying of phrases — the stuff on which battles raged and victories turned. The art of cross-examination became refined so that points scored on the courtroom floor were intellectual triumphs and there was no longer a need to seek successes on the jousting field. But the adversary process has persisted with this variation only, that the rapier has grown more awesome than the double-edged cruciform. The light touch and the swift parry — these are the techniques favored by the courtroom champion of our day. The ponderous, heavy-handed counsel no longer is the forensic ornament he once may have been. The model is the adaptable, nubile combatant, skilled in all manner of warfare and versed in the most advanced weaponry of his profession.

A lively imagination coupled with an awareness of history, a knowledge of law, and a boldness for innovation, can set the legal rafters ringing for generations. An artistic presentation will go a long way to help. Judges and jurymen must be attentive if they are to be convinced. Counsel cannot always keep them happy, but assuredly he can do a great deal to keep them awake.

I have been told that there is no place for poetry in the court room today, that jurors want fact, not fantasy and that some judges are as wary of the well-turned phrase, as of a well-turned ankle. I have never accepted either of those generalizations. Where the prosecution produces circumstantial evidence of small weight, but designed to raise suspicions, how better to round off an attack upon it than with Iago's cunning words as he takes Desdemona's handkerchief and says:

> Trifles light as air
> Are to the jealous confirmations strong
> As proofs of holy writ.[2]

Or in an action for defamation, how better to end an address to the jury than with Shakespeare's famous lines spoken out of the mouth of that self-same Iago to Othello:

> Good name in man and woman, dear my lord,
> Is the immediate jewel of their souls:
> Who steals my purse steals trash; 'tis something, nothing;
> 'Twas mine, 'tis his, and has been slave to thousands,
> But he that filches from me my good name
> Robs me of that which not enriches him,
> And makes me poor indeed.[3]

Defending an accused indicted for rape, in addressing the jury I have walked over to the witness stand, taken the court Bible and opened it and turned to Exodus, chapter 39, and read aloud the story of how Potophar's wife falsely accused her husband's servant Joseph, of forcing her to lie with him. Verses 7 to 20 graphically tell the ancient story of how an innocent man may be cast into prison by the hue and cry of a scheming woman.

The jury is still the touchstone of justice in all countries whose citizens enjoy the benefits of the English common law. Who is the jury, and why has its authority been nurtured and treasured for so many centuries? I have sometimes asked this question of the twelve men and women whom I have addressed at trial when I have summed up and invited them to consider their verdict. The answer I find most satisfying was written by Gilbert K. Chesterton after he had served for the first time as a juror in an English court. This is what he wrote:

> Our civilization had decided, and very justly decided, that determining the guilt or innocence of men is a thing too important to be trusted to trained men. When it wishes for light upon that awful matter, it asks men who know no more law than I know, but who can feel the things that I felt in the jury box. When it wants a library catalogued, or the solar system discovered, or any trifle of that kind, it uses up its specialists. But when it wishes anything done which is really serious, it collects twelve of the ordinary men standing round. The same thing was done, if I remember right, by the Founder of Christianity.[4]

The jury system provides a method of trying issues and achieving justice that is both old and new. Its roots are ancient, but it is as modern as the concept of "participatory democracy." Though it is a venerable institution, it can be made to work well if counsel play their proper role at trial with skill and grace. One of its principal virtues is that it militates against harsh and unconscionable laws and that it brings the administration of justice into harmony with the temper of the times.

Lord Justice du Parcq described the importance of the jury system upon the growth of the law when he said:

> The common law of this country has been built up not by the writings of logicians or learned jurists, but by summings up of judges of experience to juries consisting of plain men, not usually students of logic, not accustomed to subtle reasoning, but endowed, sofar as my experience goes, as a general rule, with great common sense, and if an argument has to be put in terms which only a school-man could understand, then I am always doubtful whether it can possibly be expressing the common law.[5]

It is a part of the artistry of the courtroom that counsel resist the impulse to say everything that can be said on any subject; that he avoid the temptation to produce in court every fact however remotely relevant, every exhibit, every alternate argument in support of his position. Paring is the most difficult part of preparation, but it is one of the most significant secrets of success. It is as difficult for a lawyer to slim down his case as it is for a gourmet to slenderize his form. "I apologize to the court for my sesquipedálian submission," I have had to say. "I simply did not have the time to write a short one."

A. E. Housman, in his *Letters,* tells of his encounter with the great Clarence Darrow. He writes:

> I had a visit not long ago from Clarence Darrow, the great American barrister for defending murderers. He had only a few days in England, but could not return home without seeing me, because he had so often used my poems to rescue his clients from the electric chair. Leob and Leopold owe their life sentence partly to me; and he gave me a copy of his speech, in which, sure enough, two of my pieces are misquoted."[6]

The man of law would do well to remember that if, in the heat of battle, or in the exultation of his own eloquence, he should unintentionally misquote a witness or opposing counsel, a judge or a poet, the most forgiving of all will be the poet. There was no English writer so impeccable as Housman and the three slim volumes of his work contain poems more perfectly wrought than the diamonds set in the Imperial Crown of his native land. When asked about the work he was producing, he wrote to Witter Bynner in 1910:

> The other day I had the curiosity to reckon up the complete pieces, printed and unprinted, which I have written since 1896, and they only come to 300 lines . . . In barrenness, at any rate, I hold a high place among English poets, excelling even Gray."[7]

For loquacious lawyers as for prolix poets, Housman's works have a clear message: the ability clearly to express in a few phrases the essence of a client's case in court is the highest achievement of advocacy. It is not enough to have a knowledge of all of the facts and an appreciation of all of the nuances of evidence that will go to prove those facts; neither is it enough to have mastered the many fine points of law that arise from those facts and the inferences that can be drawn from them. Most important and most difficult of all is to decide the issue that is vital to the case, and then to discard all that is merely subsidiary. It is an exercise that may sound simple, but counsel is confronted with no more agonizing ordeal. It is not only he and his junior who will ponder and debate these questions. His client will urge upon him all manner of theories and press upon him a whole wilderness of irrelevancies, demanding that they be placed before the court. These, counsel must consider, but he must also be firm enough to dismiss them if, in his considered opinion, they do not clearly advance his client's cause. For success, counsel must go for the jugular. Study, practice, and a little luck are all that is required to determine just where that vital vein lies.

Another of the most difficult skills for counsel to cultivate is a mastery of the art of understatement. The man of law often is considered among the most loquacious of the human species. The talent of silence is seldom praised. But if a man's speech be silver, he may be surprised to discover that his silence may be gold. As Sydney Smith said after sitting next to Macaulay at dinner, "He has occasional flashes of silence that make his conversation perfectly delightful." Counsel should be content to draw the broad outlines of a case, lightly sketching the salient features and leaving to the judge and jury the satisfaction of filling in the interstices with their own knowledge, experience, and imagination. The thoughts that are conjured up in his own mind by a judge or a juror are bound to carry more weight with him than any idea that is directly and obviously planted in his head by counsel. Each of us is enamoured of his own brainchildren and it is only natural that we should admire our own progeny while we may not welcome our neighbor's children; and sometimes, we may find ourselves treating them as simple nuisances.

A distinguished Italian counsel, Piero Calamandrei, some forty years ago is reported to have said: "A lawyer should be able to suggest the arguments which will win his case so subtly to the judge that the latter believes he has thought of them himself."[8] This is the finest forensic art that most perfectly conceals art.

The artistic (or the artful) counsel will therefore leave spaces in his submissions so that his listeners may be free to furnish them with familiar trappings, each fashioning his own associations out of the memory of his personal experience. Counsel will trigger the minds of a jury into action so that they will themselves conjure up their own questions and draw their own inferences. Clay cast in a mold chosen by its maker is not easily fractured by a critic of its form. So a juror, however open to conviction, is likely to hold more firmly to his own views, than to defend the arguments of counsel.

Judges and juries wish to draw inferences from facts that have not been dogmatically pounded and repounded for their edification by persistent, tedious counsel. Similarly, evidence that is led before the court must be, and must seem to be the witness's own testimony and not a mere reflection of the view of some solicitor or police officer who has schooled the witness.

The artfulness of silence also applies to the defendants. In criminal cases, most convictions are the result of statements or confessions that a suspect has given to the police or to a witness who is called by the prosecution. Mankind is a simian species, said by Darwin to have descended from the ape, and his most obvious characteristic is an inability to control his garrulous tongue. Even though his very life depends on silence, it seems impossible for him to remain mute. He needs must talk, and talking — confess. There would be fewer inmates in our prisons had they read their Shakespeare in school: "The silence, often, of pure innocence persuades when speaking fails."

Theodor Reik has written at length on *The Compulsion to Confess*. Drawing his illustrations from Freudian psychoanalysis, he concludes that "Man's self-betrayal oozes from all his pores."[9] Reik suggests that confessions represent "a kind of verbal masochistic exhibition of self-punishment in words: they may have the effect of relieving a person of an oppressive feeling of guilt. But while a confession may tell the truth, it may not tell the whole truth; much of it may be repressed and remain unknown."[10] Because a suspect must talk or burst, in more than ninety percent of the cases in which crime is investigated, the suspect condemns himself by his instinctive loquacity that ends in a signed confession.

But if ninety percent of the convictions are the result of an accused saying too much (though perhaps not all), the other ten percent are the result of his counsel (who should know better) falling into the same trap. As true for counsel as for the politician is the old maxim that it is better to remain silent and be thought a fool than to open one's mouth and remove all doubt.

Young counsel sometimes boast of their success in the criminal courts. "I got him off!" they jubilantly declare to their cronies. "The evidence against him was damning, but I got him off!"

If the man of law does not believe in the presumption of innocence — the principle that under our system of law everyone is innocent until proved guilty beyond all reasonable doubt — how can it be expected that a jury or members of the public will understand and believe in that fundamental principle of law that is the chief bulwark against arbitrary arrests and capricious convictions? There is no such thing as defense counsel "getting a client off." The entire process of the criminal law involves the prosecutor in "getting him *in*" — in proving him guilty. If the prosecutor fails, the accused wins. He is acquitted. He is *not* "gotten off."

Of the young lawyer who tells me that he got his man "off" I cannot resist asking: "If you got that man of yours 'off,' tell how many of your clients you got convicted?"

VII
CHARISMA

There is a story told of a small western town
about 1908. The railroad tracks were laid, and the first
locomotive pulled into the station. The townsfolk
came to admire this miracle of transportation. They
saw a long line of cold, sombre-looking flat beds and
freight cars attached to each other behind the
engine that was belching fire. Steam was spouting from
its sides. Suddenly, with a great roar, black clouds
of smoke poured forth, the engine started moving, and
the long line of cars jerked forward one by
one, and began moving along with it.

"Father, what do you think of this wonderful
sight?" a small boy asked the grizzled man that
held his hand.

The man appeared to be lost in thought for
a moment and then, very softly, he replied, "Look how one,
hot, fiery creation can pull along so many cold ones!"

That's charisma.

A TALE TOLD BY MY FATHER

In the field of law, as with medicine, there is so much that is unknown and unknowable that the lawyer's authority cannot rest entirely upon his knowledge, broad though it may be. Sapiential accomplishment is not enough if he is to exercise the influence he hopes to bring to those concerns that fill his working hours and often haunt his sleep: matters of life and death, freedom and prison, reputation and calumny, property and poverty, and the sense of justice and the despair of injustice. There are circumstances where sapience fails or is insufficient, but charisma may come to the rescue of the man of law when other gifts fail.

When counsel goes to the jury with his case, he has the opportunity of mounting a performance as memorable, even though it may not be so well rehearsed as the role played out by the most celebrated actors of the stage. Sir Edward Marshall Hall, one of England's great barristers, frankly admitted the similitudes of the courtroom and the theater. He said: "My profession and that of an actor are somewhat akin, except that I have no scenes to help me and no words are written for me to say. There is no black-cloth to increase the illusion. There is no curtain. But, out of the vivid, living dream of somebody else's life, I have to create an atmosphere — for that is advocacy."[1] To this, Edward Marjoribanks, Marshall Hall's biographer, describing the ideal advocate, added: "He must, then be histrionic, crafty, courageous, eloquent, quick-minded, charming, great hearted. These are the salient qualities which go to make a great advocate."

The barrister's charisma in the courtroom, rightly or wrongly, has earned the profession the kind of accolades that the conjurer and magician enjoyed wherever traveling showmen put down for the night. The crowd loved the spectacle, but they considered it all a hoax carried off by fast talk and sleight of hand. Legal folklore is not dead: there are tales of the lawyer who, sensing perjury strips a witness naked to his lies and snatches his client from the hangman's noose, or who discovers the missing murder weapon hidden in his adversary's gown with the fingerprints of the prosecutor's chief witness clearly visible on the barrel. That lawyer is still a hero who, reading the fine print of a statute under which his client stands charged, discovers a saving word that no one has noticed before and so saves his client from the prison, the jaws of which, but a moment before, threatened to lock him away from the world forever. These are the unforgettable images that still reflect some of the realities of courtroom drama. They serve to clothe the man of law with a charisma that, in an age of science and pragmatism, still persists as an indefinable but incandescent quality, marking the great advocate as a man apart.

Alas! Real life generally is less romantic!

The art of persuasion before a judge and a jury does not miraculously flow from the lips of an eloquent lawyer possessed of a pleasing personality. Talent, the facility of words, brilliance of expression — these may appear to be God-given gifts that require no effort. Nothing could be further from fact. They are a species of art that conceals art. Diligence, accuracy, research: these are the stuff out of which the authority of the true advocate is fashioned. His task is to define and distinguish, refine and explain. If he appears to fly on Pegasus over Elysian Fields, it is only because study and experience have revealed to him their every acre. If he seems to control and influence human emotion, it is because, having pursued every clue, unearthed every piece of evidence, learned every fact and plumbed every motive, he has learned everything about his client, the witnesses, and the facts that enmesh them. His charisma is not a thing that stands apart from the man of law and his world. It is the measure of his capacity to take infinite pains with infinitesimally minute details. Even so polished an orator as Winston Churchill spent many hours in the bathtub preparing his extemporaneous sallies for the House of Commons.

It is not only in court that the lawyer's charisma may shine through. It may appear in his first encounter with a client who has come to him for counsel and advice. His interview should be a graceful exercise in learning what is beneficial to both of them. It is not always so. Oftentimes, at the very outset, the interview may develop into a battle between solicitor and client. Some lawyers consider it necessary, early in the game, to test their clients in the crucible of cross-examination. To determine a client's credibility and character may be desirable, indeed necessary, to discover his reactions to unexpected questions. It is certainly safer and more productive to proceed with the hard-line operation early in the relationship rather than later, since, however wary he may be, counsel tends gradually to identify with his client's position and then it may become too late to examine his evidence as critically as may be necessary. The consequences of a turbulent introduction, of course, may be traumatic and leave scars that impair the confidentiality and trust that are essential to a successful professional relationship. If the charismatic qualities of counsel can be transmitted to a client, that lawyer has gone a long way in assuring success to his cause. The miracle of inspiring confidence in the pusillanimous and imparting strength in the fainthearted is often performed by counsel whose charismatic qualities are so contagious that they infect a client and his cause with optimism, and this can prove to be a significant aid to success.

Sometimes the process operates in reverse. Counsel may appear diffident to the strident claims of a client. He may lack enthusiasm for the case or he may simply be tired. In this event an understanding and perceptive client may so stimulate his curiosity and fire his imagination as to impart into the performance of a pedestrian counsel a measure of genuine brilliance. A client must always furnish the body of the case. On some occasions he or she is capable of also providing its spirit. Client and counsel interact one upon the other like an actor on stage with his audience. A successful performance, therefore, depends upon the behavior of both in the special relationship that has brought them together.

Charisma does not emerge out of the naked personality of the man of law. If he is the shaman in an Age of Reason, his sorcery flows from his address, and the words he speaks are his amulets. While human thought may shape those words, the words themselves will generate fresh thoughts. Whether communicated across the courtroom floor or across the centuries, there are words that command men's minds and charge their conduct.

Charisma, therefore, is born of language. Astronomers have told us that a newly designed electronic telescope has discovered sounds that were generated billions of years ago when matter first exploded and brought the universe into being. Genesis need no longer serve as the source of the story of creation: the facts can now be explored in the echoes of the sounds generated out of the Big Bang, the cataclysmic explosion in which the universe was born twenty billion years ago. To earthbound creatures who stand only a little lower than the angels, the idea that sounds never really disappear but somehow, continue to exist in space forever, is at once a fascinating and unnerving idea.

If what the physicists and astronomers tell us is true, they join with the poet in saying that "nothing is lost out of nature," and that nothing is really changed though everything be altered. The words I speak today, whether they knock around the court house corridors or go reverberating in space are never lost, but continue their existence forever. The thought is sobering enough to remind me (though not sufficiently often) that when I do not speak a word, I remain its master; but once I express it, I am forever its slave. It may haunt me forever.

What this discovery may mean is that every thought given utterance by human beings since the beginning of time, is stored in a great universal sound bank, there to remain forever like an infinitely vast hoard of electro-magnetic tapes locked in the grandest computer of them all.

Just think! Every word you have ever spoken to yourself or your wife or your neighbor, to your colleague, friend, or enemy — every telephone conversation you have had, every letter you have dictated, every private piece of pillow talk — all of your words, sense and nonsense alike, every statement you made in public, every whisper in private, every bit of evidence you attested to in court, every sound you have expressed, from the first babblings of infancy to the last dissonant snorings that murder sleep at midnight are, and forever will remain a part of the great universal scheme of things, there to be preserved in stellar warehouses until the last syllable of recorded time!

Omar Khayyam knew nothing of the computers or the electronic telescopes of our time, yet he sensed the truth that contemporary science has confirmed: nothing is lost out of nature and nothing that is said may ever be recalled:

> The Moving Finger writes; and, having writ
> Moves on: nor all your piety nor wit
> Shall lure it back to cancel half a line
> Nor all your tears wash out a word of it.[2]

For this reason, it is an important element of charisma that every word spoken at trial should be truthful, that every phrase aptly reflect the facts as they were observed by a witness at the time relevant to the action, and that counsel in his address to the court depart not a whit from the testimony of the witness he is describing. In lands where the common law of England prevails, each witness at a trial must swear to tell "the truth, the whole truth and nothing but the truth." The purpose is to bind the conscience of the deponent and to assure, so far as it is humanly possible, that he will not lie or mislead the court. Man's yearning for justice is so great and the stakes in litigation so high that from earliest times it has been recognized that justice can no more be born from falsehood than a baby emerge from a garden cabbage.

Oaths vary. The Hebrew swears on the Old Testament, the Mohammedan on the Koran. A porcelain plate may be broken before a Buddhist who invokes divine providence to strike him down and shatter him like a piece of clay should he give false testimony. The "Scotch oath" is available to those who do not wish to invoke the name of the diety in affairs profane, a sentiment the Scot shares with the Hebrew who, a mere mortal, is enjoined from uttering the name of the Ineffible. Paradoxically, the Scotch affirmation is available as well to the atheist who claims there is no God, and to those who are agnostics and do not know. Such persons may affirm and, without holding or kissing any sacred book or thing, they may raise a hand and declare that they will tell the truth. Notwithstanding the materialism of our times, when a witness appears in our courts to testify, he is expected to bind his conscience to say only what he knows to be true.

Some suggest the courtroom Bible that has always lain close to the witness stand is an archaic prop that ought to be banished. "After all," it is said, "few people believe in an afterlife or in the damnation that awaits the souls of those who swear falsely and lie on the witness stand. If witnesses tell the truth, they do so only because they fear they will be prosecuted for perjury and locked up for their crime. Why bother to invite God to sit in at a trial? Why not simply read from the Criminal Code and remind witnesses that the penalty for perjury is prison?"

There are many reasons to invoke the diety, not the least significant of which is that justice itself is a godlike quality.

The skeptic may smile and say that the law, like God, "passeth all understanding." Yet he will be among the first to claim his right to a fair trial and to assert the law's guarantee of the first principle of natural justice, that no man be condemned unheard. As authority for that important principle, early English judges relied on the reluctance even of God to condemn either Adam or Eve without giving them an opportunity to defend themselves. When God learned that they had eaten of the tree of knowledge, He called them to Him and asked whether it was true they had disobeyed his law. Of Adam he asked, "Hast thou eaten of the tree, whereof I commanded thee that thou shouldst not eat?" And Adam, who was not a very brave man, passed the buck and said, "The woman whom Thou gavest to be with me, she gave me of the tree, and I did eat." Then God gave Eve an opportunity to defend herself: "And the Lord said unto the woman, what is this that thou hast done? And the woman answered and said, "the serpent beguiled me, and I did eat." Then God gave judgment and meted out his punishment. He condemned Eve forever to bring forth children in sorrow. He sentenced Adam to live by the sweat of his brow. For his part in the affair, the serpent was condemned to crawl forever on his belly. It has always troubled me that while God gave the man and the woman a fair hearing and an opportunity to defend themselves and speak to sentence, the serpent was denied a hearing and had no chance to speak in his own defense. Moreover, he was without counsel. Little wonder that, like a disgruntled litigant, he has been hissing venomously at God's world ever since!

I have interviewed hundreds of potential witnesses and I try to keep careful notes of what they tell me. Almost without exception, each of them, consciously or unconsciously seeks to make as favorable an impression as he can. But when, in the courtroom that same person steps into the witness box and testifies on oath, it comes as no great surprise to me to hear evidence that bears only a vague resemblance to the story he told in my office. The new evidence may distress me; but save in rare cases, I have had little doubt as to the truthfulness of the witness on the stand. I am convinced that the facts to which a witness testifies in court are more accurately described by him than at any other time.

There are fewer lies told in the witness box than anywhere else. The stakes are higher than anywhere else. A man's property, his reputation, his freedom, indeed, his very life may be in jeopardy. It is tempting to lie in defense of any of these. But the solemnity of the traditional courtroom, its elevated bench of oak or walnut, the Royal Coat of Arms above the judge's chair, and the robes worn by the judges, by counsel, and the clerk have a way of saying to a witness that where the gravest matters are being decided, law and truth can never be strangers. Here, justice must rule and truth prevail.

In a world in which lies and half-truths are commonplace, and deception passes for advertising, and prevarication for what is politic, why should one feel that the courtroom is a specially isolated shrine of probity and truth? This again is a matter of charisma. It may be the solemnity of the oath and the fear that punishment and retribution will be the liar's lot by divine intervention. It may be a justifiable apprehension of prosecution for perjury. Or perhaps it is the subconscious knowledge that the testimony a witness has publicly uttered will reverberate through the infinite spaces of the universe, there to follow and haunt him forever, neither "his piety nor wit" ever to "lure it back to cancel half a line."

Nowhere, save in the lawyer's world, is the word, whether spoken or written, so closely examined or so highly prized. Ali Baba's was not the only treasure unlocked by the key of magic words. It has been suggested that "syllables govern the world"[3] Because so much depends upon it to change men's fortunes, language remains the litigant's Aladdin's lamp, just as it has always been the lawyer's friendliest genie.

Until a century ago, when more than three hundred crimes carried with them the death penalty, English law recognized how easily an accused might be seduced to lie. An accused, therefore, was forbidden to testify in his own behalf lest in his zeal to save his life, he commit perjury and so condemn to purgatory his immortal soul. Only with the decline of ecclesiastical influence was the rule relaxed and an accused permitted to take the stand in his own defense. But so entrenched is the ancient principle that a man ought not to be tempted to lie, that the law throws a mantle over those who choose not to testify, and protects witnesses against self-crimination. No one may be compelled to give testimony at his own trial. It is a benign rule that exists only where the English common law traditions prevail. But it is as much a stranger to continental courts as to regimes in the totalitarian states behind the Iron Curtain and in China, the Middle East, and many of the African countries. There, the inquisitorial system is applied. Judges are employed to ferret out offenders and to prosecute as well as punish those whom they find guilty. In these lands there exists no right to remain mute; neither does there exist the right "to be let alone." Under such circumstances, judicial impartiality is a chimera — and justice, at best, a fortuitous coincidence.

What may seem charismatic to the spectator in the courtroom is, in fact, the result of careful management by counsel of the participants at the trial. The arrangements should be as painstakingly planned and carried off in the courtroom as onstage at the Grand Theater. Models may be brought into the courtroom to serve as "properties," the better to demonstrate a fact. I have used a mannequin to illustrate how a garment may have been torn, a rifle to show how it might be accidentally triggered, and model cars to show the likely results of a motor vehicle collision. Witnesses must be called. They are the *dramatis personae* that make their entries and their exits on stage. The lines they speak become the record of the evidence that judges and juries must hear and winnow and weigh. What is not produced in evidence in the courtroom is not fact. For purposes of the issues to be decided, it simply does not exist. In civil matters counsel's duty is to bring all relevant documents into court; in criminal matters prosecuting counsel's duty extends to bringing all witnesses who have knowledge of the events into court for defense counsel to examine or cross-examine at trial.

What of the lines that the characters in court come to speak? Some clients wish to discuss the evidence they will be giving at trial on every occasion they meet their counsel. It is my practice to consider with my client (and with other witnesses I interview) the principal facts that are relevant but not the detailed questions that will be asked or the precise answers that are likely to be given. Premature discussion with a client of the specific questions he is likely to be asked at trial is not particularly helpful. Often it makes the witness apprehensive; it encourages memorization and rehearsal, and so destroys the ring of sincerity that even the most truthful answer must carry if it is to be believed. As Lord Mansfield said, "Plain truth, dear Murray, needs no flow'rs of speech."[4]

Just before trial, I go over the facts with each witness whose brief of evidence I have already before me. I tell the witness:

1. You are present in court to answer questions that are put to you. Your first duty therefore, is not to talk, but to listen. Be sure you understand the question. If you do not understand it, say so, and it will be repeated or rephrased.

2. When you are sure you understand the question, your duty then is to give information to the court on the subject raised by the question. If you are being examined, you will be on familiar ground and will know the area which your answer should cover. Cover it — slowly, clearly, so that whoever hears what you are saying will understand what you mean. Then stop.

3. On cross-examination, after you are certain you understand the question, answer the question and only the question, directly, clearly, and briefly. Don't wander.

4. If you do not know the answer to a question, do not be ashamed to say so. Don't make up an answer simply because you think you *should* know.

5. Be yourself. Tell the truth. It is important that the court believe you and be convinced that you are sincere. There is no better way of conveying your sincerity than to be yourself and tell the truth.

6. Don't exaggerate, even in a little matter. If your taxi bills to the doctor's offices totalled $37.50, don't say they were $50.

7. Don't lose your cool. It may lose you your suit.

8. Don't try to argue with cross-examining counsel. If he is unfair, I will speak for you, or the judge may intervene.

9. Whatever the temptation, hold back that smart remark. Even a brilliant raconteur like Oscar Wilde came to grief exchanging witticisms with that plodding, thorough cross-examiner, Edward Carson.

10. Don't try to play lawyer. Advocacy is for your counsel, not for you.

11. Dress properly for court; be neither slovenly nor gaudily attired. Know how to address the court. In the witness box, if possible, stand; do not sit. A witness's voice carries better when he stands, and he appears more upright on his feet than on his buttocks.

12. Don't drink before coming into court; don't take drugs unless they are specifically prescribed for you for the day you testify.

13. Don't bring bad breath with you into the courtroom.

14. Don't chew tobacco or gum — especially bubble gum!

15. Avoid cheap perfumes and offensive new-made scents. The ventilation of a courtroom is generally bad enough without them. A woman can usually select a perfume that enhances her personality, but a man — never!

16. Before court convenes, open the valves and relieve your bladder.

These are the most pedestrian of matters, to be sure. But they are the common stuff out of which the charisma of trial counsel is made, just as the shaman's powers emanate from bits of stone and pieces of bone, of the skin of seals and ivory, and the hair of the great white polar bear. They help to place counsel in command of his team of witnesses, experts, and clerks. Although the judge conducts the court, it is counsel who conducts his case. It is counsel, therefore, who may set the tempo of the trial, he who can, within limits, select the issues and coin the key phrases that will be remembered.

Counsel, who, like Disraeli's Egremonts, have never said anything that is remembered, or done anything that can be recalled, are likely to have lacked not only charisma, but a clientele.

VIII

OBLIGATION

The law — it has honoured us; may we honour it.

DANIEL WEBSTER, "A TOAST FOR THE LAW", 1847

I hold every man a debtor to his profession
from the which as men of course do seek to receive
countenance and profit, so ought they of duty,
to endeavour themselves by way of amends, to be a
help and ornament thereto.

FRANCIS BACON, *ESSAYS*

It is the common fate of the indolent to see
their rights become prey to the active. The condition
upon which God hath given liberty to man
is eternal vigilance.

JOHN P. CURRAN, "SPEECH ON THE RIGHT OF ELECTION;"
JULY 10, 1790

OBLIGATION

Every lawyer is a debtor to the law and to the profession that has enriched him with its knowledge and traditions. The model man of law enjoys the profession's intellectual challenge. He is improved by the dignity and independence it offers. He is strengthened by his brothers at the bar — their competence, competition, and cooperation. He is blessed by the warm friendships that are forged and the happy companionships that are created within its magic circle. It is therefore natural that the lawyer should sense an obligation to the law and should feel that in some measure it can be repaid by conserving and perpetuating its genius and applying its techniques to the age in which he lives. To improve the effectiveness of the judicial system is one of his desires; but to all of this, mastery of that system and an understanding of its nuances, is an obvious prerequisite.

The lawyer whose professional thoughts begin and end with his own clients is something less than a complete man of law. Only by diligently seeking to improve the law can he practice in the grand manner. As Justice Holmes of the Supreme Court of the United States said, "Happiness cannot be won simply by being counsel and having a large income. An intellect good enough to win the prize needs other food besides success."[1]

The lawyer, be he practitioner or academic, an employee of a corporation or a man engaged in research, is obliged to consider the law not simply as a tool to enable him to earn his livelihood but as a body of knowledge and a code of conduct that concern him as a human being and as a citizen. By virtue of the knowledge he has acquired in his training and the experience he has gained in his profession, almost every lawyer is capable of making some contribution to the total of legal literature and to its fuller understanding. His obligation, too, is to enlighten his clients concerning the law and its purpose. As a professional, his client looks to him not only for advice on points of law but for guidance on prickly political and economic questions. A lawyer's influence upon the people who consult him extends far beyond the four corners of the statute that may have brought them into his office.

The man of law will never content himself with being rich in rule any more than a musician will be satisfied with reading notes or studying an orchestral score. If he is to be a musician, he must do more than learn the literature: he must master an instrument and make music. So will the model man of law use the rules he learns to advance the interests of his client, his profession, and his country. He will speak forthrightly in his chambers. He will champion his client's cause in the courtroom. He will assert the virtues of the law in public places. He will preserve the ancient principles of law and strive to improve them. It is his obligation to do so.

A Saskatchewan lawyer, having undertaken to defend a client charged with a serious criminal offence, failed to appear at the opening of the trial. Instead, he sent a junior to advise the court that he had ceased to represent the accused because he had not received his fee. In New York, lawyers who had not been "fee'd" in advance in a criminal case (as it is their right to be) for years adopted the custom of advising the presiding judge that they had not yet succeeded in establishing contact with a material witness in the case, "Mr. Green, by name." They then asked the indulgence of the court to grant an appropriate adjournment to enable counsel to find the elusive witness. "Mr. Green," of course, was the code word for "greenbacks." Understanding judges generally complied. The funds were found and the trial proceeded. But in the Saskatchewan case, the jury array had already been summoned and was in court, all sixty of them waiting to be challenged or empanelled. Crown witnesses had been subpoenaed expecting to be called to testify. To fail to appear under such circumstances was unquestionably a serious matter, and Mr. Justice R. A. MacDonald who presided, regarded it precisely so. He summoned counsel to appear before him to show cause why he ought not to be committed for contempt of court. In due course, the unhappy lawyer appeared and explained, as best he could, his dilemma. The judge reprimanded him for his "monumental error in judgment" but found that he had not intended to act contemptuously toward the court and so simply ordered him to pay the court costs incurred by his absence. But Mr. Justice MacDonald wisely chose the opportunity to remind lawyers that their obligation to their clients and the court is a heavy one rooted in sound and ancient precept. And so he quoted *Luke* xii:14:

> For unto whomsoever much is given, of him shall be much required; and to whom men have committed much, of him they will ask more.

In his novel, *Joseph Andrews*, Fielding mercifully expressed the corollary: "To whom *nothing* is given, *nothing* can be required."[2]

There was a time when the improvement of the law through concerted effort at legal reform was stoutly resisted by the profession. The *Edinburgh Review*, referred to the hostility of the judges to matters of reform, their principal interest being to preserve existing procedures. It concluded that such judges were blind to the defects of the law because "there is no task so repulsive as that of unlearning in old age the lessons of our youth." Lord Ellenborough stated the case against law reform in a few, very candid words: "If that rule were to be changed, a lawyer who is well stored with these rules would be no better than any other man is without them."[3]

That was a hundred and twenty years ago. The pendulum has since swung far and appears now to have reached the opposite extreme.

Law reform is very much in vogue. The Law Reform Commission of Canada has vigorously pursued its work of research. And its studies and recommendations for change in the fields of criminal law and evidence, family law, and commercial law have been published widely among members of the profession. Acting upon the Domino Theory, almost every province has set up its counterpart, and commissions with varying degrees of competence and imagination have churned out papers on a variety of subjects, all recommending fundamental changes in the law covering a spectrum as wide as the law itself.

In the arena of contention where counsel meet as adversaries and each presses for a particular and opposite result, there emerges from the contest a microcosm of nature in which competition is the law of life. Without conflict and debate, the progenitors of a new theory may become so enamoured by it that they tend to develop an inflexible bias in its favor and thus ignore its weaknesses. No one with the slightest knowledge of human nature (even though his experience of the law be small) would suggest that a decision for change having wide public consequences should be made without debate. The reasons for the adversary procedures at trial derive from man's knowledge that it is dangerous to apply the law or its sanctions to even one person without a careful assessment of all sides of the question by competent and impartial men. If the writing of a judgment that deals with the application of the law to one specific set of facts affecting but a single individual requires such great caution, how much greater is our duty to take care that new principles of law which may have universal application long into the future, should be debated at least as fully and pondered at least as carefully by men as competent as the judges who sit in our highest courts.

For any law reformer to believe that he can really "simplify" the law in a society that daily grows more complex, is a vain hope. The great Justice Learned Hand said: "Law has always been unintelligible, and I might say that perhaps it ought to be and I will tell you why, because I don't want to deal in paradoxes. It ought to be unintelligible because it ought to be in words — and words are utterly inadequate to deal with the fantastically multiform occasions which come up in human life."[4]

Simplistic "solutions" are always attractive to the law reformer. The less he knows about the "problem," the simpler the "solution" will naturally be. In the western world we are, for the most part, optimists. We believe that wherever there appears to be a difficulty or a "problem," there *must* be a solution available somewhere. Preferably an instant solution. And, fashionably, a legalistic one. The reason is obvious. There is nothing cheaper today than to pass a law. It requires only a small majority in Parliament, a few sheets of paper and a little ink to enact a whole legion of laws and to send them marching through the land with orders to change human nature. There is nothing more futile and few things more mischievous than indiscriminately printing and passing new laws, unless it be the unbridled printing and passing of money.

Yet many a legislator and law reformer takes seriously the comic-operatic ditty of Gilbert and Sullivan's Lord Chancellor:

The Law is the true embodiment
Of everything that's excellent
It has no kind of fault or flaw
And I, my Lords, embody the Law.

The law can shape no simple formula to solve society's ills. To expect the law to produce more wealth, to distribute human talents more "fairly," or to equalize differences of geography is to embrace the false hopes of the medieval alchemist who sought in vain to change bronze to gold.

There are many who believe that life is a great arithmetic book with problems set out in each chapter under neatly collected titles; that we must work away at the "problem" and quickly find the solution; and if we cannot work it out ourselves, we need only turn to the back of the book to find the answers. But life is not an arithmetic book. And there are no answers that God has neatly collected in an appendix for our convenience. There are many uncomfortable conditions that simply cannot be regarded as "problems" for which any solutions can be expected to be found. More often, there are *situations*. There are *conditions* that do not lend themselves to a ready answer. If statute books could cure human ills we would be the healthiest nation on earth. But laws are like medicine. The more of them we take, the more dependent we become upon them. A surfeit of laws, like an overdose of medicine, produces a malaise in a nation no less than in a patient.

Innovation is not necessarily reformation. The wise law reformer applies common sense to his sense of obligation to "improve" the laws. If he lacks common sense he is bound to make a bad situation worse. Our experience with what euphemistically passed for "tax reform" has amply demonstrated to a long line of Finance Ministers that the time comes when the tax collector's pluckings at the feathers of the public goose yield more hisses than down. It is then that the band strikes up and the old game of musical chairs starts once again.

A law that may seem popular, may not be morally just, economically sound, or physically feasible. It is a simple thing to pass a law repealing Newton's law of gravity or Einstein's law of energy, $E = MC^2$, or Gresham's law of money, but passing the hurdles of Parliament does not mean that such legislation will pass the tests of common sense and reason or that it can ever repeal a single law of nature.

It was the observation of Edmund Burke that "laws, like houses, lean on one another." The legislator must therefore be wary in making new laws and in altering the old, lest changes in one remove the effect of others. There are principles of architecture in the construction of laws just as there is art in the building of an edifice. The architect takes pains carefully to instruct the engineers and surveyors whose task it is to lay out new structures for human habitation. The laws under which men live, no less than the roofs under which they dwell, require high skills in their construction and vigilant management in their maintenance. It is to the man of law that the nation turns for direction, not as mere mechanic, but as architect. The professional law reformer often falls into error in repeating the misleading maxims that "new is better than old" and "more is better than less." Reality shows quite the opposite to be true, and nowhere so clearly as in the law. "The art of governing," say the ancient Chinese, "is like the art of cooking a fish: don't overdo it."

There is a natural and obvious presumption that ancient laws under which a people has succeeded in surviving are sound. A law is a living, vibrant organism. Like a sentient human being, there exists a presumption that it has the right of continuity. If it is to be banished or put to death, the burden rests upon those who would condemn the law, to prove beyond all reasonable doubt that to perpetuate it is to do injury to the individual, to the community, or to the nation.

To offer new lamps for old is the right of every common hawker on city streets. But the moral of Aladdin's magic lamp should not be lost. That tale should remind every generation that it is not the superficial glitter of gilt that creates the lantern's light. Its magic is never obvious. The lustre lies within. So, the genius of the common law and all the light it sheds are not impulsively to be traded for the mass-produced statutes that promise through codification, instantaneous illumination of the land with immaculate light that will lead everyone to his heart's desire.

From time to time, changes in the law are of course necessary. A blind faith that everything that is old must, *ipso facto*, be better than what is new is just as doltish as the worship of reform for its own sake.

In a free society that exists on the premise that all that is *not* forbidden is allowed, the perimeters of the law must be strictly drawn lest they so circumscribe the areas in which man may move, as to make of him a caged and confined creature. By definition, laws reflect the character and wishes of the people whom they serve. When they purport to do more, whether for "good" or for "ill," the laws themselves are jeopardized because free men will not long tolerate a tyranny of laws. Cicero declared us to be "in bondage to the law so that we may be free." But never, for a moment, did he condone laws that deliberately imposed bondage upon free men.

The man of law knows better than most, that however its terms be couched, and whether it be designed to punish mercilessly or to reward munificently, no law can make the ignorant learned, the idle industrious, the thoughtless loving, or the drunken sober. It is not the law that changes man's nature. It is man that changes the nature of the law. If it be our hope that man's ways may improve, let it be remembered that changes in the human state have always been slow to evolve, and that laws passed to achieve "obvious" improvements in human conduct are more likely to produce the opposite result.

Our zeal to change the rules that govern the game and the vanity that persuades us that we can direct humans, like trained seals, to obey our commands have often made legislators believe that men and women can no longer govern their own lives. But experience has a way of reasserting itself and confirming the fact that every person must make his own choices and accept responsibility for what he may produce. If there is a measure of sadness in the familiar lines of the *Shropshire Lad*, there is no despair in them. In a very personal sense they reflect the law's traditional concern, not to make men good, but to contain and diminish evil:

> Therefore, since the world has still,
> Much good, but much less good than ill,
> And while the sun and moon endure
> Luck's a chance, but trouble's sure,
> I'd face it as a wise man would,
> And train for ill and not for good.[5]

Change in the law can best be accomplished piecemeal when a significant abuse becomes apparent, or when disorder strikes, or when a lacuna in an existing section of a statute appears, or where unintended conflict arises between clauses that were meant to supplement each other but, upon closer examination, are shown to be at odds. If the people are to rule, then changes should be made only when there arises a clear and specific public demand for changes in the law. It is not the business of civil servants to manipulate the statutes to serve their own convenience or to enhance their personal powers. If changes become so numerous as to outstrip the conscious recognition of citizens that certain amendments are justified, the public will be alienated from the known and from what is familiar and comfortable to them, and so be made strangers in their own house. In the end citizens will grow hostile to the regime that pays no heed to its desires, and ultimately they may come to destroy it. The case of Louis Riel, the Metis rebel of the nineteenth century whose personality has cast a long shadow over Canada's twentieth, should remind us that tragedy stalks the over-zealous law reformer who, with the best intentions in the world, can stir up suspicion, hatred, and violence. A federal survey of the lands in Manitoba that threatened the native population's ancient way of life was sufficient to ignite a rebellion and fire tempers that have yet to cool.

Let it not be forgotten that among the prime purposes of laws are predictability and stability. Thoughtfully conceived, they render it possible for people to inform themselves and know in advance, the consequences of their acts. They ought to create the conditions that render it possible for each of us, as individuals, to plan for the future and to make provision for the security of ourselves and our families. If there is to be any measure of certainty in human relations, it is not to be found in financial dependence upon the state. Its soundest foundation is the law that does not shift. The law's purpose is to strengthen the individual's capacity to withstand the storms that nature visits upon mankind. It ought not to change with every shifting wind, but like Polaris; it should remain constant, and so serve as a faithful guide to the mariners of planet earth.

Should politicians adopt the practice of repealing laws that have long served society's needs simply because a vocal minority finds them irksome, the concept of law as a guarantee of order and continuity, will ultimately fall into disrepute. The question will be asked (as many are already asking it): If lawmakers regard the law as a mere passing show, transient and unsettled, why should law-breakers regard the law more reverently?

The law reformer who promotes his pet model on the premise that it will save the public time and money is seldom vindicated. Newly drafted legislation too often abandons the terminologies and definitions that have been settled after decades of costly litigation, simply because the history of their legal application is unknown to the authors or, in their zeal to sever all ties with the past, they draw upon vocabularies ill-suited to give effect to legal concepts that impose mandatory strictures upon human conduct, all of which requires the clearest and most precise language. The vague, subjective jargon of the social scientist is not equal to the task of defining legal rights and legal obligations. Since it is to be assumed that the draftsman of laws and regulations desires to communicate thought and not obscure it, he will employ words and phrases that will be recognized and understood in precisely the same sense by himself and by the person he wishes to reach. He will use language that is likely to be familiar to the reader; and if it concerns a subject that may be new or unfamiliar, old phrases will, so far as possible, be adopted. Professor F. Reed Dickerson has said, "You shouldn't define a word in a sense significantly different from the way it is understood by the persons to whom the legislation is primarily addressed. This is a fundamental principle of communication, and it is one of the shames of the legal profession that draftsmen so flagrantly violate it."[6]

When the tested terminologies of the law are abandoned, the new supports may be found inadequate to bear the stresses of the freshly conceived structure. In the testing process of the new timbers, the members of the public most concerned with the effect of the revised laws will not only find themselves suspended in a limbo of uncertainty, but will for many years, be put to great expense litigating the fresh issues that legislators have so casually created. When this happens, the whole process of judicial interpretation must begin afresh upon unknown and shifting soil. In due course, ambiguities will be detected in the new terminology. The uncertainties of the past will be compounded. Were greater care taken to preserve the tried and established principles and vocabularies of the law, ordinary litigants would be spared the ordeal of being made the unwitting victims of the legal vivisectionists.

The recently enacted laws governing the rights of a married person to share in the property of a spouse will generate decades of bitter, costly conflict in the courts, not because the principles of sharing are unjust, but because newly enacted statutes in certain of the provinces, are not content to regard the judge as an adjudicator of rights and obligations. They seek to make of him an accountant, tax collector, social worker, probation officer, and occult medium. The common law and the rules of equity, coupled with the statutory discretion accorded Superior Court judges to deal with this area of the law have operated reasonably well for many years. Unfortunately, an ill-conceived lawsuit like the <u>Murdoch</u> case[7] that is given wide publicity in the information media, may create the unwarranted impression that the law requires overhauling, when all that really needed to be changed in that particular case was the concept of the action to be tried and the language in which the pleadings and argument in court were couched.

The man of law, by virtue of his training and his daily work, is congenitally wary of change for its own sake. His acceptance of history and his respect for the precedents of the past do not derive

125

from any lack of imagination or sympathy for the high expectations of the new generations that make their appearance upon the scene. He is aware of all of these. But he knows also that each generation that is born is a fresh barbarian invasion, and that if children are not civilized by their parents and teachers according to the laws of the land into which they are born, it will not be long before that land will become the sanctum of savages.

Peering into the unknown from the sixteenth century, Sir Francis Bacon recognized the value of precedents and said: "It were good ... that men in their innovations would follow the example of time itself; which indeed innovateth greatly, but quietly, by degrees scarce to be perceived. ... It is good also not to try experiments in states except the necessity be urgent, or the utility evident; and well to beware that it be the reformation (of the individual) that draweth on the change, and not the desire of change that pretendeth the reformation."[8]

If Bacon's counsel were read and heeded by the men of law who sit today in Canada's Parliament and in Quebec's Assembly, the law would not be made an instrument to change man's nature, his language, or his domicile. The agonies of national bifurcation would be allowed to heal naturally, slowly, without the surgeon's knife. The panacea sought through instant linguistic immersion and metric conversion would be abandoned as being abrasive and unsettling, and the Draconian francophonic laws would be repealed.

The competition of tongues and tempers is not new to the affairs of mankind. It was inevitable that England's military victory on the Plains of Abraham in 1759 should have brought about changes in the laws and languages of the country. This was not the first time a conqueror influenced the culture of the people he overcame. Six hundred and ninety-three years before Wolfe scaled the cliffs overhanging the St. Lawrence, William of Normandy landed in Pevesney in Northern England and later fought the Battle of Hastings where the English were defeated. William — the bastard son of "Robert the Devil," Duke of Normandy, and a Frenchman — became King of England, and as Normans came to occupy positions of importance in court and church, so French words and phrases and ideas infiltrated the land and became an integral part of a new language. Only lawyers who have read the earliest reports of legal proceedings after the Norman Conquest can appreciate how great the French influence upon the language of the courts of England has been. The French fact in English law is still very much alive. One example of the French contribution to English legalese appears as late as the seventeenth century in the case of *LeRoy* v. *Starling Alderman de London et 16 Autres:*[9] a prosecution for conspiring to withhold lawfully levied taxes.

The case has so contemporary a ring, it confirms John Dryden's observation that "mankind is ever the same, and nothing lost out of Nature, though everything is altered."[10]

In Charles's time, there was no need for two languages. The judges became masters of Saxon English and Norman French and so wrote learned judgments that drew on both vocabularies, and these were understood by men and women with only a smattering of ignorance in either language.

Here is the report of Starling's case, verbatim:

LE ROY versus STARLING ALDERMAND DE LONDON, & 16 AUTRES.

Information pur impoverishing les farmors de excise.

Information fuit perferr vers S. & les auters, brewers de Lond' pur ceo que ils fueront de confederacy & ont conspire pur deprender le gallon trade (que est ceo per que les povers sont supply) & pur cause les povers de mutiny vers les fermors del excise, et l'information ouster recite que lou l'excise est settle sur le Roy per Act de Parliament & part de son revenue les defendants ont per combination & confederacy endeavour depauperate les fermors del excise, et sur rien culp fuit trye in London & jury trove les defendants culp de rien forsque le conspiration pur depauperate les fermors del excise, et fuit move pur quash cel information.

1. Pur ceo que nest vi & armis, mes ceo fuit over-rule per Curiam car est bone sans vi & armis intant que confederacies & conspiracies ne sont properment ove force mes secret & occult sans overt poyar, et la sont plusors informations in Lexchequer pur tiels misdemeanors san vi & armis.

2. Fuit move que les defendants icy ne sont trope culp dascun offence, car sont acquit de tout per le verdict forsque l'impoverishing del fermors & nest ascun offence punishable per nostre ley pur depauperate auter al intent de inrich moy

127

mesme come per vender commodities al cheaper rates. Et tiel general charge ne poet estre ascun offence in les defendants come appiert 29 Ass. 45. Stamford 95 F. Mes apres several debates fuit adjudge per Curiam que ceo est bone verdict sur que judgment serra done pur le Roy, car le verdict relate al information & l'information recite coment l'excise est parcell del revenue del Roy & pur impoverish eux voil fair eux incapable de render al Roy son revenue, et coment la ne poit estre conspiracy sans ascun overt act de plusors uncore ils touts agree que le confederacy icy est act punishable pur que judgment serra done pur le Roy, et puis ils fueront fine in 2000 marks, scil. chescun forsque est 100 marks & il 500.

Nota fuit move pur le Roy que evidence poet estre done in Court del manner del confederacy al intent que le fine serra pluis haut mes le Court ne voet oye ceo.

Mr. Justice Kenneth C. MacKay of the Superior Court of Quebec tells a story which he admits may be apocryphal. An English-speaking judge of the Court of Appeal wrote in his reasons for judgment that one of the parties to the appeal that was a company, had reneged on an agreement because "it had a change of heart." When the official French version of the judgment was published, the expression became: "Elle avait eu une transplantation cardiaque."

About the same time that the decision in Starling's case was written in England in legal "franglaise," Frenchmen in Canada were wrestling with the laws of New France. One settler wrote to his family:

I will not say that justice is more chaste and disinterested here than in France; but at least, if she is sold, she is sold cheaper. We do not pass through the clutches of advocates, the talons of attorneys, and the claws of clerks. These vermin do not infest Canada yet.[11]

Happily, they never came to "infest Canada". Of course, the cost of legal services was as much a matter of concern in the seventeenth century as it is in the twentieth. It is not the client alone who worries over costs.

The lawyer, whose profession brings him into the closest of relationships with his client, is ever mindful of the burdens that a heavy financial commitment may place upon the man whose cause he has undertaken to champion. When he advances his client's interests, the man of law seeks to secure for him all of the benefits that it lies within his power to command. He may be retained to consider only a single problem or to negotiate or consummate only a single transaction for his client; or he may represent him in all of his business affairs. Whatever he does, be it great or small, complex or simple, his duty is the same: to use all of his skills, knowledge, and energy for the advancement of his client's interest and welfare, and to do nothing that he can foresee which may cause him injury or harm. This carries with it the obligation to incur such costs and make such charges of his client as are fair and reasonable.

"How is he to determine all of that?" you may ask. He must give consideration to a great many factors, and these will include the importance of the matter in hand, the result which he has achieved for the benefit of his client, the skill and expertise that he commands and that he exercised in achieving the result, the difficulty and complexity of the issues of the case, and the time that he and his associates devoted to the task. These elements vary from case to case. There exists no easy formula for determining a fair fee for legal services that are rendered, save in the simplest of cases. At the outset, when a lawyer first meets with his client to listen to his problem he hears only one side of the story, and at best only a small part of that story. Only after digging into all of the facts of the case and learning what others who have a knowledge of the events and circumstances have to say about the matter, can the lawyer acquire any genuine appreciation of the issues in dispute. So long as the facts are not clear and the issues remain in contention, it is not possible to advise a client with any certainty as to the outcome of the dispute or as to the exact costs that will be incurred. All he can do is to express his opinion as to the result, and his estimate as to the costs. He can give no guarantees save that he will apply his best efforts to succeed and that his fees will be calculated according to a formula upon which the lawyer and his client may agree in advance.

Traditionally, lawyers have not advertised their presence in the marketplace because it has never been possible to publish a list of the services they render with a price neatly set opposite each, like a merchant who advertises the butter and cheese, the beans and the bacon he offers for sale to the public. It is a simple matter for the butcher, the baker, and even the undertaker to advertise his wares or services, and simple, too, for the customer to examine what each of them has to offer before he buys. But legal services cannot be examined in advance by a prospective customer; such services can neither be weighed nor measured, sniffed or squeezed like a turkey or turbot or a melon or cheese. Were he to advertise, the lawyer would have to praise, not his merchandise, but himself. How could he ever become a crier who hawks his wares on the streets — pricing and praising and puffing them — without promising to do more than anyone else can do for a client he has never seen, in respect of a problem he has never considered, opposing parties he does not know, and in a court or forum as yet undetermined?

More often than not, the man of law is not consulted by an individual who requires that he do a specific job or perform a specific piece of work, any more than a dentist is asked to extract a particular molar or bicuspid or fill a designated cavity or insert a special bridge. The patient generally confronts his dentist with a problem of loose or lost or aching teeth, and asks his advice as to how he can be made well. If the patient has demanded that two incisors be removed, the dentist will not act upon these instructions alone. He will first carry out his own examination and diagnosis, and then he will advise the patient what should be done. If the patient agrees with the treatment recommended, the dentist will proceed with his work. But should the patient disagree and decide not to follow his dentist's advice, the relationship will obviously end, since it would be wrong for the dentist to treat the patient in a manner that he considers improper or inappropriate, and it would be unprofessional to carry out any operation contrary to the patient's instructions. A patient in the dental chair is not a motorist at the service station who can order the attendant to "fill 'er up" and pay him for the gas at the price posted, and drive off. Neither is the client sitting in the lawyer's office to discuss a suit for damages arising out of a personal injury in a motor car accident, a mere customer shopping for a suit of clothes at the department store. Garages and service stations and haberdashers are able to communicate useful information to the public concerning their merchandise and their services because what they offer for sale has been predetermined and the information they publish can be precise.

Commercial advertising of a personal nature has been avoided over the years by lawyers who appreciate that he who blows his own horn is likely to inflate the sense of his own importance and to mislead others as to his ability and merit. His comments are likely to draw or infer comparisons between himself and others in his profession and in so doing, it is virtually impossible for him to be

130

objective. It is not that competition among lawyers is to be discouraged. On the contrary, the adversary system of the law depends upon competition, and there is no profession more thoroughly schooled in it. The simple fact is that the most unlikely place to measure the ability and competence of any man of law is in the advertising sections of our daily newspapers and periodicals, or during the commercials that are heard and seen on the electronic media.

Undoubtedly, the merits of counsel will continue to be judged by the public just as their ancestors assessed them when they watched the champions battle a client's cause on the jousting fields of medieval England. A contest in court where the issue is justice, the weaponry the law, and the prize, a client's success, will reveal a host of truths about the champions. But in a publicity contest that is sparked by narcissism, fired by the self-laudatory language of the participants, in which the prize is the patronage of the uninformed or gullible, merit and truth are likely to lose the day.

It is paradoxical that in recent years, consumer organizations, spurred on by Ralph Nader's "raiders" of the United States and Canada, should criticize members of the legal profession for their reluctance to advertise. In the past, such groups have never relented in their sharp condemnation of every organization, from the producers of soaps, detergents, and deodorants to the manufacturers of automobiles, motor boats, and chewing gum for the great sums of money spent by them on advertising. They have been tireless in pointing out how large a percentage of the price paid for mass-produced goods goes to Madison Avenue, and how the consumer and not the producer or distributor or retailer pays. Advertising, it has been claimed, is simply another rip-off of the consumer by the economic establishment. And yet, these associations have inexplicably convinced governments that a professional association that discourages its members from advertising is guilty of restraining trade and violating the rights of its members to engage in free speech.

Touting or advertising for legal business traditionally have been avoided if not actively reproved for a very sound and simple reason. By virtue of the fact that the barrister is a gladiator who does battle for those who employ him, a large part of his life is lived in controversy and contention. And because of the intimate and confidential relationship that exists between the lawyer and his client, and the high trust that a client reposes in his counsel, the lawyer occupies the unique position in which he is capable of strongly influencing his client's decisions and course of conduct. The man of law is naturally reluctant to volunteer his services and advice to others lest such gestures appear importunate and may be interpreted as designed to benefit the lawyer and not the client. Since it is the client's interest that must be served and not the lawyer's, the man of law is naturally reluctant to do anything which may place his personal interest above his client's.

But there is another reason why it is in the best interests, not only of the lawyer, but of society, that the man of law ought not to be forward in his search for business.

The prime reason for the existence of laws is to preserve peace and tranquillity in the communities of the country so far as that is possible to achieve through human institutions. To commit a breach of "the King's peace" or "to stir up disaffection among His Majesty's loyal subjects" have always been regarded as crimes. Because the man of law, of all citizens, is in a position to issue writs and serve summonses, begin lawsuits and apply for mandatory orders and injunctions, and generally so to utilize the courts to initiate litigation as to jeopardize lives, liberty, reputation and property, it was always important that his influence and power should be exercised for the purpose of promoting peace and contentment, and not to stir up animosity, hatred, and discontent.

For that reason, it is the practice of lawyers, wherever possible, to make every effort to settle disputes between contending parties rather than immediately to rush to the court house to issue a writ. The model man of law seeks to lay contention to rest and not to promote or exacerbate it. He does not inspire or promote litigation, but first seeks out alternatives to achieve his client's desired result.

For a lawyer (and particularly a young lawyer) to make his presence known, and declare his interest in meeting the public, some of whom may avail themselves of his knowledge and expertise, is not only natural but desirable. For that reason, announcement cards that a lawyer is engaged in the practice of law, and that his special expertise lies in a particular field are always acceptable. Informational advertisements by the law society or bar association that represents all lawyers, indicating the particular areas of practice in which its members engage is helpful to the public, and cannot be misinterpreted as an egoistic, aggressive assault on the public for custom. These practices will provide the prospective client with the limited measure of guidance he requires to find the lawyer's door where he will receive the kind of advice that will serve him best.

Samuel Johnson's view on legal advertising was not wholly acceptable to the lawyer Boswell, but it was full of good sense, and it remains instructive after two hundred years:

> **Johnson:** Sir, it is wrong to stir up law-suits; but once it is certain that a law-suit is going on, there is nothing wrong in a lawyer's endeavoring that he shall benefit rather than another.
>
> **Boswell:** You would not solicit employment, Sir, if you were a lawyer?
>
> **Johnson:** No, Sir, but not because I should think it wrong, but because I should disdain it. However, I would not have a lawyer to be wanting to himself in using fair means. I would have him inject a little hint now and then to prevent his being overlooked.[12]

My model cannot be complete unless he has been touched and quickened by the wit of Edmund Burke who spoke so eloquently of the common law lawyer of England. "The study of law," he said, "renders men acute, inquisitive, dextrous, prompt in attack, ready in defence, full of resources. In other countries, the people, more simple, and of a less mercurial cast, judge of an ill principle in government only by an actual grievance; here they anticipate the evil and judge of the pressure of the grievance by the badness of the principle. They augur misgovernment at a distance, and snuff the approach of tyranny in every tainted breeze."[13]

To serve these ends in each century of time, let every citizen and every student of the law, and every man who loves the law, remember his obligations. Let each of them grow a nose long enough to make the public business his business; sharp enough to smell the first stench of slavery, masked though it may be by the perfumery of bureaucratic benevolence or the promise of political philanthropy; and ubiquitous enough to be seen and felt in every courtroom and every assembly and in all places where power resides and is employed in the governance of men. This, and nothing less, is the lawyer's obligation to his country and his profession.

IX

JUDGMENT

Give therefore to thy servant an understanding
heart, to judge people, and discern between good and evil.

"SOLOMON'S PRAYER FOR WISDOM," 3 *KINGS* 3:9

And eke men seyn that thilke juge is wys that
soone understandeth a matiere juggeth by leyser.
A good judge conceives quickly, judges slowly.

GEOFFREY CHAUCER, 1386

TO DO JUSTLY
AND TO LOVE MERCY
AND TO WALK HUMBLY
WITH THY GOD

JUDGMENT

J udgment is not a faculty reserved exclusively for the man of law who sits on the bench. It is a quality as essential to the character of the lawyer as sapience, for knowledge without judgment renders the man of law as destitute as one who, having the capacity to walk, lacks the ability to balance.

If the lawyer who sits at his desk and advises clients lacks judgment, that is a misfortune. But if the lawyer who sits on the bench and judges his fellow man lacks judgment, that is a calamity.

Benjamin Disraeli was once asked what difference there was between a misfortune and a calamity. "If William Gladstone," he said, "were to fall into the River Thames, that would be a misfortune. But if anyone were to pull him out, that would be a calamity!"

In his role as solicitor, the man of law must exercise his judgment as selflessly and express his opinion as cautiously as a judge adjudicating a cause that is argued before him. He must familiarize himself with the facts, refresh his knowledge of the law bearing upon those facts, and putting aside all personal interest (be it the desire to earn a large fee by litigating or the subconscious hope to enhance his personal reputation by counselling court proceedings that may attract publicity and advancement), he must honestly advise his client on the course of action that is most likely best to advance his client's interests. Not only material interests are of concern. The psychological effects of litigation, for example, are of great relevance, as are the elements of time and the simple human wear-and-tear of the contest. The lawyer who fails to take these peripheral factors into account may find that he has labored hard and long for what may well prove to be a dissatisfied, irate client.

The solicitor in his office may seem more remote from the judge than the barrister pleading his case in a court of law. But the distinction is only superficial, and of a physical kind. For a client regards his solicitor as the adjudicator of his rights and obligations, and the sensitive lawyer always bears in mind the fact that his client hearkens to his words and relies upon his opinions as though he were a judge speaking *ex cathedra* from the bench.

The lawyer's advice is generally accepted, and the client acts upon it as though it were the fiat of the court, albeit more expeditiously and less expensively come by. The client, if he is wise, will avoid litigation, just as the solicitor, if he is experienced, will counsel against it whenever he can. The lawyer recommends a law suit as reluctantly as a physician recommends surgery. It is the remedy of last resort — as diligently to be eschewed as a declaration of war; but to be pursued as vigorously, once embarked upon.

Every statement of claim that is issued out of the registry office of a court of law is the opening artillery barrage of a battle in which the power of the law is set in motion. It is an awesome force to let loose, and an expensive one. Happily, the mere fact that it is there, and the knowledge of its potential, are generally sufficient to move men and women to modify their behavior, to act more reasonably and to conform with the law. With the exception of petitions for divorce, only a very small fraction of the writs and statements of claim issued in civil cases culminate in trials. The threat of a lawsuit is often sufficient to bring a recalcitrant debtor to heel. The pre-trial steps that must be taken often have an equally astringent effect.

When a defendant finds he must produce and deliver to the person suing him, *all* letters and agreements and all other documents that bear on the dispute, he is sometimes sufficiently shaken to admit his obligations and keep his papers to himself. After both parties have submitted to searching "examinations for discovery" at which they must answer on oath, all questions put to them, they often come to assess the weaknesses as well as the strengths of both sides and this has the salutary effect of often leading to a compromise and a satisfactory settlement. On the court house steps on the very day of trial, litigants sometimes choose to become judges in their own cause and with counsel, they work out their own settlements. These are better than any judgment that could be imposed upon them by a judge or jury. At the time they are concluded, such settlements may seem to be the result of oppression or duress, but these are elements arising from their own personal relationships and are not instruments of the law. Judges and lawyers encourage such settlements, for the purpose of the law is to lay contention to rest and not to perpetuate conflict.

Lawsuits reveal the pathology of human conduct, not its norm. They may be constructive and life-supporting or they may be destructive and debilitating, and while total success in a lawsuit is not necessarily the rule, what is one party's gain is obviously the other's loss. Everyone views the scene differently depending upon where he sits. In the kingdom of the cannibals, it is said that after a long famine, when there is nothing to eat, the cannibal medicine man praises providence for ultimately sending his tribe a nice plump missionary.

It is small wonder that Justice Learned Hand of New York remarked, "As a litigant I should dread a law suit beyond almost anything else short of sickness and death." It is when the citizen finds himself in that much-dreaded position exhibited at court in the claw of the law, that he prays with Sir Thomas Talfourd that the seats of justice be filled "with good men, not so absolute in goodness as to forget what human frailty is."

That model appeared when Chief Justice Ted Culliton was appointed to the Court of Appeal of Saskatchewan. Appellants behind prison bars no less than counsel at the bar of his court, came to know and admire the brilliant mind that was moved by an understanding heart. Prisoners often filed notices of appeal simply to have someone to whom to tell their troubles. Culliton never failed to listen, never failed to ponder, never failed to remember that he had before him not a file, but a man. Recidivism was a phenomenon he deplored; yet, he made it an opportunity to discover how appellants whose sentences he had reviewed months or years before, were now faring. Especially if they were natives. "How's your young brother Clement?" he would ask a prisoner after he had made his representations to the court. "Has he got a job yet? I'm glad he's been staying out of trouble." Or to the prisoner himself, "You're having a tough time to learn, eh? We'll see that you are released in time to get you back to school to write your exams. . . . See that you pass them, eh?"

When a man of law is elevated to the bench, he forsakes his clients — the rich and the poor, the powerful and the obscure, the immoral, the respectable, the stubborn and the tractable, the hostile and the lovable, the tremulous and garrulous, the silent, the mystic and the fatuous, the guilty and the innocent, the scholars and the ignorant, those happy and of ill content — all clients who, if not his friends, were certainly the sustinence of a practice that trained and qualified him for his new role.

Upon his "elevation to the bench," a phrase still cherished by lawyers who wish to show respect for their colleagues newly appointed to the judiciary,[1] the man of law also renounces his ties with governments, especially with the government that appointed him to his high office. Thenceforth, he has only one client, and that client is the law. He has only one cause, and that cause is justice. He acknowledges only one debt, and that is the debt he owes to his predecessors who developed the law and his brethren on the bench and counsel at the bar who will assist him in interpreting and applying it.

The life of the man of law as counsel in court is much affected by the sense of fairness, the temperament, and the sensitivity of his "brother-in-law" who sits as presiding judge. Counsel's reputation, his success and his peace of mind, rise and fall as the judicial instruments are tuned and played according to the *tempi* of the court conductor's baton.

Except in a very small community, lawyers and litigants are not wedded to a single judge. Normally, there are a number of judges who sit on a rotating basis in each judicial centre. It is often possible for counsel so to arrange his schedule as to assure with reasonable certainty that a particular judge will try his case, or more importantly, that a certain judge will *not* try it. The process is sometimes pejoratively called "judge-hopping," but it involves no clandestine or improper maneuvering by a lawyer. It is a sensible procedure since counsel has both the right and the duty to advance his client's cause by selecting the most appropriate court and the most perceptive judge to hear his plaint.

The judge's singular function, briefly and starkly stated, is simply to discover the facts, to interpret the law, and then to administer it. About 400 B.C. Socrates said that in carrying out these duties, the judge should hear courteously, answer wisely, consider soberly, and decide impartially. In 2400 years, these directions have not been improved upon.

It is not the Goddess of Justice alone who is painted blind. Judges, on occasion, are oblivious of the effect their demeanour may have upon the parties who appear before them. There is a surprising consensus among lawyers, wherever they may practice, concerning the manners, erudition, and sense of fairness of judges. The judge that a plaintiff's lawyer favors for his understanding is generally the judge that the defendant's lawyer will also prefer for his moderation. The trial judge whose work load is heavy, like the lawyer whose calendar is full, may feel assured that he enjoys the confidence of the bar. A heavy calendar is a high, albeit an unsolicited compliment that a judge graciously receives. On the other hand, when a judge's trial list evaporates at the opening of a sitting, that judge should reflect that he, too, may profitably learn from his brethren at the bar and may well benefit from some quiet introspection into the acceptability of his courtroom demeanor, of his industry, or of the principles of law upon which his judgments rest. The classic opening of an appellant's argument in the Court of Appeal of Saskatchewan, at one time began: "This is an appeal from the judgment of the Honourable Mr. Justice Taylor. But, my Lords, on this appeal, I have other grounds as well." The lawyers of every jurisdiction have their own cryptic counterpart.

The judge only interprets the laws. He does not make them. Couched as most statutes are, in general terms, it becomes the judge's duty to concentrate upon the specific dispute he must resolve, particularizing the general, and so personalizing the law to fit the circumstances of the case that is before him. It is in this process that the wisdom and practicality of the law undergo their severest tests. What may seem to be a perfectly reasonable principle when stated in general terms, often becomes a monstrous anomaly when applied to a particular set of facts. Justice Holmes stated many years ago that "experience, not logic, is the life of the law," but in my view, both are elements without which the law can neither subsist nor grow. Experience furnishes the inductive elements of the law, and logic or reason its deductive fiber, and like the warp and the woof of a tapestry, not only are both necessary, they are inseparable. It then becomes the duty of the judge to interpret the statute before him sensibly, analyzing not only the individual words of the enactment, but considering the purpose the statute seeks to accomplish and the end result that his adjudication is likely to produce. He will compare it with other statutes in which the same or similar phrases are used, and he will relate it to earlier laws that the new statute is designed to replace or to supplement. Logic, reason, and experience all have a role to play in the adjudicative process.

It has been said that law is the common sense of the ordinary man as it is modified by the legislature. That may have been true when statute books were thin and common sense a strong and robust thing. Now that legislation has grown so gross, and pays little heed to the common sense of the ordinary man, it would be more accurate to say that law has become the enactment of the legislature, modified by the experience and good sense of judges.

No one, least of all learned counsel at the bar, suggests that the judge is omniscient, although he may at times, appear omnipotent. Having done his best to reach a fair result, the judge is not surprised when he is criticized by lawyers, laymen and newspeople, some, perhaps more learned in their respective fields than he.

The judgments and conduct of every judge are subject to the

criticism of the press and of lay persons, just as they are subject to the scrutiny and comment of other judges and lawyers. And rightly so, for the judgments of the men of law are matters that lie within the public domain, and they must be capable of standing close scrutiny. Criticism is to be encouraged. But all such criticism must be constructive and expressed in the interests of the administration of justice and not for the purpose of discrediting the judge or subverting or undermining the rule of law itself. An attack *ad hominem* in which a judge is personally assailed for what some may believe to be an unwise or unwarranted decision is improper because, as Sir Winston Churchill observed, "Judges are required to lead a form of life and conduct far more severe and restricted than that of ordinary people." It is difficult, if not impossible, for a judge to enter the public arena of controversy to defend his judgments against unfair attack — just as difficult as it would be for a referee to explain to an excited, bottle-throwing crowd of baseball fans why he called a batter out on first.

Speaking for the members of the Supreme Court of Canada in 1978, Chief Justice Laskin said: "We certainly must expect, and indeed, even welcome scholarly criticism of our decisions. Such criticism is in the tradition of our law, but it is voiced or expressed without charging the court with bias. It is the decision that is always open to question and to criticism, but not the integrity of the judge."[2]

A judge ought not to resent the fact that other judges sitting in higher courts reverse his decisions, reduce sentences, or even question his common sense or his reasoning. The duty of a judge is to adjudicate a dispute and to determine the rights and obligations of the parties who stand before him. He may do nothing less. But on occasion, there is more that is required of him. "It is not the court's function to legislate or to lay down broad, general principles to tie the hands of courts in future cases," Chief Justice Culliton of Saskatchewan has often said. "It is the judge's duty to define the point of law that is appropriate to the problem and to apply that law to the facts and come to a conclusion on the specific issue before him. When a judge strays far afield enunciating broad general principles, he is almost certain to create more difficulties tomorrow than he is likely to solve today." In the result, with an economy of words that is the envy of his brethren, Culliton's lean judgments have a way of sweeping away the deadwood, leaving only a well-pruned principle to stand. His influence, particularly upon the criminal law of Canada, has been to simplify many difficult concepts, such as "intent" and the defenses of insanity, drunkenness, and automatism.

The regenerating strength of the bench arises from the fact that the man of law, whether barrister, solicitor, or judge, is one of a company unique among the learned professions, for there is no other in which superiors so publicly criticize the apparent shortcomings of their inferiors, and inferiors so zealously (if less publicly) criticize the patent imperfections of their superiors. I hasten to add that "superior" and "inferior" are intended by men of law to refer (as is the custom) to the jurisdiction of the *court* in which the judge sits and not to the judge's intellectual capacity or his legal or literary attainments.

In a speech to the members of the Canadian Bar Association meeting at Banff, Alberta, in 1963, Sir Richard Diplock told of Queen Victoria's opening of the Royal Courts of Justice in London in the year 1882. The judges of the High Court had met to agree upon a suitable address to Her Majesty for the occasion. The presentation began humbly with the words, "Conscious as we are of our manifold defects ..." Lord Jessel objected to what he regarded as an unnecessarily abject view of the abilities of the judges. It was then that Lord Bowen suggested the classical alternative that proved acceptable to all: "Conscious as we are of *one another's* many imperfections ..." The Queen graciously accepted the address, doubtless reassured that her judges would ever be as mindful of the sensibilities of her loyal subjects as of their own.

In court and in the law reports, the examination and reexamination, assessment, revision, criticism and correction of judicial decisions go on continuously, all "with the utmost respect" according to the settled traditions of the bar. In the law journals and in academic communities, the criticism is often less restrained. The reason is obvious. In court, the battle of wits is a duel — an affair of honor carried on at close range. The legal writer, researcher, and teacher, on the other hand, may lob his shells over the hedges of academe secure in the knowledge that his fire is unlikely ever to be returned. Wherever the sortie may originate, every man of law knows that his views are never sheltered from *bona fide* criticism and attack.

We have seen that the statutes of Parliament and the rules and regulations of the hydra-headed hierarchies of the state are the "law written," and fixed. They cover thousands of acres of printed paper proliferating every conceivable human activity. The man of law may influence those who write the law, but he cannot control the content of the statute books or the volume of the delegated legislation those books spawn. The judge, on the other hand, gives expression to the text of the law. He is the "law speaking." It is he who breathes the breath of life into the inert mass of black letters that constitute the written body of the law, refining its generalities, infusing common sense into its ambiguities, reconciling its inconsistencies, and applying the substance of the law to the facts of the specific case that, as judge, he must decide. If legislatures are the composers of the notes that orchestrate the law, judges are the conductors who read those notes and translate them into sound and sometimes fury. Wherever possible, they will make those notes signify something. In the performance, the judge interprets the notes according to his capacity, his sagacity, and experience. It is to be expected, therefore, that there will be eminences of the bench just as there are the virtuosi of the concert stage. No two are alike.

One can never be certain that a man tried on a criminal indictment before Judge "A" will receive the same verdict were he tried on the same charge before Judge "B". And it goes without saying that the twelve persons who sit as Jury "Y" might deliver quite a different verdict than will be delivered by the twelve persons who constitute Jury "Z", hearing the same evidence as it affects the same accused. In human affairs the camera records forever all that has transpired, and there can be no retake of any scene. A trial may be a drama, but it is no movie set. One can only speculate what might have been, had a different judge presided or a different counsel defended, or the principal witness talked a little less. Cynics might call the law a lottery and the courtroom a gaming house. All of this may be true, but only in the sense that being born at all is to find oneself a one-in-a-billion winner in the great game of genes. And when and how we make our quietus (statisticians notwithstanding) is likewise bound to remain, until the very end, a benign mystery.

I once put a question to Lord Hailsham of Marylebone when we appeared as adversaries in the Judicial Committee of the Privy Council in London in 1952 — years before he became Lord Chancellor of England and ornamented the woolsack in the House of Lords. I said to him: "Here we are in the highest court of the Commonwealth. Its judges are not bound by precedent; the principle of *stare decisis* has no application in this place. By what process do you think the Law Lords reach their decisions?"

Anticipating, perhaps, his future role in the highest of all courts of the Commonwealth, Hailsham with the certitude of the brilliant lawyer he was, though he had not yet taken silk nor been elevated to the bench, said that such a judge would study all the evidence in the case with care. And then, after weighing and pondering it, he would ask himself two questions:

First, as a matter of fairness and justice, what result does my conscience move me to reach? Once I have decided this, then I must ask myself the second question: Is there any existing rule of law or of equity that prevents me from reaching that result? If there is, I must follow the rule. If there is no rule that prevents me from holding what my sense of justice directs me to do, I would give judgment according the sense of justice that my conscience reveals.

Justice Benjamin N. Cardozo described that same judicial process in different language:

When the legislature has spoken, and declared one interest superior to another, the judge must subordinate his personal or subjective estimate of value to the estimate thus declared. ... Even when the legislature has not spoken, he is to regulate his estimate of values by objective rather than subjective standards, by the thought and will of the community rather than by his own idiosyncrasies of conduct and belief ... [I]f the communal thought or will is different, there will be neither statute nor custom nor other external token to declare or define the difference. The judge will then have no standard of value available except his own. In such circumstances ... the axiology that is to guide him will be his own and not another's.[3]

The judgment which is declaratory of new values establishes principles that find their way into the law and have the effect, not only of amending existing principles of law but of influencing human conduct in the future. The judgment of a court of law may not only crystallize the contemporary conscience of the community, but may enliven and animate it, guide it, and lead it. Justice Cardozo illustrates this phenomenon by asking whether anyone can doubt that "courts of equity in enforcing the great principle that a trustee shall not profit by his trust nor even place himself in a position where his private interest may collide with his fiduciary duty, have raised the level of business honour, and kept awake a conscience that might otherwise have slumbered?"[4]

The process is a never-ending one and judges today are as capable of giving expression to high standards of conduct as they were in the time of Bracton and Blackstone and Mansfield. Mr. Justice William G. Morrow, sitting in the Northwest Territories, tried an Indian charged with drinking whiskey off his reserve. He questioned whether the law could deny a Treaty Indian the prosaic right to drink on the same terms as any other citizen. In digging into the prohibitions of the *Indian Act*, Morrow cast up the dry bones of the *Canadian Bill of Rights* and resurrected them and gave new life to the principle that no federal law may be interpreted to discriminate against any man because of his racial or ethnic origin.[5] It is true that Morrow was a justice of the Supreme Court of the Yukon Territories when he tried Drybones. But it is also true that, possessed of like learning and industry, the man of law, upon whatever chair he sits, may so stimulate the growth of the law as to cause it to flourish as a tree under which every man may sit, and no one make him afraid.

In a country in which legislative powers are divided between a central federal parliament on the one hand, and state or provincial legislatures on the other (as in Canada, the United States, and Australia) the Supreme Court must act as adjudicator and ultimate arbiter of the validity of the laws that are passed by all rule-making bodies. To the judges of the Supreme Court is entrusted the highest responsibility of all: that of interpreting the constitution of the nation and applying its general principles to the specific people and problems that seek judgment in that court. The task is not a static one, merely to preserve the phrases enshrined in our national monuments and declarations and *Bills of Rights*. It is a never-ending work of creation and regeneration to which the justices of these, our highest courts, dedicate their lives with monkish devotion. In their role as appellate judges, they review the decisions that lower courts have made in specific cases involving disputes, many of them of a seemingly pedestrian nature: employer-employee contracts, family property, drunken driving, the exhibition of movies, making a confession to a police officer, adopting a child, selecting a school. In this role, the court may declare unconstitutional a law duly enacted by a majority of the popularly elected representatives of the people of a province or state, or indeed of the whole nation, should that law offend the constitution.

Where sovereignty does not reside in a single man or a single body of men but is divided among numerous governments — federal, provincial, and municipal — authority must somewhere find its ultimate resting place. No government, provincial or federal, may ride roughshod over the law-making areas that the constitution carves out for the other. To permit such public trespass would be to condone an invasion by the federal Parliament into the territories of the provinces. Conversely, to permit a province to extend its powers by enactments encroaching upon federal law-making areas would be to condone or encourage an invasion by the provinces into the exclusively determined federal domain. The courts are the domestic peace-keeping forces forever on the alert within our land. They preside in peace and war. They are the watchdogs and the guardians at the gates. They stand not only at the arches of our cities, but at the portals of our oceans and our national boundaries, at the entrance-ways to our provinces, and at the doors of our temples, and the porticos of our homes. As the highest tribunal in the land, the judgments of the Supreme Court of Canada declare the law more precisely than any act of Parliament or any pronouncement of a Prime Minister. It may be said that in a federal state true sovereignty resides in its highest court.

In matters of constitutional interpretation, judges are mindful of public opinion; but unlike politicians who feel they must bow to popular pressures, judges remain independent because they are not elected to their positions. They do not run for public office and they cannot be ruled by any political party. Public policy is too unruly a horse for any judge to mount. The judge's duty it not to do what may seem popular but to do what the law proclaims to be right. It is as true today as it was in 1617 when Sir Francis Bacon made the strident statement that "a popular judge is a deformed thing: and plaudits are fitter for players than magistrates."

The parliamentarian may (if that be his philosophy) pursue the mass applause of the public, for upon its approbation his office depends. His duty is to interpret the public will, reduce it to reasonable terms, having regard to his own knowledge and experience, and, where appropriate, to give it legislative expression by the repeal of those laws that are ill-conceived or incapable of useful administration, and the enactment, sparingly, of those laws that are necessary to liberate the energies and abilities of citizens so that they may live fuller lives, and the nation reap greater benefits from their skills and their industry.

While the justices of the Supreme Court are the ultimate referees in judicial contests between the central authority and the provincial legislatures, they may not act capriciously. Rightly understood, it is not the judges who are supreme, but the constitution. But since the constitution does not speak for itself, the judges must declare what it has to say on each question that is asked of them. Omniscience is not a quality that is ever claimed by any judge, but the court in which he sits may well claim infallibility — not because its judges are infallible but because, like the Supreme Court of Canada or the Supreme Court of the United States, under the constitution it is made the court of last resort.

Chief Justice Laskin described the adjudicative process on constitutional questions in more complex terms. Answering the criticism that the members of the Supreme Court of Canada have freedom to express their personal predilections and thus give effect to political preferences, he said:

We have no such freedom, and it is a disservice to the present members of this Court and to the work of those who have gone before us to suggest a federal bias because of federal appointment. Do we lean? Of course, we do, in the direction in which the commands of the constitution take us, according to our individual understandings. I do not say that we respond mechanically; that would be to deny our intellectuality and our contribution of judgment to the issues that come before us. Interpretation and application of constitutional directives involve judgment on factual issues as preliminary to the assessment of constitutional propriety. I do not believe in abstract constitutionalism, in the divorce of constitutional interpretation from a factual underpinning. The statute that governs our jurisdiction is rooted in a healthy pragmatism, a realization of experience that judicial issues, in whatever branch of the law they arise, involve a meshing of the factual and the legal, a mix of fact and law.[6]

In the final analysis, when a cause reaches the highest court of the land, there exists no guarantee of justice except that it be found in the personality and integrity of the judges themselves. This ideal was expressed by Rufus Choate, the great American counsel, who said to his junior who was rising to object to what he felt was an improper ruling of Chief Justice Shaw of Massachusetts: "Let it go. Sit down. Life, liberty and property are always safe in his hands!" Happily, I have felt confident enough to experience that same remarkable sentiment when I have sat at counsel's table before almost all of the superior court judges before whom I have appeared over a period of thirty-five years to try my clients' cases.

Sitting in appeal with two — or as many as eight — other learned judges is a humbling experience, since no one judge can dominate the others, and even the Chief Justice who presides is only one among equals. In the result, each judge of an appellate court forms his own view of the evidence; each judge considers the law. Consensus, that pale and flaccid concept, currently so fashionable in the make-believe world of the social scientist, occupies space of small consequence in the judgment-making process of appellate justices. Argument, debate, persuasion: these weapons, grown so familiar to the man of law in his forensic forays in the courts, are not allowed to grow rusty when the lawyer climbs out of the arena and occupies a place on the judge's bench. In court and in the conference room to which judges retire to consider their decision, each remains an individual, jealous of his independence, and dedicated to the adversary system which he recognizes to be the most effective means of searching for and discovering truth, and so reaching a sound, sensible, pragmatic, and principled result.

The wise and curious judge will therefore encourage argument in court. He will question counsel on his position and discourage him from reading or reciting his submissions as if by rote. Assuming counsel is presenting his case with some knowledge of the points at issue as disclosed in the pleadings, the judge will frankly tell him what his chief concerns are and upon what points he would like counsel's assistance by way of authority and precedent. The process of argument in court between well-briefed counsel and a keen-minded judge is a creative one. Each stimulates the mind of the other.

I have had the experience of arguing a case in successive appeals from the Court of Queen's Bench, ultimately to the Judicial Committee of the Privy Council. No two experiences were ever the same. The oral tradition (as compared with the practice of filing voluminous written briefs, very much in vogue in the United States) still persists in our courts. As a result, questions put by judges to counsel have a way of stimulating new, and often better, thoughts. A fresh phrase from the bench may plant a new idea and produce a surprising insight into the application of a statute that has been read and studied a hundred times. The questions and answers that move between bench and bar, the thrust and parry of debate, are the hammers that strike down upon the smithy's anvil, fashioning the heated iron into a shape that best fits the hoof of the horse to be shod. In the process, there will be sparks, and these often light the way to a more profound perception of ancient law, or reveal the path to a new concept that will find its place in the growing body of contemporary jurisprudence.

The decision of an appellate court is the decision of a majority of the judges who sit. Each judge may state the reasons for the conclusions he has reached, orally or in writing. No law specifically requires a judge to give reasons for a judgment. But it would be unthinkable for such a court to dispose of a case of any consequence without stating the reasons for its decision in order that all may be assured that the judges have heard and understood the case advanced by all parties to the proceedings, that they fully considered the facts and the law, and that they have reached their conclusions and given their judgment by a proper exercise of their authority in accordance with the law. As Chief Justice Holt stated many years ago, "The reason of a resolution is more to be considered than the resolution itself."[7]

If an appeal is dismissed, the judges (or a majority) may of course state quite simply that they agree with the decision and the reasons "given below." Having nothing to add, that of itself, obviously, is a statement of the appellate court's opinion. But where the issues to be decided are complex, or where opinion is divided, or where the matter is of great public interest and importance, appellate court judges invariably take great pains to explain the reasons why they have reached their conclusions. Earlier decisions of other courts and other judges are cited, examined and adopted, or they are distinguished from the case under consideration. Where the court's conclusions may appear to depart from established practice, distinctions are drawn in order that all who wish to examine the judgment may be convinced not only that a just result has been achieved, but that the result has been achieved by reason, and not caprice. It is a well-established principle of English law that finds its source in folk wisdom and common sense, that it is not enough that justice be done. It is necessary also, that it be made apparent to all that justice has been done. In an age in which intuitions, primitive practices, and the occult are idealized by some as native virtues more precious than knowledge and reason, the wisdom of the Roman lawyer Marcus Tullius Cicero serves as a sobering guide to the man of law today: "Wise men are instructed by reason; men of less understanding by experience; the most ignorant by necessity; and beasts by nature."

Let it not be thought that the judicial process can automatically assure a just and satisfactory result to all parties in every case. Opinions of the judges of every appellate court, from time to time, will differ. If there be a single requisite above all others that a judge insists upon, it is his right to complete independence — not for the sake of flattering his personal vanity, but to enhance his competence and influence in serving the public that trusts *him* and reposes confidence in *his* integrity. An appellate court is not a committee that is designed to diminish the personal responsibility of each member who serves upon it. Every judge bears the heavy burdens of his office alone. Numbers do not diminish duty. They only serve to assure that no evidence be overlooked, no argument be ignored, and that whatever has merit be measured on the balances of justice.

The final judgment of a court of last resort may not always be a model of clarity. Its *ratio decidendi*, or ruling principle, may be clouded by dissenting opinions or embellished by *obiter dicta*. Since the Right Honorable Bora Laskin became Chief Justice of Canada in 1974, nine judges have sat upon almost all appeals, and there has been no dearth of dissent, the greatest dissenter of all being the Chief Justice himself. These are signs, not of weakness in the court, but of strength. A dissenting judge is a thinking judge. And a judge who writes a majority judgment in the face of strong dissenters, faced by his colleagues' fire, is forced to concentrate his mind wonderfully. Dissent is the triumph of the adversary system enthroned on the bench where the majority opinion rules, but the minority view, biding its time, may see the day when, ultimately, it will be accepted as the rule.

Judges sitting in the appellate courts do not reach their decisions in the rarified atmosphere of the ivory tower. More of them are former academicians than ever before. But they cannot remain theorists balancing words and phrases in the allegorical scales of justice. Theirs to despatch, is the nation's most practical, pressing business. It is not the effect of their decisions upon the parties to the appeal alone that must be considered. Appellate judges must ever be mindful of the result which the principles they propound will have upon succeeding litigants and upon the countless others who will never appear in court but will nevertheless be bound by the cases that have been litigated. No decision dies with the judgment that lays a cause of contention to rest. The principle expressed in an appeal, like John Brown's body, goes marching on for decades and generations. In this sense, judges are more than mere adjudicators of the quarrels of litigants. The by-product of the judgment in any trial is the principle that is refined out of the mass of material that the millstones of the law have ground out of the evidence. The principle then becomes a rule as binding upon all members of society as any valid statute that Parliament may pass.

Samuel Johnson, that prolific lay commentator on the law, so much of whose conversation was the epitome of good sense, said:

Every just law is dictated by reason; and . . . the practice of every legal court is regulated by equity. It is the quality of reason to be invariable and constant; and of equity, to give every man what, in the same case, is given to another. The advantage which humanity derives from law is this: that the law gives every man a rule of action, and prescribes a mode of conduct which shall entitle him to the support and protection of society. That the law may be a rule of action, it is necessary that it be known, it is necessary that it be permanent and stable. The law is the measure of civil right, but if the measure be changeable, the extent of the thing measured never can be settled.[8]

In very recent years, judges have taken to meeting together in formal seminars at regular intervals to exchange views and establish principles they might apply uniformly within their respective jurisdictions. Discussion among professionals is generally assumed to be a useful and desireable exercise. But judges occupy a unique position in which personal independence is their chief virtue and the citizens' principal guarantee of justice. When judges reach a consensus among themselves concerning the manner in which they will in future deal with any class of cases as to the admission of evidence, the imposition of sentences, or any similar matter, there arises a very real danger that the principle agreed upon may override the considerations that ought to be weighed in every particular case that comes before each judge when he has heard the evidence. Laying down "policy" in advance may result in prejudging an accused or in anticipating an argument that counsel may present on his behalf. The judge who declares, "Henceforth I shall sentence everyone convicted of impaired driving to at least fourteen days in jail" impairs that judge's ability, if not fully and fairly to hear the evidence, then at least impartially to adjudicate upon the sentence to be meted out to an accused whom he has convicted. For a judge to make such a pronouncement, is, in effect, to disqualify himself from sitting on such cases. Where the general principle overrides the particular circumstances of the case, justice will have a bitter struggle to prevail. It is true that sentences vary considerably and press reports often convey to the public the impression that some citizens receive more favorable treatment from a judge, than others. Newspaper stories of trials are no longer full, fair reports of what has transpired in court. They are vignettes. A phrase that has caught the reporter's fancy may be all of the substance that may reach the press or the television screen, and the outsider is more likely to be titillated by what he sees or hears, than informed. Simply comparing sentences meted out for offenses passed under the same penal provisions of a statute will never convey the reasons why one man may have been sentenced to twenty years and another to two years for manslaughter (the maximum penalty for which is life imprisonment). Only one who has sat in court and witnessed the whole of the proceedings is able fairly to judge whether a conviction or a sentence imposed by the court is just and appropriate having regard to all of the circumstances. A desire to achieve "uniformity" simply to satisfy the statistician or to please the populist, may make individuals victim of grave injustices. The Procrustean bed that every wayfarer is made to fit is a crude and vulgar substitute for the concerned judgment of an informed, impartial judge.

Why are the courts able generally to fulfill the unique function of holding the scales of justice evenly between the competing interests of the litigants who seek judgment? The answer is not simply that the judges who sit on the benches of our courts are men learned in the law and experienced in its administration. It is also the fact that judges bring to their task a singular dedication to the principles of the law, that overrides all other loyalties. The lawyer, for whom the law has always been a jealous and an overweening mistress, when he is elevated to the bench, is expected to take her to his couch as his one and only lawful wife, foresaking all other passions. Sir John Simon, a great Lord Chancellor of England, once said, "We have put the judge in the position in our constitution where the only possible object of his honourable ambition is to leave a reputation for impartiality. He has nothing else to gain." In no other calling does a man, when he reaches the apex of his energies and his intellectual powers, so clearly abandon self-interest and enthrone altruism as the dominant force of his life.

Fortunate is the nation whose judges have not departed from these high standards. John Marshall expressed the sentiment of all who cherish the crucial role of the model man of law sitting as judge. "I always thought from my earliest youth till now," he said, "that the greatest scourge of an angry heaven ever inflicted on an ungrateful and sinning people, was an ignorant, a corrupt or a dependent judiciary."[9]

The ancient injunction of Micah applies to every man of law, but to the lawyer who sits as judge it is the highest precept of all. It might well be added to the oath that every judge takes upon his elevation to the bench in which he will solemnly swear "to do justly and to love mercy, and to walk humbly with [my]God."[10]

But how can anyone do justice and love mercy unless he first has knowledge? Centuries ago, Sir John Fortescue said that knowledge must be won and had, for "nothing can be loved except it be known."[11] And even when the law seems to be known, there still persists the overwhelming "agony of decision" that is the lot of every man who decides anything according to his conscience and the law.[12]

There was a time when King James I, erudite as he was, argued that since all law was founded upon reason, the sovereign was able to decide questions of law as well as any of his judges. To this, Coke, with the greatest of respect to his monarch, replied:

True it was that God hath endowed His Majesty with excellent science, and great endowments of nature; but his Majesty was not learned in the laws of His realm of England, and causes which concern the life, or inheritance, or goods, or fortunes of His subjects, are not to be decided by natural reason but by the artificial reason and judgment of law, which law is an act which requires long study and experience, before man can attain to the cognizance of it.[13]

The old Testament prophet said: "Thou shalt appoint the judges and the magistrates at all thy gates . . . that they may judge the people with just judgment."[14]

How may one find judges who will bless the people with "just judgments"? Learning the laws may not be an easy exercise today, but it is simple compared with the task of judging people with "just judgment."

Sir Matthew Hale, sitting as a judge in the seventeenth century,[15] set out the practical rules he sought to follow religiously in reaching just judgments. "I must remember," he said:

1. That in the administration of justice I am entrusted for God, the king and country; and therefore,

2. That it be done, first, uprightly; secondly, deliberately; thirdly, resolutely.

3. That I rest not upon my own understanding or strength, but implore and rest upon the direction and strength of God.

4. That in the execution of judgment, I carefully lay aside my own passions and do not give way to them, however provoked.

5. That I be wholly intent upon the business I am about, remitting all other cares and thoughts as unseasonable, and interruptions.

6. That I suffer not myself to be prepossessed with any judgment at all, till the whole business and both parties be heard.

7. That in business capital, though my nature prompt me to pity; yet, to consider that there is also a pity due to the country.

8. That I be not too rigid in matters purely conscientious, where all the harm is diversity of judgment.

9. That I be not biased with compassion to the poor or favour to the rich, in point of justice.

10. That popular or court applause or distaste have no influence in any thing I do, in point of distribution of justice.

11. Not to be solicitous what men will say or think, so long as I keep myself exactly according to the rules of justice.

Sir Francis Bacon expressed a similar view in his essay "On Judicature." He wrote:

A Judge ought to prepare his way to a just sentence as God useth to prepare his way, by raising valleys and taking down hills: so when there appearth on either side, high hand, violent prosecution, cunning advantages taken, combination, power, great counsel, then is the virtue of a Judge seen to make inequality equal; that he may plant his judgment as upon an even ground . . . in causes of life and death, judges ought (as far as the law permitteth) in justice to remember mercy; and to cast a severe eye upon the example, but a merciful eye upon the person.[16]

Counsel appearing before a court should expect to be the beneficiaries of courtesy and of the understanding judicial heart no less than litigants. The judge's respect for counsel is as important as the respect that counsel is duty-bound to accord to the judge. So Bacon warned judges that "Patience and gravity of hearing, are an essential part of justice; and an overspeaking judge is no well-tuned cymbal. It is no grace to a judge, first to find that which he might have heard in due time from the bar; or to show quickness of conceit, in cutting off evidence or counsel too short; or to prevent information by questions, though pertinent."[17]

In the fourteenth and fifteenth centuries, it is said that the justices of England sat for only three hours each day, from eight to eleven o'clock in the forenoon. Sir John Fortescue, in describing the afternoons of the King's judges, tells us why:

After they have taken their reflection, [they] doe passe and restore all the residue of the day in the study of the laws, in reading of Holy Scripture and using other kind of contemplation . . . so that their life may seem more contemplative than active. And thus do they lead a quiet life, discharged of all worldly cares and troubles."[18]

The judge's life is more active today. He will travel more, hear more, observe more, and judge more of worldly affairs than his ancient predecessors. There are no ivory towers and few cloistered gardens in which he may find asylum. But he will be as contemplative as Sir John's medieval judge. He will have no special, personal interest in the parties before him, but he will know everything about the case he must decide. He will withdraw himself, not from the world, but from active participation in its affairs. He may isolate himself from his old associates and brothers at the bar, not because he fears he might be influenced by old friendships but because he wishes that it be apparent to all that he will not be so influenced. The judge's life may therefore be a lonely one at times. But his detachment from the immediate and the contempoary enables him to view events more dispassionately and to observe the people who play a role in those events more compassionately.

Every judge recognizes that justice cannot be done when he is personally involved in an issue. Hence the maxim, "no man may be judge in his own cause." Personal involvement obscures vision. An ancient sage once said, "A penny will hide the biggest star in the universe if you hold it close enough to your eye." By eschewing the mundane and embracing the universal, the judge's view of the world will be refined and his writing may then capture something of the brightness of that biggest star.

From earliest times, the law was believed to have had its origin in the divine order of things. Cicero[19] held that law is the distillation of the highest reason implanted in man, the pervasive nature of which commands what ought to be done and forbids what may not be done. The intervening centuries have demonstrated that the law is not a dead body of parchment precepts. John Buchan described it more appropriately as an elastic tissue which clothes the living body of society.[20]

The law has always drawn its viability and vitality from society itself. No one has recognized this natural quality of the law more frequently nor expressed it with greater perception than Chief Justice Bora Laskin. "The law," he has said, "is not a still pool merely to be tended and occasionally skimmed of accumulated debris; rather it should be looked upon as a running stream, carrying society's hopes, and reflecting all its values, and hence requiring constant attention to its tributaries that are the social and natural sciences, to see all they feed in sustaining elements."

If it be true that society feeds the law and nourishes it, it is also true that the law sustains society and shapes it. Legislators may write the text on the nature and growth of the social order like a Doctor Spock writing on *Child Care*. But it is the judge who must apply that text to the men and women in society, understanding their nature, fostering their growth, guiding them, and sometimes chastising them like a firm but kindly parent. But always according to the law. For judges "are the depositaries of the laws; the living oracles, who must decide in all cases of doubt, and who are bound by an oath to decide according to the law of the land."[21]

X
HUMOR

True wit is nature to advantage dress'd,
What oft was thought, but ne'er so well express'd.

ALEXANDER POPE, "ESSAY ON CRITICISM"

I know you all, and will awhile uphold
The unyok'd humour of your idleness.

WILLIAM SHAKESPEARE,
KING HENRY IV, PART I, I, ii, 154

And that Nisi Prius nuisance, who just now is rather rife,
The Judicial Humourist — I've got him on the list!
All funny fellows, comic men, and clowns of private life —
They'd none of 'em be missed — they'd none of 'em be missed.

WILLIAM S. GILBERT, *THE MIKADO,* I

We have seen that trials had their origins in battle and battles have never been laughing matters. In the beginning, individuals who were unable to settle their differences amicably, resorted to violence. The survivor won the day, the argument, the fair damsel and all. As men grew more civilized, their brawling was supervised by neighbors who judged foul from fair, and declared the survivor who abided the rules as victor. Ultimately, the disputants chose champions to do battle for them. Their descendents are members of the legal profession.

To this day, a trial remains very much of a battle. It is still no laughing matter — even for the victor. For a trial is a contest, the outcome of which remains as uncertain as a horserace or a football game. Generally, they are costly affairs even for the parties who win the purse. Mr. Justice Riddell of the Ontario High Court appropriately said: "A jury trial is a fight and not an afternoon tea."[1] It is no treat for the effete. It is, however, a place *non pareil* where the able gladiator and the happy warrior find their true *metier.*

Who is the happy warrior? Who is he
That every man of law should wish to be?
He is the generous spirit, who, when brought
Among the tasks of life, has wrought
The plan that pleased his new-found thought.
'Tis he when called upon to face
Some awful moment for his brief's disgrace,
Joining great issues, good or bad, when fired,
Is happy as a lover. Then attired
With sudden brightness, like a man inspired
Through all the heat of conflict keeps the law
In calmness, and awaits to see what he foresaw.[2]

There are some who say there is no place for laughter in the courtroom. I regard such people as disciples of melancholy who have lacked an experienced mentor to light their gloomy way. Even Schopenhauer justified laughter among mankind. Man's lot, he said, is so miserable, he is the only animal whom nature found it necessary to endow with the capacity to laugh.

Every warrior has need for laughter to lighten his load. Whether he sits upon the bench or stands many years at the bar hoping to be offered a seat, the courtroom lawyer greets wit as a freshener that raises the spirit and eases the tensions of trial. An apt phrase in court can be more therapeutic than loosening shoe laces that have grown too tight after standing for three hours before a demanding judge.

As Reginald Hine, that "un-common attorney" confessed, "Lawyers are not professional wits, but there is a good deal of wit flying about the profession."[3] So much solemnity hedges the lawyer's life! His gown, the trappings of the courtroom, the demeanor of the judge, the subject matter of most trials — death, imprisonment, and money — that it is natural for the man of law to unburden himself with frivolity and laughter.

At dinner, the ancient self-serving toast may still be heard in praise of the lawyer-shy public:

> When a festive occasion our spirit unbends
> Let us always recall the profession's best friends,
> So pass 'round the ale and a large bumper fill
> For the jolly testator who makes his own will!

Mock arguments are still made at the lawyer's supper table about the merits of a defense of contributory negligence to an action for seduction or a paternity claim, and the question is still put: "Does the expression *en ventre sa mere* mean the same thing as *in loco parentis?*

The judge in court may be the butt of caustic comment. But not often. For he who derides a presiding judge runs the risk of finding a humorless judge calling upon him to show cause why he ought not to be committed for contempt of court. Counsel and client therefore do well to allow a judge the last word and hope that he may not extend it into a long sentence.

Because the courtroom is a place of grief, humor is a welcome visitor: has it not been said that laughter is God's hand upon a troubled world?

Gallows humor more often emanates from the bench than from the bar. In earlier days, judges were known to have deprived jurors of "fire, food, and drink" to speed them to their verdict. Alexander Pope had this in mind when, in "The Rape of the Lock," he wrote:

The hungry judges soon the sentence sign,
And wretches hang that jurymen may dine.

Now that the country provides appetizing meals for members of the jury while they are considering a verdict, defense counsel awaiting their return count not the hours they are out, but the meals, and they pray these are sufficiently laced with wine to keep the jury in good spirits. A happy jury is not a convicting jury.

In Bacon's *Apothegms* it is reported:

Sir Nicholas Bacon ... by one of the malefactors mightily importuned for to save his life ... on account of kindred. "Prithee," said my lord judge, "how came that in?"

"Why, if it please you my lord, your name is Bacon and mine is Hog, and in all ages Hog and Bacon have been so near kindred, that they cannot be separated!"

"Nay," replied Judge Bacon, "you and I cannot be kindred, except you be hanged; for Hog is not Bacon until it be well hanged."

Executions of a different kind concern our courts today. The story is told that when John Friesen sat as a District Court Judge in Regina, he tried an unfortunate citizen charged with evasion of income tax. The evidence was damning. The accused had kept two sets of books, one for his own purposes, and one for the Revenue. At the close of the case, the accused stood and, raising his hand, said: "As God is my judge I am not guilty." To which Judge Friesen is reported to have cryptically replied: "He is not. I am. You are."

My old friend, Mr. Justice Alan Cullen of the Trial Division of the Supreme Court of Alberta, now in God's hand, enjoyed delivering speeches full of good humor. One of these he entitled "Sausages and Sailboats" because, he said, it contained very little meat and a whole lot of wind. Cullen succeeded in tickling the funny bone of the law when litigants before him were under great tension. If wind there were, it helped to bring to port many a leaky vessel that otherwise would have certainly been lost at sea.

Mr. Justice "Bud" Estey, shortly after he was elevated to the Supreme Court of Canada, improved upon Cullen's quip. Of an applicant for leave to appeal, who was drawing the finest distinctions between a leading Supreme Court decision and the case he argued, that learned judge waggishly asked counsel, "Are you slicing the meat so thin because you hope it won't look like baloney?"

What is baloney to one judge may look like rib roast to another. A young counsel, with the natural inventiveness of a Ronald Barclay, snatched success from the jaws of defeat when he defended an accused charged with breaking and entering a dwelling by night. Counsel argued that his client had not broken into the house at all. "He found the parlour window open and merely inserted his right arm and removed a few trifling articles," he said. "Now, my client's arm is not himself, and I submit that you cannot punish the whole person for an offense committed by one of his limbs only." He asked that his client be acquitted.

The judge considered the novel argument for a few moments, and then replied: "Your argument is very well put. Following it logically, I sentence the arm of the accused to one year's imprisonment. He can accompany it or not, as he chooses." The accused smiled, and with his lawyer's assistance, he unscrewed his bionic arm. Leaving it in the prisoner's dock, he walked out of court a free man.

Legal lore tells of another counsel who was defending a man charged with assault. It was alleged that the accused bit the complainant's ear off in a street fight. Only one witness appeared at trial and when defense counsel rose to cross-examine, he remembered the Roman maxim: *Testis unus testis nullus* — one witness is no witness. He fixed the witness in the box with a penetrating eye and sternly said to him: "Now you did not actually *see* my client bite the complainant's ear off, did you?"

"No sir," said the witness, "I did not."

Counsel preened himself in pleasure. Not content with this perfectly satisfactory answer, and determined to pin the witness like a butterfly, he boldly marched on: "Sir, if you didn't see my client bite the complainant's ear off, how can you say that he *did* bite his ear off?"

"Well, sir," said the witness calmly, "I seen him spit it out!"

The hearsay rule of evidence is believed by some lawyers to be expressed in the injunction: "Believe only half of what you see and

164

nothing of what you hear!" This principle obviously has no application where an ear not only hears but is also seen.

How often counsel has wished he had bitten his tongue rather than have asked that extra question! The great bard expressed the cross examiner's irresistible urge to ask just one more question in words that should be written large on every lawyer's shirtcuff: "Striving to better, oft we mar what's well."

It is axiomatic that most people accused of crime are convicted out of their own mouths. While speech is indeed a gift of the gods, to speak too much can raise the very devil. Indeed, a hyperactive tongue has carried many a man who lacked the wit to remain silent, directly to the gallows. Had police officers to rely only upon physical clues or upon the eyes and ears of witnesses and their own ingenuity, they would be as helpless as grasshoppers stuck to windshields in an automatic car wash. But the laws of nature come to the rescue of the police. Unbridled tongues have a way of bringing suspects galloping into the R.C.M.P. barracks, there to waggle out confessions of crime the police would have known little or nothing about, if only those frenetic tongues had stayed at home enjoying a quiet evening of pretzels and beer.

If ninety percent of the country's convicts fall into the net as a result of their own loquacity, the balance who are found guilty may have reached their unhappy state because of the verbosity and volubility of their counsel. There is tragedy stalking the overspeaking lawyer — for his client, that is! But counsel's performance oftentimes is not without humor, the formula for which is simple. It has been demonstrated by the most effective public speakers, from Mark Twain to Tommy Douglas: "See what fools we are — and look at me, heading the whole procession!"

The overspeaking lawyer may sit in any part of the courtroom. He may sit at counsel's table for the defense or for the plaintiff or the prosecution. Lawyers, male and female, are chatterers. In *All's Well that Ends Well*, the immortal bard said: "She is a woman. When she thinks, she needs must talk." To which I would add the corollary: He is a man. When he thinks not, talk seems his greatest need.

N. Ross Craig, K.C., one of Saskatchewan's most able lawyers, was acting for the defendant in a damage action heard in Regina about 1910. The trial, held in February, brought a farm boy of fourteen to testify for the plaintiff who alleged he had been kicked by the defendant's horse. The young lad came to court with his father on a very cold, snow-bound morning. The two had traveled together by horse-sled from their farm near Moose Jaw and, partially thawed out, they now sat in the courtroom waiting to be called.

When the young lad came forward and stood in the witness box, he was duly sworn to tell "the truth, the whole truth and nothing but the truth." He gave strong evidence in favor of the plaintiff. Craig, for the defendant, cross-examined him carefully and at great length. It became apparent that the lad could not be shaken on a single material point.

As a last resort, Craig, toying with his gold watch chain said, intimidatingly, "I suppose, when you and your father traveled to Regina this morning, the two of you talked about the case?"

"That's right, sir," said the boy.

"I see, I see!" said the cross-examining counsel, much encouraged by the answer. "And tell me, young man, did your father tell you what to say on the witness stand this morning?"

"Yes sir," the boy said, "he did."

"Well, let's have it! Tell us what your father told you to say!" urged Craig, dramatically, expectantly ...

To which the young witness paused not a second to reply: "He told me, sir, to tell the truth."

Obviously, it is not with the hand alone that a pair of deuces can be overplayed. Over-encouragement to a witness in a cross-examination may imperil not only a client's case, but counsel as well.

A husky young man was charged with assault occasioning grievous bodily harm. Notwithstanding an especially severe cross-examination, the accused stoutly maintained that he had merely pushed the complainant "a weeny bit."

The prosecutor persisted and asked again and again, "Well, about how hard?"

"Oh, just a wee bit," the accused insisted.

"Now," said the prosecutor, "for the benefit of the judge, will you please step down here and, with me for the subject, illustrate just how hard you mean."

The accused descended from the witness stand and approached the lawyer. When he reached him, the spectators were astonished to see him slap the lawyer in the face, kick him in the shins, seize him bodily, and, finally, with a supreme effort, lift him from the floor and hurl him prostrate across the table.

Turning from the bewildered prosecutor, he faced the judge and said mildly: "Your honor, about one-tenth that hard!"

It is not only the prosecutor in a criminal trial that may be abused. All counsel who work in the field of criminal law are in jeopardy, especially if they practice in a small town. A motorist drove into Weyburn, Saskatchewan, one day. On the outskirts, the young driver unfortunately struck a bicycle ridden by a small girl. She lay on the pavement badly hurt. The girl was rushed to hospital. Thoroughly shaken and worried over the charges he might face, the driver hurried into town to see what could be done. He decided that the first and best thing to do was to consult a lawyer, so he went to the hotel beer parlor and appoached a table where three or four locals were spending the afternoon. Without much in the way of introductions, the ashen-faced stranger earnestly asked them: "Tell me, have you got a criminal lawyer here in town?"

A silence descended over the table. All of the regulars looked down into their beer. Then the most grisly among them spat his tobacco juice into the brass spitoon; he looked up at the stranger thoughtfully and deliberately. "Well," he slowly drawled, weighing his words with care, "we reckon we got one here all right, but we just ain't got enough evidence on him yet." (When Harry Walsh of Winnipeg, one of the most learned and brilliant common law lawyers practicing in the criminal courts, refers to a colleague or an adversary as a "criminal lawyer," with his usual caution he insists on adding, "I use that phrase in the gerundial and not in an adjectival sense.")

In the same town, and at the same hotel, another visitor was sitting with the esteemed regulars. They were a taciturn lot. No one said anything much to anybody else. The silence was unnerving. Finally, in desperation, the uneasy visitor asked, "Is there a law against talking in this town?"

"No law against it," answered one of them. "But there's an understanding here that no one's to speak unless he's sure he can improve on silence."

Laymen often measure a lawyer's effectiveness by his physical stature, a problem which my friend Larry Kyle early in his career succeeded in overcoming.

The story is told of a diminutive lawyer who himself appeared in the altered role of a witness in court. He was cross-examined by a gigantic counselor with a correspondingly stentorian voice.

"What is your profession?" opposing counsel boomed out.

"I am a lawyer," said the little man meekly.

"You a lawyer!" exclaimed the giant counsel. "Why I could put you in my vest pocket."

"Very likely you could," quietly said the witness. "But if you did, you would have more law in your vest pocket than you ever had in your head!"

Few lawyers or judges are as well versed in the classics today as their predecessors of a generation or two ago. English literature has fallen victim to the television tube and the "adult movie" (geared to the intelligence of slow-learning children) and accordingly, the literate litigant is becoming a rarity in the courts.

An elderly man of convivial habits was hailed before the bar of justice at Moosomin for the eighth time in the space of a year.

"You are charged with being drunk and disorderly in a public place," recited the magistrate. "How do you plead?"

"I suppose I was drunk," began the accused. "Man's inhumanity to man makes countless thousands mourn," he continued in a flight of oratory. "But I am not so debased as Poe, so profligate as Byron, so ungrateful as Keats, so intemperate as Burns, so timid as Tennyson, so vulgar as Shakespeare, so . . ."

"That'll do, that'll do," interrupted the presiding magistrate impatiently. "$50.00 or seven days in jail. And, constable, take down that list of names he mentioned and keep an eye on them. I expect they're just as bad as he is!"

Police officers often furnish the comic relief that eases the tension of a tragic and dramatic trial. Sometimes they play the role of fool, each to his own King Lear.

The evidence in a case involving cruelty to a horse turned upon the fact that the animal, identified as the property of the accused, was found dead at the intersection of Thirteenth Avenue and Elphinstone Street in Regina. The defense had evidence that the beast had actually been picked up by the city dump truck on Thirteenth Avenue and Angus Street.

The story (apocryphal I am sure) has it that the investigating constable was called to the stand and asked whether it were true that the horse was found, not on Elphinstone, but on Angus Street.

"Well, it's this way, your honor," said Dan Magee, one of Regina's finest, and the noblest specimen I ever encountered of the shrewd detective and the tender Irish policeman, "I first did see that horse a-lyin' sorry and dead on Elphinstone Street but for the love o' God, when it came to writing out my report at the station I couldn't for the life of me spell Elphinstone. I bicycled out to Thirteenth Avenue and dragged the poor beastie two blocks down the road and left him at Angus Street, and then, so help me, I cycled back to the station and made out my report and spelled out Angus Street without a hitch, and there it is just as ye see it here, and no harm done!"

Among the memorable yarns Dan Magee regaled me with is the scenario laid on another street corner — this time in Belfast. A man standing there feels the cold, hard press of steel at the small of his back. A cold sweat breaks over his body as he fears he is about to become another victim of the long "disorders." A harsh, menacing voice demands of him, "What are ye, tell me? A Protestant or a Catholic?" Frightened to death, but thinking fast, the victim says, "I'm a, I'm a Ju . . . Ju . . . I'm a Jew!" To which the merciless voice crushingly responds, "Praise Allah! I gotta be the luckiest Arab today in all of Ulster!"

Things are much the same among policemen the world over. A Muscovite who escaped to the new world and settled in Canada decided, after thirty years, to return to the Soviet Union as a tourist. He found few changes. The gloom had not lifted from the city; there were still shortages of all things, still the long queues at the stores, still the lack of goods on the shelves. He did notice, however, that Moscow's police officers, who in former days had patrolled the streets singly or in twos, now walked about in *troika*. Wondering why there were no shortages of policemen in the U.S.S.R., the visitor stopped a Muscovite and asked:

"As I remember the old days, comrade, Russian policemen used to walk the street in 'ones and twos'. Now, they walk everywhere in 'threes'. Why is it that the rules have been so changed?"

The old man thought a moment and said, "I will try to explain it to you, comrade. You see, the first policeman over there — he can read but he cannot write. The second policeman, he can write but he cannot read. Now the third policeman, he is a reliable cop. He is a good party man. His job is to keep an eye on those other two intellectuals."

In Leningrad, a man was denouncing Soviet policies before a crowd, and he condemned a system of justice that consigned counter-revolutionaries to Siberia and dissenters to mental hospitals. Three police officers came up and arrested him. People began to plead, "Leave him alone, you can see he is nothing but crazy."

"He may be crazy," replied one of the policemen, "but the trouble is he's telling the truth!"

In New York's Columbus Circle, soapbox orators for years were accorded the right to give free-expression to their views, however true or false they might be. One afternoon a particularly articulate speaker was holding forth loud and long, condemning the government, exhorting the president to change the economic system, and calling upon all who would listen to join his crusade for change. Two of New York's finest approached him angrily, and said, "Hey you! You've no business talking like that here! We don't want no communists in this country! Get going or you're under arrest!"

"But, Mr, Policeman," expostulated the speaker. "I'm an anti-communist!"

"I don't care what in hell kind of a communist you are," shouted one of the officers. "Just get going!"

The English bobby is more sophisticated.

Near Marble Arch in London's Hyde Park, free speech is a way of life that has flourished from the time that condemned felons mounted the gallows and addressed their last defiant words to the crowd of adoring women and curious men that came to witness the macabre spectacle that ended with the featured performer swinging grotesquely in the air at the end of a rope. To defy authority is still fashionable in this most fertile cradle of free speech and no gibbet is necessary to strike the sparks of eloquence.

A fiery speaker was seeking and, indeed, gaining the attention of a crowd of passers-by one Sunday afternoon. He described to those who would listen the shameful plight of Londoners who were without a place to live. Even if they could find a miserable flat, they had no money to pay the rent. As a result of the controls of the welfare state, apartments were not being built, houses were filled to capacity, and rents were sky-high.

The speaker then turned to the gathering crowd and incongruously shouted: "You see over there, maties! There's Buckingham Palace. In there lives Queen Elizabeth and her husband Philip and their four kiddies. There's a hundred and thirty bedrooms in Buckingham Palace and most of them are empty! And you and I have no place to sleep! Are we going to allow this sort of bleedin' scandal to go on in a free country when there's no place to live for you and me and our kiddies? Blimey no! Not if I can help it, we won't! Now maties, here's the time to do something about it!" he shouted. "I tell you what we'll do: let's us go and burn Buckingham Palace! Burn it to the ground. Today! Now!"

By this time a large crowd had gathered, so large, in fact, that all traffic was stopped. Two or three bobbies watched impassively as excitement mounted and as many angrily agreed with the speaker and began raising their fists. Sensing the rising hostility of the crowd, one of the bobbies stepped forward and said: "All right, all right gentlemen! One moment please. Some favors burning the palace and some doesn't. Now here's how we do it. Them as wants to burn Buckingham Palace move over here on the left, please. And them as don't wants to burn Buckingham Palace, you move over there on the right, please. But all of ye, please let the traffic get by. There's a good fellow!" And so they did until it was tea time and a good hour to go home: a classic example of the supremacy of law over paw.

French civil law and the English common law differ in many important respects, but the principles are similar. In Canada, it is significant that no serious problems have arisen out of the fact that commercial transactions in Quebec are governed by one body of law, and in Canada's other nine provinces and the Territories, they are governed by another. Lawyers and businessmen are able to accommodate to these variations and it is to their credit that the law has not become a *casus belli* in the *separatiste* debate. There are, of course, differences in temperament and approach.

The Parisian's attitude to the administration of justice has sometimes differed from the Londoner's. The story is told of a winemaker from the Loire Valley who brought an action in the Court of Queen's Bench of the United Kingdom claiming damages from an English concern that allegedly was infringing the use of a trade name that the Frenchman's family had used in marketing their wines for centuries. The Frenchman consulted a leading London solicitor who, in turn, retained a barrister of great eminence in anticipation of the litigation.

In due course, the matter was set down for trial. A few days before the opening of court, the French plaintiff visited his solicitor and asked if he knew who the trial judge would be. He was told that it was likely to be Mr. Justice So-and-So. The Frenchman asked where the judge resided. Surprised at such a question, the solicitor inquired why he would wish to have such information. "But sir, of course," said the Frenchman, "it is my wish to send to the judge three or four cases of my most distinguished wines of great vintage."

"Good Lord!" exclaimed the solicitor. "No one in his right mind would ever dare to do any such thing in this country! Why, if you were to do that, you would certainly lose your lawsuit — and rightly so! Judgment would likely go to the defendant. Whoever sent the wine would likely be charged with bribery, and he would, no doubt, be convicted and go to prison to boot! Now go home and forget about it!"

The Frenchman, not a little chastened and very much confused, departed the solicitor's chambers in mortification and silence.

The litigation went well. At trial, the evidence led was favorable to the plaintiff. It was only perfunctorily challenged by the defendant and his witnesses. In due course, judgment was delivered awarding the French plaintiff sizeable damages and granting an injunction that forbade the English defendant from using the plaintiff's family name in relation to his products.

The grateful client appeared at his solicitor's chambers to thank him for his services and to pay his fee.

"Are you not happy, now," inquired the solicitor, "that you took my advice and did not send the judge any of your wine before the trial?"

"Indeed, I am grateful to you for your good advice," said the client. "However, the fact is that I did send him six cases of wine."

"You did what?" exclaimed the lawyer, nonplussed at the very thought of the enormity of the crime his client had just admitted to.

"Yes, indeed I did," said the client. "I sent six cases of fine wine to the judge. But of course, the wine I sent was the defendant's brand, and the card accompanying it bore his name."

Attempts to influence judges of Canadian courts is so rare that even anecdotes and fanciful stories on the subject are virtually non-existent. There is a story told of a Texan judge who, a few days prior to the commencement of an important trial, received from the plaintiff an envelope containing five thousand dollars in cash. On the day following he received an envelope from the defendant containing ten thousand dollars in cash. When the trial opened, the judge announced to the parties and their counsel that his was a court of justice and he a man of integrity. "Justice," he said, "cannot be bought or sold here. I must tell you that I have received from the plaintiff in this case the sum of five thousand dollars. I have also received from the defendant in the same case the sum of ten thousand dollars. I am now returning the sum of five thousand dollars to the defendant." The judge then handed an envelope containing the money to his clerk to pass on to the defendant. "And now," the judge continued, "let the trial begin. The scales of justice are once again evenly balanced and the parties may be assured that neither will be given any special advantage by me!"

Some lawyers, like some politicians have been linked with the long-winded, the platitudinous, and the tedious. There have been occasions, I am sure, when a presiding judge has been sorely tempted to compliment my eloquacity with Biblical allusion, saying, "Your argument is like the love of God, it passeth all understanding; and like His mercy, I thought it would go on forever."

It is reminiscent of Winston Churchill who once distributed to his fellow M.P.'s a book containing a collection of his speeches. A Labour member wrote to him to say, "Thank you for the copy of your speeches delivered in the House of Commons. To quote the late Lord Beaconsfield, 'I shall lose no time in reading them.'"

The *double entendre* is by no means the darling of the House of Commons alone. It engages the members of the judiciary as well. The presiding judge of the Queen's Bench was soundly criticizing counsel for presenting an argument which, in the opinion of the court, was wholly without merit. Learned counsel listened patiently to the judicial tirade. When finally the judge had done, counsel courteously bowed low to the bench and said in his most ingratiating tone, "Your Lordship is right and I am wrong . . . as Your Lordship usually is."

Under somewhat similar circumstances, when a judge had upbraided counsel mercilessly, the lawyer smiled sweetly and said: "I am not so great a fool as your Lordship . . . (long pause) believes me to be." Whereupon the judge, red-faced but composed said, "In future, Sir, I advise you to place your words closer together!"

Young counsel are sometimes given to inflating their factums in the Court of Appeal by lengthy quotations relating to the most elementary principles of the law. It is said that on one occasion Chief Justice Samuel Freedman of Manitoba was not only presented with such a brief but was being regaled by counsel with a long catalogue of classical authorities. "But Mr. Brodsky," he said in his most kindly manner, "you must give this court credit for knowing something of the law." To which counsel tersely replied, "That's exactly the mistake I made in the court below."

Addresses to the jury today are not generally so brilliant nor so highly embellished with classical allusions as they were a few decades ago. One searches in vain for the eloquence and rhetoric that brought audiences to the courtroom in droves, rivalling in numbers the paid attendance at the local theater. Today, addresses tend to be arid and somnolent. Of a speech to the jury by Crown counsel in a false pretences case in Regina, there was so much hesitancy in the presentation that I could not resist the comment that the best that could be said for it was that "it contained some brilliant flashes of silence."

An apt and modest way of which William Haddad, now of the Alberta Court of Appeal approves, to begin an address is to say to the jury: "Ladies and Gentlemen. My job is to talk to you. Your job is to listen to me. If you happen to finish your job first, I'd be mighty obliged if you would just let me know."

Juries are frequently the butt of gallows humor at the bar. I remember an old codger who, because the sheriff liked him and he had little else to do, appeared on jury panels with great regularity. Once I asked that old juror by whom he felt he was most influenced. By the lawyers? By the judge? By the witnesses?

"Well," he said. "I'll just tell you. I'm a clear reasoning man. I'm not influenced by anything the lawyers say; I'm not influenced by what the judge says. No sir, I'm not influenced by what the witnesses say either! What I do is this: I just look at the man in the dock and I ask myself the question, 'If he ain't done nothing wrong why is he here then?' So I bring 'em all in guilty."

Unfortunately, it is not only jurors who sometimes take this view, but judges. The story is told that in a murder case, a jury, after deliberating three hours, brought in a verdict of "not guilty of murder." Not impressed, the judge turned indignantly to the jury and said: "What reason do you have for acquitting the prisoner of murder?"

The foreman of the jury said, "Insanity."

To which the judge wryly asked: "What? All twelve of you?"

In paternity suits, judges frequently regard it as their inherent right to bring a little levity into otherwise grave, monotonous, and highly strained, and emotionally-charged proceedings. The judge, in one such suit, heard the story of the young lady-complainant. She said she had known the accused for two years; they had been intimate on numerous occasions; he was the only man with whom she had had sexual relations during the whole of her post-virginal life. The young man then gave evidence, frankly admitting that while he had, indeed, had sexual relations with the young lady, he was in fact sterile and could not possibly be the father of the child.

The learned judge listened carefully to all that was said. He pondered the evidence after counsel were done with their arguments. Then he reached into his vest pocket, pulled out a cigar, handed it to the defendant and said to him, "Congratulations! You have just become a father!"

Whatever might have been the disabilites of that young man, it is obvious the complainant in the paternity suit was not suffering from the same condition. Neither was she troubled by the physical condition that a group of women were animatedly discussing in a quiet restaurant at lunch one day. A lawyer sat at the next table and could not help overhearing their conversation.

"Poor Marjorie," one of the ladies said. "The doctor has told her she can't have any babies. She seems impregnable." The second giggled. "That's not the word, my dear. The correct term is impenetrable." The third was indignant. "What ignoramuses you are! What you really mean is that she is inconceivable." The fourth raised her voice and her nose and said, "Nonsense! You really mean that she is unbearable." Unable to contain himself, the lawyer leaned toward their table and said, "Ladies, ladies! Excuse me, but the word you are all looking for is inscrutable."

While at the dinner table such comments, though unforgettable, are forgivable, in actions in which a wife seeks maintenance and support from a husband who has deserted her, judges and lawyers appreciate that they must restrain their natural inclination to interject with comments that might be considered frivolous.

At the end of a long hearing of a wife's action for maintenance and support, the presiding judge turned to the defendant husband and said, "I have heard all of the evidence and considered it carefully. I have decided to give your wife $200.00 a month for her support." To which the husband, with an appreciative smile upon his face said, "I think that is very fair of you, your honor. If you do that, I'll do my best to throw in about $25.00 or so, a month myself, just to sweeten the kitty."

Generally the entertaining moments arising out of domestic litigation are few and far between. Too much bitterness and acrimony occupy the lives of married folk seeking liberation to open even a chink to release their bile and allow a little humor to enter their lives.

On one occasion, I met my client in court before her petition for divorce was to be heard. It had been several months since I had last interviewed her and she seemed to have taken on weight in the interim. She had been separated from her husband for more than three years. Looking at her distended abdomen and distressed that my client may have been litigating by day but surreptitiously copulating with her spouse by night, I asked: "Tell me, Mrs. Merryweather, are you pregnant?"

"Oh no," said she. "I am just carrying this for a friend."

Quite a different case was one in which a wise teacher noticed that the brightest student in his class was obviously dejected and seriously disturbed. "What troubles you, my son?" he asked.

Reluctantly, the young man said, "rabbi, my wife gave birth to a child last night. A boy."

"Congratulations!" said the teacher. "But why do you seem so unhappy? This should be a cause for great celebration!"

"One thing troubles me," said the young man. "Rebecca and I have been married only three months, and I have studied and learned that it takes nine months to have a baby. It is that which troubles me deeply."

"Well now," said the rabbi sympathetically, "let's consider the facts. How long did you say you have been married to Rebecca?"

"Three months."

"And how long has Rebecca been married to you?"

"Three months."

"And how long have you been married to each other?"

"Three months."

"Well," said the wise man, "three months plus three months plus three months. That makes nine months in all."

"That's right," said the boy.

"Well, then," said the rabbi encouragingly, "what have you got to worry about?"

Men of law often come to hold a cynical view of marriage since they invariably must cope with the very worst side of it. Weddings and wedding anniversaries are as pleasant for lawyers as for any other guest who attends. I recall the words a hard-headed judge said to me, "Whenever I go to a wedding I give the happy pair about three years." When I asked him why, he said, "It doesn't matter whom a man marries, he is sure to find the next morning he has married someone else."

But for all that, after long and vexatious debate that lasted a lifetime, Dr. Johnson concluded that "marriage has many pains, but celibacy has no pleasures."

Definition sections in statutes often create strange bed fellows. A statute may define "cattle" as including "horses, pigs, sheep, swine, and fowl." To provide a common handle for this polyglot of domestic animals is convenient. But to retain a sense of reality in a lawsuit it is necessary for lawyers occasionally to hearken back to the simple but real facts of life. No one was more effective in so doing than Abraham Lincoln in his role as a man of law. He was arguing a point with opposing counsel, but with very little success. Lincoln finally turned to his opponent and said: "Well, let us see now — how many legs has a cow?" Counsel opposite answered, "Four, of course."

Lincoln agreed that that was quite correct. He then said, "Now let us call a cow's tail a leg. How many legs would a cow then have?"

Opposing counsel answered, "Five legs, of course."

"Now," said Lincoln, "that is where you are wrong. Simply calling a cow's tail a leg does not make it a leg, does it?"

The draftsmen of the *Income Tax Act* who invented the notion of "deemed income" and the ministers who tax it as such, probably never saw a live cow — or many people producing *real* income. . . .

No lawyer and no president of the United States spun more uncommon yarns or spoke more common sense than Abraham Lincoln. One of the most celebrated courts-martial during the Civil War concerned Franklin W. Smith and his brother, who were convicted of defrauding the government. The men had borne a high character for integrity. At this time, however, courts-martial were seldom invoked for any other purpose than to convict the accused, and the Smiths shared the usual fate of persons whose cases came before that body. The two men were kept in prison, their papers seized, their business destroyed, and their reputations ruined.

The finding of the court was submitted to Lincoln who, after careful investigation, disapproved the judgment and set it aside in these words:

Whereas, Franklin W. Smith and his brother had transactions with the Navy Department to the amount of a million and quarter of dollars; and

Whereas, they had a chance to steal at least a quarter of a million and were only charged with stealing twenty-two hundred dollars, and the question now is about their stealing one hundred, I don't believe they stole anything at all.

Therefore, the record and findings are disapproved, declared null and void and the defendants are fully discharged.

Problems always seem to grow most critical in the early hours of a sleepless morning. Worries become magnified and difficulties reach crisis dimensions in the dark. Like many other lawyers, I receive bizarre telephone calls at two and three in the morning asking advice upon matters that were better left to normal waking hours. Then, monsters are less likely to walk abroad or lurk among apprehensive clients, and clients are more likely to allow sleeping dogs like me to rest.

Late-night callers who ask advice by telephone at outrageous hours are generally strangers. Frequently, they refuse to give even their names, determined as they are only to unburden themselves of their anxieties by heaping them on anyone who will listen. These denizens of the night may be divided into two classes. The first is made up of anxious, apprehensive people who fret over the errant ways of their absent spouses or errant lovers. They then make sudden demands upon the police, the legal profession, or the fire department to compel the loved one to make immediate amends on pain of dire retribution. Often, these demands strain not only their own personal marital relations but the marital serenity of the lawyers and doctors and police officers and firemen whom they favor with their nocturnal alarms.

A woman wakened me with her persistent telephone ringing at an unseemly hour and told me that her husband was philandering. She demanded that something be done about it at once. She said that matters had become intolerable. "At this very moment," she cried, "I know my husband is in bed with his secretary, and this is not the first time! He's been carrying on with her night after night after night!"

I asked how long it was that he had been unfaithful to her.

"At least a year," she said, "and come to think of it, a whole lot longer than that! He's been philandering for at least two years — night after night after night."

"And have you seen a lawyer since you first learned of it?" I asked.

"No," she said. "I want to talk to you about it. What should we do?"

"You know what I think we ought to do?" I asked after a pregnant pause.

"What?"

"Since he's been philandering for two years now, let's you and I let him philander for just one night more. Then come and see me in the morning."

The response was silence and then a sudden slam of the telephone.

The second class of late-night caller consists of the inebriates who have been picked up by the police and asked to provide a sample of their breath to determine whether their ability to drive a motor vehicle is impaired by alcohol. It is a criminal offense to refuse to comply with such a demand if properly made by a peace officer. But the courts have held that the *Canadian Bill of Rights* requires that every such suspect must be accorded an opportunity to consult his lawyer and be advised of his rights, if he so requests, before deciding whether to comply with the demand.

The breathalyzer reading is only circumstantial evidence of impairment of a suspect's ability to drive, just as the observations made by a police officer of a suspect's ability to walk and talk are circumstantial evidence of the amount of liquor he has imbibed. But when transcribed onto a piece of paper and called a "certificate," the reading becomes sufficient evidence to convict a citizen under the Criminal Code and fine him, deprive him of his driver's license, and send him to prison. Recent legislation has converted what traditionally was merely a piece of circumstantial evidence into a *prima facie* case upon which a conviction may be entered for a serious substantive offense. A reading on a specially approved breathalyzer machine, showing .08 percent of alcohol in the blood of a person suspected of driving a motor vehicle, itself has become a criminal offense without proof of the driver's actual impairment.

The purpose of this, and similar legislation recently enacted, is to discourage drinking and driving. But it has not achieved this end. It has simply made it easier for the police to secure convictions of drivers with a strong smell of liquor about them. The unhappy motorist, finding himself in the police detachment betwixt the devil of a conviction for "refusal," and the deep blue sea that a breath test presents, asks the most ingenious of questions: "If I smoke, will it confuse the machine?" *Answer:* "Yes." *Question:* "If I can down a couple of drinks just before the test, will that invalidate the reading?" *Answer:* "If you can, yes." *Question:* "If I can stall off the test for two hours, will that save me?" *Answer:* "Possibly, yes." *Question:* "If I knock the machine off the table and bust it up, what will happen?" *Answer:* "You'll probably be busted too, though perhaps not for 'refusal'."

In the middle of the night the lawyer who is called to the telephone to advise a perfect stranger, sight unseen, as to his "rights," is torn between his natural reflex to help a person who is in jeopardy, and his consciousness that to give advice by phone on facts that cannot possibly be made fully known to him is perilous. Especially if he is roused from sleep and unlikely to be able to make notes of his conversation. It has been suggested by some zealous police officers that a lawyer who advises a client not to submit to a test demanded by a police officer constitutes the crime of "aiding and abetting," and that the lawyer who so advises may be counselling the commission of an offense and could be prosecuted as a party to the main offense. A pusillanimous solicitor might be deterred by such a threat, but no competent counsel would ever be intimidated or influenced by it. The right of a suspect or an accused to legal advice from counsel must override the sophist's argument that providing such advice amounts to a constructive crime.

It is a human trait, as unhappy as it is common, to think the worse rather than the better of one's fellow man. Even the legal presumption of innocence that purports to repeal that sad law of human nature is not sufficient to alter this nasty proclivity. An accused may be legally wrapped in the law's mantle of innocence from the time that a criminal charge is laid upon him to the time the jury pronounces its verdict. But it cannot ensure against the hasty, unreliable, and unwarranted conclusions in suspicious and ill-disciplined minds that the mantle of innocence really hides a guilty man. Since everyone talks about the presumption of innocence but so few understand its deep significance, it falls to the man of law to explain its benign meaning and to illustrate its beneficence — not as a weapon for the guilty but as a shield for the innocent. Since no one can be sure who are guilty and who guiltless, it must offer equal shelter to all.

The presumption that everyone is guilty may stem from the ancient Christian idea that all of us are conceived in sin. Whatever this ecclesiastical doctrine may be, in my view it has no place in the courts of the land, and this is recognized by the simplest of men. The president of the Ladies' Aid Society of a small western town sought out the municipality's handyman and loudly criticized him for his habits. "Really, my good man," she said, "you drink too much! It can't be good for your health, and it must be a great hardship to your family."

"But I'm no great drinker, ma'am," he protested.

"How can you say that, when you were in the Red Fox Beverage Room all last night?"

"But I wasn't," he said.

"But you were. I saw your motorbike outside the bar yesterday afternoon and it was still there this morning," she said.

The handyman said nothing more. He left. That afternoon, before going home, he carefully placed his bike outside the door of the house of the president of the Ladies' Aid Society and left for the night. . . .

Machines have not improved on the human brain in determining guilt or innocence; neither are machines or their location without prejudice.

The new electronic technology was designed to simplify human relations and expedite the performance of tedious tasks. Instead, it has everywhere seized control over human relations and it threatens to dehumanize our lives. Radar is summoned to declare its omniscient measurement of speed. Computers spew out their monotonous miles of printed forms and figures coded to obfuscate the obvious and confuse the commonplace. Breath machines are by statute declared to be robot judges that are made to preside at trials conducted in the police station at all hours of the day and night, and all *in camera*, as in some modern starless chamber. Their verdicts are seldom appealable. The legal prerequisite to "His Honor Judge Breathalyzer's" jursidiction is that the citizen who is to be tried by him must first be considered by the police officer who has observed him, to have impaired his ability to drive a motor vehicle through drink. Such a proposition would have moved even Bloody Judge Jeffreys to declare an accused in such condition to be unfit to stand his trial.

Happily, the machines have their limitations, as most lawyers and judges recognize. The trouble with them is that they are robots: they've no judgment and no discretion and in the judicial scale of measurements they are cretins. It should require no mathematician or physicist or statistician to convince a court of the fallibility of an automaton. Even Dorothy Parker appreciated the limitations of the equine creature that traditionally has been associated with good common sense. She was asked to use the word "horticulture" in a sentence. Hesitating not a moment she said: "You can lead a horticulture but you cannot make her think."

The Swiss have ingeniously come to the rescue of those who insist on drinking and driving. It appears that they have invented a powder made of fructose, glucose, chlorophyll, and something that speeds by several hundred percent the disappearance of alcohol from the bloodstream and thereby thwarts the breathalyzer in its tests. Already, the powder has found its way into France which has the highest per capita consumption of alcohol in the world, and also the highest per vehicle number of automobile accidents. Confronted with a challenge to the enforcement of legislation designed to remove drinking drivers from its highways, the French have produced a simple new law: it is an offense to sell the powder for the purpose of confusing the breathalyzer. It may only be sold for dietary use.

Drink has produced events that have spawned a vast body of law in Canada, of concern not only to drinkers and drunks but to all citizens. The criminal law has taken cognizance of drunkenness as a defense to an indictment for murder: it may reduce the offense to manslaughter where the accused was so intoxicated as to be incapable of forming the specific intent to kill. Liquor laws have enriched not only the distillers of booze and the brewers of beer, but bootleggers and bureaucrats at every level. Booze has produced important principles.

In *Nat Bell's* famous case[4] the Privy Council not only enlarged provincial legislative powers in respect of the sale of liquor, but also defined the principles governing the documents that may be examined by a superior court in reviewing the decisions of lower courts in *certiorari* proceedings. The "trade and commerce power" of Parliament and the apparently overlapping power of the provinces to legislate in respect of "property and civil rights" in the province, were considered by the Privy Council in a long line of liquor litigation that was inspired by the lucrative trade. *Russell* v. *The Queen,*[5] *Hodge* v. *The Queen,*[6] *Re Canada Temperance Act*[7] and the Manitoba Licence Holders Association Case[8] resulted in an expansion of the powers of the provinces at the expense of the federal parliament. By the early 1930s, the net result appeared to be that the Parliament of Canada could control the liquor trade only if and when drunkenness has succeeded in creating a crisis or a national emergency.

In the early part of the century judges imposed severe strictures

upon peace officers in their enforcement of provincial prohibition laws by searching persons and premises and seizing and forfeiting liquor. Because prohibition was unpopular, public policy favored the citizen who fell victim to the law. And because judges, among others, liked their convivial cup, they were less than enthusiastic about convicting persons accused of liquor violations. As a result, citizens caught on the pricks of the law, stood a good chance of having their convictions quashed by the Superior courts. A body of law, sympathetic to those accused of liquor-related crimes, developed in the unpopular atmosphere of prohibition. To the legislators who ground out laws to prosecute the boozer, the public responded with a backlash of speakeasies, hidden stills, home brew, and bootlegging. The great experiment generated a body of law that supported the Englishman's traditional right to regard his home as his castle and so resist arbitrary searches. It frowned on extra-judicial seizures and asserted the presumption of innocence.

I have often wondered what the effect upon the law would have been had prohibition been directed not against liquor, but against the use and abuse of drugs such as marijuana, hashish, and cocaine. While many lawyers and judges have been known to enjoy their liquor, I know of none who have ever taken to drugs. Would that have made any difference in the interpretation and growth of the law? Who can tell?

Mr. Justice H. F. Thomson of the Queen's Bench of Saskatchewan was well-known for his intransigent views on demon rum. During prohibition days, as a young barrister, he prosecuted thousands of ordinary tipplers and hundreds of pharmacists who offered succor to the thirsty on the strength of a "medicinal prescription" which the law allowed and which physicians were quite willing to provide to all who made their need known. He also prosecuted the ubiquitous home brew artists whom many regarded as the aristocracy of the wild west and of whom A. E. Housman might have been thinking when he observed that

> . . . many a Peer of England brews
> Livelier liquor than the muse,
> And ale can do far more than Milton can
> To justify God's ways to man.
> 'Tis thinking lays lads underground.[9]

Long after the days of prohibition ended and citizens were free to drink the fermented nectar of the grape of which governments became the exclusive purveyors and peddlers, Mr. Justice Thomson held tenaciously to his stern views on alcohol. He became a great judge, learned and sound, but the slightest evidence before him of whiskey breath from an accused, whatever the charge he might be facing, was certain to result in conviction.

At a reception on a hot summer's day, Thomson was approached by his hostess. "I see you are drinking coffee, Judge," she said. "Why don't you try something cooling? Did you ever try gin and ginger ale?"

"No," said Judge Thomson wryly, "But I've tried many a fellow who has."

It was suggested, during prohibition days, that the Moose Jaw Public Library remove the *Encyclopaedia Britannica* from its shelves because the first volume contained a formula and described the procedure for distilling whiskey. Several chemistry textbooks are also said to have come under fire. But people's preferences prevailed even in the face of great odds, and the law came to their rescue.

A perceptive entrepreneur, with the advice of a young lawyer, went into the business of packaging the ingredients required for brewing beer at home. The packages were offered for sale by city grocers and at general stores in many rural parts of the west. The whole package sold for about $2.00. It was capable of producing a five-gallon crock of fine beer. The instructions on the label of the package were the lawyer's *volte-face* and read as follows:

TAKE NOTICE!

Anyone placing 4 gallons of water at room temperature in a 5 gallon crock or other container, adding thereto the full contents of this package, stirring well, and thereafter adding 1 small cake of yeast, covering the crock or other container and placing the same in a quiet sequestered place at a temperature of 72°F, and allowing the said contents to stand and so remain for 3 weeks, stirring occasionally; then syphoning the fluid, placing the same in pint bottles and firmly capping the said bottles and storing for use at appropriate intervals, is guilty of an offence and liable, on summary conviction to a fine not exceeding $500. or imprisonment for a term not exceeding 6 months, or to both.

Since a sense of humor is a *sine qua non* if one is to be a sane and happy warrior practicing at the bar, it is desirable that the gift, if it exists at all, be cultivated early in one's career — preferably at school, but no later than as a student at law school.

How much law a student need know in order to pass his examinations has always been a matter of conjecture. At one time, fifty percent was acceptable as a passing grade. The percentage has since risen, and one likes to believe that standards have followed suit. If this were so, it would be an exception to the rule that universities have been following ever since my own graduation. That, of course, is not an unusual view to entertain. Even Jonathan Swift said of the schools of his day that a university is a place of great learning because, since most students bring a little learning with them and so few take any away, the stuff just naturally accumulates.

In a criminal law examination for third year law students at the university recently, it is reported that only two questions were asked: First, "Define capital murder." The candidate answered: "Capital murder is culpable homicide that is commited in any capital city like Ottawa or Washington." The second question was: "What is the rule of circumstantial evidence in the field of criminal law?" To this, the student answered, "I don't know." His first answer was wrong. But obviously, his second answer was correct. He received a mark of fifty percent and passed.

It must have been that very same law student, who, upon graduating, hung out his shingle and reported to his father that he was qualified and available to the public to accept briefs upon all matters that might come before him. "Now that I have placed my name outside my office door," the young lawyer said, "I feel I ought to place a label on my forehead for all to see, with the words 'To Let,' and make myself available to anyone who is prepared to pay for my advice!"

"Right, Tom! Right!" said his father. "But don't forget to add, 'Unfurnished'!"

Justices of the peace performed most judicial functions in the early days of western Canada. Many of them, like "necessity," knew no law. That inhibited them in the performance of their duties not a whit! It is said that during the hunting season in the year 1908 in the Battleford area of Saskatchewan, a local sportsman wished to get to the north end of a slough to position himself more advantageously for his shoot as the ducks came down to water. Having no raft, he informally borrowed a boat that lay on shore and rowed himself out into the shallow waters, a distance of about a thousand yards, and there took cover in some reeds. His shoot was highly successful. When he rowed back with his boat full of birds, he was met by a member of the local constabulary who charged him with stealing the boat. The officer at once took the unfortunate hunter into custody and swore out an information against him. The nimrod had, indeed, deprived the owner of possession of his rowboat for a matter of about four hours; and he had no permission to take it. He was fully aware of what he was doing, of the nature and quality of the act, and that it was wrong. And so there appeared to be no apparent defense to the charge — not even insanity.

The unfortunate felon was brought before the local J.P. who was the only living creature that resembled a judicial officer in the district. After hearing the evidence, he searched his Criminal Code for some reference to "theft of a rowboat." He could find none. The index contained no reference to the theft of boats or vessels, rafts or canoes. But "piracy" was clearly defined as an indictable offense relating to sailing vessels. The Code clearly provided for the conviction and punishment of anyone who, "while in or out of Canada . . . steals a British ship."

The learned J.P. verified the fact that the owner of the boat was a citizen of the United Kingdom. He then directed that the information be amended. It was duly resworn by the complainant charging what the marginal note of the statute described as "piracy." This done, the accused was speedily found guilty as charged. The J.P. then consulted his Code to determine the penalty he must impose. He found that the punishment for piracy was death. There was no other. Then and there, the J.P. solemnly sentenced the hapless prisoner to be hanged by the neck until dead and invoked the Deity to receive the unfortunate man's soul when ferried across the River Styx. The prisoner was returned to the local lockup, there to be indifferently guarded awaiting the fateful day.

At once, the conscientious Justice of the Peace communicated with the Department of Justice in Ottawa and requested that the official hangman be despatched to Battleford as expeditiously as possible, there to carry out the law's just but gruesome sentence. Meanwhile, he directed that a gibbet be constructed for the execution.

Before complying with the request, the Minister of Justice reviewed the case. It occurred to him that the J.P. may have exceeded his jurisdiction, for capital offenses were required to be tried by a judge and jury. After some weeks, the case was brought before a higher court upon an application for *certiorari*. The J.P.'s judgment was quashed. The gibbet was never completed. The hangman never appeared. Neither did the prisoner. He had taken wings and migrated south with the birds.

Miscarriages of justice have not been confined to J.P.'s. Judge C. B. Rouleau, in whose memory a Saskatchewan village near Regina is named, about the year 1905, found a Chinese guilty of pick-pocketing. After sentencing him to two year's imprisonment, Rouleau is reported to have said to the unhappy prisoner: "If I really thought you were guilty, Charlie, I would have given you ten years!"

Outlandish though that may have been, the story has its contemporary counterpart in a proceeding before a Regina magistrate with a penchant to convict practically everyone who appears before him. From time to time, he is said to have applied the standard of "reasonable doubt" in a somewhat novel fashion. It is a well-established rule, of course, that in a criminal prosecution, where there exists reasonable doubt upon any issue of fact or of law, that doubt must be resolved in favor of the accused. If such doubt exists in respect of any ingredient of the offense or upon a consideration of all of the evidence, an accused is entitled to an acquittal. The magistrate applied this rule, but only after he had found the accused guilty. "I find you guilty and I am imposing a light sentence upon you consisting of a fine of $25.00," he said, "because I must say, I have had real doubts about your guilt."

Both anecdotes have their Russian counterpart. It is told that a new convict arrived at a Siberian prison camp. The inmates began questioning him about the length of his sentence.

"Twenty-five years," replied the newcomer.

"What for?"

"Nothing. I didn't do a thing. I am innocent."

"Don't give us that garbage! The innocent only get *ten* years!"

We like to believe that the motto of the R.C.M.P. is still "Give us the charge and we will find the man." The official policy of the K.G.B. in the U.S.S.R., on the other hand, is simpler: "Give us a man and we will find him a charge."

Stalin is said to have mislaid his pipe, and after a long and thorough search, he decided that someone had stolen it. He summoned a guard to find it. Some time later, he accidentally stumbled over his pipe in his bedroom and so he notified the guard to drop the matter.

"We can't," replied the guard, "we have arrested six suspects."

"Release them," ordered Stalin.

"We can't," the guard replied.

"Why not?" asked Stalin.

"Because four of the suspects have already voluntarily signed written confessions."

Sentencing a prisoner is always a difficult task for the conscientious judge, and many agonize over it, weighing as they must, the purposes of punishment which in themselves are inconsistent and contradictory. Locking a convict away in a cell to protect society may be necessary in some cases, and this can be a simple yardstick to measure penalties. But such cases are rare, and there are additional factors that must invariably be considered. Deterrence to others is one of them. Discouraging an offender from repeating his offense is an important matter to the accused and to his friends and relations. This cannot be achieved by a term in an institution that provides all of the amenities of a safe and secure home with no obligation to maintain and pay for any part of it by hard work. Reformation of the convicted is an objective that has long ranked highest in the minds of judges. If sincerely pursued, this desirable end can in some cases be achieved, but it is said to be possible only with an indeterminate sentence which is a cul-de-sac that deprives a prisoner of the certainty of release after he has paid his debt in terms of time for his misdeeds. Today, neither judge nor counsel favors lengthy sentences except where the law provides for a minimum period of incarceration and there is no alternative. Where the crime has been especially heinous, a judge may find it necessary to consider the feelings of the victim and his family. The idea of retribution is sometimes said to have died with Sigmund Freud and since his time, it has not been a popular basis for penal conviction. But there does persist the view that members of a community expect retribution to be visited upon those of their peers who have breached the rules and mores of the group. They will not feel secure, neither will their sense of injustice be assuaged unless a punishment commensurate with the gravity of the crime, be meted out to the criminal.

An English judge very much aware of his duty, sentenced an elderly man who had been convicted of burglary, to seven years in Brixton prison. "Don't you think that's a very long time for an old man like me to spend in Brixton prison?" he asked of the judge before the next case was called. The judge thought a moment or two and then replied, "I see your point, Sir, but I really cannot see how you can complain. After all, everyone must expect to be *somewhere* all of the time."

More serious was the case of the woman who no longer could stand her husband, and so she determined to "do him in." For his birthday she baked a tasty layer cake. To the cake she added not only candles but a generous helping of strychnine. As she expected, her husband ate supper heartily and enjoyed the cake immensely. But shortly before midnight he lay sprawled on the floor, dead as old Pharoah. In due course, the lady was arrested by Scotland Yard. She was charged with murder, tried at the Old Bailey, and ultimately convicted and sentenced to die. The judge pronounced sentence. She was to be taken to Brixton, there to remain until the day of her execution, then to be hanged by the neck until dead. The accused being female, the Home Secretary was troubled about sending her to the gallows, and so he directed that she submit to a psychiatric examination. It was discovered that the unhappy lady was insane and so, exercising his prerogative, the Home Secretary speedily sent a messenger to the prison. The day before the scheduled execution, the courier arrived. He announced to the unfortunate lady that the Home Secretary had seen fit to direct that her sentence of death be commuted — that she was to be at once removed from prison and sent to Broadmoor, "there to remain for the King's pleasure."

"Well, well," said the aging widow, a twinkle in her eye. "I really thought I'd grown too old for that sort of thing — but then, one lives and learns!"

It has been said that lawyers live well but die poor. So busy are they advancing their client's interests that they usually take precious little time to consider their own. Cobblers' children are not the only proverbial youngsters who go barefoot. The lawyer assuredly advises his clients to make a will, but strangely and not infrequently he himself neglects to draw one for himself. Friends and relations are often shocked to learn that the leading lawyer in their life has died without so much as a scrap of paper that would pass as a testamentary devise. In Dublin many years ago, Patrick O'Brien, an elderly barrister who had been highly regarded by his colleagues and by his fellow citizens, died alone in his chambers. Knowing that he had no wife or family nor any next of kin, his colleagues considered it their duty to give him proper burial. But there was no money in the lawyer's bank account and it was found that he had died virtually penniless.

His friends then decided to take up a public subscription among members of the bench and bar to bury their departed brother. A committee of the benchers canvassed from office to office. They approached the judiciary. At the court house, the lawyers told the Chief Justice of the fate of poor O'Brien. Would the learned judge be so kind as to contribute a shilling toward his burial?

"What?" exclaimed the judge indignantly. "A shilling to bury a barrister? Here, sir; here is a guinea . . . Go bury one-and-twenty of them!"

The play between bench and bar has sired scores of classical stories that lawyers love to recount. A young barrister prepared a most carefully reasoned argument, replete with every recent judicial decision, all buttressed by hosts of textbooks and excerpts from learned periodicals. A great fortress of books surrounded him at counsel's table, and from these he cited impeccably as he proceeded with his interminable argument. When he finally concluded, the presiding judge advised him that he proposed to deliver judgment at once. Without reserving the matter for further consideration, in few words, the judge dismissed the client's claim without reasons and without referring to a single authority.

So shocked was the young lawyer, he seized one of the large calf-bound law reports on the table and hurled it directly at the judge's head. At that very moment, it so happened that the judge's pen dropped to the floor. He bent low beneath the bench to retrieve it. As he came up, out of the corner of his eye, he saw the heavy tome go sailing within a hair's breadth of his head. By sheerest chance, it missed its target and fell noisily to the floor.

The presiding judge looked menacingly at the lawyer. The young man, visibly blanched, suddenly realized the enormity of what, in the heat of passion, he had done.

Fixing him with a stern eye, the judge shook his finger and said, "Counsel! I have every justification to commit you for contempt of court for your reprehensible act. If you had no explanation (and I can conceive of none you might have) I would be justified in committing

you to prison for a substantial term. This, most certainly I would do
... had I been an upright judge."

E. C. Leslie, Q.C. of Regina had genuine justification to heave a
heavy volume of the English Reprints at a judge before whom he
appeared many years ago, and I with him as junior counsel. It was a
constitutional case in which Canadian Pacific was testing in the
Court of Queen's Bench the applicability to railways of provincial
labor legislation. Presiding was Mr. Justice H. V. Bigelow.

The trial had droned on for several days and Harry Green, Q.C.,
of Winnipeg, for Canadian Pacific, concluded his argument on the
Friday afternoon. Leslie had barely embarked upon his presentation
when the presiding judge adjourned court to the following Monday
morning at ten. When court reconvened, Leslie continued his
well-documented argument, sat down at about a quarter to twelve,
and Green then briefly replied.

It was the sort of case that obviously required a reasoned written
judgment, and all counsel expected the court to reserve its decision
to give time to consider the numerous authorities that had been cited
by both sides. But to everyone's amazement, Bigelow reached down
below the bench, drew forth several *typewritten* sheets of paper, and
proceeded to read them. His judgment had all been written and
typed over the weekend before he had heard anything but the
outline of the facts in Leslie's argument. Bigelow came down against
the Attorney General whom Leslie and I were representing.

The judge left the bench before Leslie had a chance to express his
well-justified homicidal reaction to the judge's cavalier conduct. In
the barrister's room he swore he would never argue another case in
Bigelow's court; and later, as we drowned our colossal contempt in
soporific scotch whiskey, hearing but not heeding the conciliatory
words of his all-too-reasonable wife, Frankie, Leslie declared that if
his arguments were not worth considering (and this appeared to be
Bigelow's assessment of them), he would abandon the law forever
and take to the road as a Fuller Brush salesman. For a full week he
absented himself from his office. It seemed that he really meant what
he had said, and that he was, indeed, determined to dedicate his
forensic gifts to Fuller and forever to brush off and banish the bigots
and the Bigelows of the bench. While he was a persuasive enough
man to have made a first-class Fuller Brush salesman, Leslie in due
course returned, as we all knew he would, to the battlefield he
understood and loved best, to fight and win many a splendid victory.
Ultimately, he became one of the outstanding presidents of the

Canadian Bar Association. He would have made a great appellate court judge, but he was lost to the bench because, it is said, at the crucial time, he failed to inject sufficient fervor into a pre-election broadcast in support of his colleague who was about to become Prime Minister Diefenbaker.

My friend and classmate, William A. McGillivray, now Alberta's Chief Justice, a model of forensic discretion when he practiced at the bar, observed that it is an unfortunate fact that judges sometimes show discourtesy to counsel. It is true that counsel occasionally may invite a harsh reply, but provocation ought never to trip a judge into the trap of rudeness or cruelty. The advantages that his position naturally accords a judge, are of such plenitude, there exists no reason why he should have need to fortify himself with the verbiage of sarcasm, ridicule, deprecation, or abuse. McGillivray tells of reading a transcript of proceedings which had reached the Supreme Court of Canada. At trial, the appeal book showed that there had been a very lengthy argument by counsel, little of it either relevant or enlightening. After many pages, these words stood out from the text:

Counsel: I now turn to the well-known case of *Rylands* versus *Fletcher.*

The Court: Jesus Christ!

In *Regina* v. *Harcock*[10] the court held that while discourtesy could not be condoned, it did not, in that particular instance, invalidate a trial unless it could be said that what occurred had unfairly influenced the jury. It appears that after some argument by counsel, the learned judge said in a loud voice: "Oh, God!" (laying his head across his arms and commencing to make groaning noises).

If judges experience a sense of frustration and despair while hearing counsel, it must be remembered that the barrister may feel a good deal worse hearing judgment pronounced upon his client, or when listening to his client after it is over.

Before the advent of "legal aid," the "dock brief" was the standard route by which an indigent could retain counsel to defend him in a criminal trial. Those lawyers who were free to serve as defense counsel would sit in court, and from their number, the presiding judge would designate one among them to represent the accused. He might ask the accused himself to make the choice. The lawyer was bound to accept any brief that came to him — a principle that still has much to commend it, since it is not for counsel to judge in advance the merits of a cause. This was the "dock brief" — the "dock" being the closet in which the prisoner sits. The system worked reasonably well. To young counsel, it afforded experience, and to older counsel with no case to argue on the day he appeared, it offered occupation and the satisfaction that comes with serving a client in need, without money, and without price. I know of no lawyer who, under these circumstances, ever shirked from so serving.

If an accused felt embarrassed at having, in open court, to select a lawyer whom he would not be paying, there also existed the possibility that the "dock brief" lawyer might also be embarrassed. One morning, the judge told a prisoner who appeared without counsel that he might choose either Mr. Williamson or Mr. Johnson, both of whom were sitting in court and were free to accept a brief. Or, the presiding judge stated, the prisoner might have Mr. Fredrickson as his lawyer who, at that moment, was in the corridor.

The accused looked at Mr. Williamson; he then looked at Mr. Johnson. Then he turned to the presiding judge and said, "I think I'll take Mr. Fredrickson."

Like "legal aid," lady barristers are relatively new to the courtroom. They have come to appear more frequently and with ever-increasing success. As prosecutors, I have found them more tenacious and often more aggressive than most male barristers. There may be truth in the view that, like the widow spider, the female lawyer is indeed the deadlier of the species. They are as dedicated to the law as they are to their lovers; and as they sometimes may be over-attentive to their loved ones, so they may be over-zealous servants of their clients.

Without disrespect to the lady lawyers whom I greatly admire, I cannot resist referring to the ribald report of the female barrister who, not enjoying much success in that particular role, is said to have dropped her briefs and become a very successful solicitor.

It is sometimes appropriate that before a case is tried, counsel for the plaintiff will address either the jury or the presiding judge, briefly outlining the facts which he hopes to prove. He will also indicate the plaintiff's theory of his claim. Chief Justice McGillivray, tells of a nervous young barrister who appeared before the presiding judge and began his opening remarks, saying: "My Lord, . . . my . . . my . . . my unfortunate . . . uh . . . client . . . my unfortunate uh . . . client my . . . uh unfortunate . . . uh client uh . . ."

Counsel's stutter simply stuck him dead at that point. He could not go on. Whereupon the presiding judge came to his rescue and very kindly said: "Please proceed, Mr. Jameson . . . so far, I entirely agree with you . . ."

Mr. Justice Andre Dechene of the Alberta Trial Division is reported to have presided at a case in which the accused was charged with "living on the avails of prostitution." Counsel for the defense approached the bench and apologized for the fact that, because of the frost, his client was late in appearing and hoped that the court would permit him a reasonable adjournment to assure his atten-dance.

The learned judge reviewed the information before him and noted that there had been innumerable remands granted over a period of something exceeding one year. And so he turned to counsel and said, "I do not know whether I can at this stage accede to your request, Mr. Blackstone. It seems to me that this case is getting altogether too hoary."

When he was counsel at the bar, Chief Justice J. V. H. Milvain of the Trial Division of the Supreme Court of Alberta asked his witness to tell the court the date on which he had carried out the installation of certain electrical equipment. The witness replied:

"To answer that question truthfully would be a lie . . . I don't re-member."

His answer at least had the virtue of brevity — a quality that some counsel shun like leprosy.

Some accused are convicted of loquacity and go to jail for it. A man was charged with unlawful possession of home brew. He appeared before a magistrate who was known for the serious view he took of intemperate habits. Fearful of a jail sentence, counsel for the accused advised his client that he had no obligation to give evidence, and admonished him that in court, under no circumstances should he say anything. After a plea of guilty, his counsel argued that the appropriate sentence would be a fine, and accordingly the magistrate ordered him to pay $100.00 and costs.

Unable to contain his deep relief and satisfaction, the accused said, "That's fine, Your Worship. I've got that $100.00 right here in my arse pocket!"

To which the miffed magistrate said, ". . . and thirty days in the Lethbridge jail. Have you got that in your arse pocket too?"

If counsel were on his toes, he would have the thirty-day sentence quashed by a higher court. Once having imposed a sentence, the judge is *functus* — finished — and he is allowed no afterthoughts which may move him to vary that sentence.

Effective cross-examination is often regarded as the hallmark of the champion at the bar. It is my view that the preparation and presentation of a careful examination-in-chief generally requires greater skill and dexterity than cross-examination. It is true that the drama of the unknown stalks every moment of any cross-examination, and therefore it is capable of producing high drama. But there is a world of difference when it is carried out, on the one hand, by a lawyer of great skill and experience who has prepared himself for the performance, and on the other hand by a lawyer who trusts Lady Luck and his intuition to provide the right questions. The success of a cross-examination, depends, in large measure, upon the element of surprise. The unexpected question may seem to emerge as a brilliant gem from the forensic arsenal of the successful advocate. On the other hand, a witness's surprising answer may shatter that jewel or flaw its perfect facets. Those who embark upon cross-examination without careful preparation will discover that it is an exercise more often suicidal than homicidal.[11]

For brevity and wit, a cross-examination of Alberta's redoubtable counsel, Paddy Nolan, remains unique. Nolan was cross-examining the young complainant in a rape case. Her story was simple. She was a dairy-maid working on a farm. After the evening milking, she left the barn and was returning to the house when the accused jumped out of the bushes and suddenly attacked her.

This was Nolan's cross-examination:

Question: How much milk were you carrying?

Answer: About a gallon.

Question: How big was the pail?

Answer: A gallon-pail.

Question: Was the pail full?

Answer: Yes.

Question:	Did you lose any of your milk?
Answer:	No.

That ended the brief cross-examination.

After all of the evidence was in, Nolan's address to the jury consisted of only two sentences: "Gentlemen of the Jury, the girl lost her virtue but kept her milk. Do you believe she was attacked?"

The accused was acquitted.

No good purpose is ever served by a cross-examination that simply threshes the straw that examining counsel has raked up at trial. There is only one exception I can think of. The case involved a little girl's claim for damages she suffered while playing on the defendant company's railway track. The girl told her story in her own way, and it was all highly damaging to the company. She was a charming little girl and obviously made a great impression on the jury. Opposing counsel did not really cross-examine her at all. He simply said, "Marion, dear — tell it to us all over again — that's a good girl!" She repeated the story, letter perfect — and obviously so, for it was revealed for what it was — a well-memorized and clearly manufactured story.

In another classic case, Sir Edward Carson was cross-examining a hostile witness.

Question:	Do you drink?
Answer:	That's my business.
Question:	Do you have any other business?

The thrust and parry of the examination and cross-examination lie at the very heart of the adversary trial proceeding because they test not the skill of the examiner but the veracity of the witness, and that is the purpose of the trial. There is no substitute for the cross-examiner's probe. Neither the polygraphic lie detector nor the psychologist's sorcery can compare with the weaponry of the skilled and resourceful counsel. His perceptions must not flag for a moment; his ear must hear every syllable; he must perceive the witness's every nerve impulse. His only vacation is the space between the question he puts to a witness and the answer he gets back.

If the barrister's forensic arsenal is to be complete, he must not only be blessed with a keen eye, a sensitive ear, and a ready tongue, he must also possess empathy — the rare ability to place himself in another man's shoes. What would the witness do in the position it is alleged he found himself? What is the reaction one might expect of a complainant? What would a victim be likely to say? Leading questions based upon an appreciation of human nature may go a long way in eliciting hidden facts or half-forgotten events.

The famous Bob Edwards, founder and editor of the *Calgary Eye Opener*, was a contemporary of Paddy Nolan. One of Edwards's favorite characters was a legendary remittance man, one McGillicutty, the ne'er-do-well scion of an English baronet. Calgary had many of these colorful characters, who were sent off to the colonies after the turn of the century so that they might be of no further embarrassment to their families in the Old Country. The quarterly stipend they received (along with their tobacco and the "British Mail" they picked up from their special boxes each week at Harry Smith's News and Tobacco Shop on Eighth Avenue — augmented, of course, by booze that was then cheap and plentiful) assured them of a frontier variety of *il dolce vita*. Occasionally they got into trouble. McGillicutty was seldom free of it. After many scrapes and scaldings, he came into his most serious conflict with the law. He was indicted for cattle rustling, "cattle" as it was then defined, being a horse. In due course, he was tried, convicted, and hanged for his crime. His lawyer (apocrypha has it that he was Paddy Nolan) was charged with the delicate task of informing the unfortunate man's noble father of his son's untimely demise. The lawyer's letter was short and to the point, but kindly in its intent and assuasive in its content:

> My Lord:
> I regret that I have to inform you that your son met his death last Friday morning whilst taking part as a principal in an important public ceremony. Unhappily, the platform on which he was standing gave way.
>
> I have the honour to remain, Sir,
>
> > Your most obedient servant, etc.

One of Nolan's contemporaries was Richard Bedford Bennett, the ambitious young Conservative lawyer who became Canada's Prime Minister just in time to take the blame for the economic depression of the 1930s. He reversed the course of immigration by moving to

England after his defeat, became an English peer, and died leaving no one to inherit his title. In his early years, Bennett was the Calgary solicitor of the Canadian Pacific Railway and defended the company in most of the damage actions brought against it by farmers who had lost cattle on their right of way, and by Calgarians who were injured in train wrecks and by the heirs of those who lost their lives. Edwards made a point of giving prominence to these claims, and he embellished the stories with photographs of train derailments and damaged cars. The pictures became a source of embarrassment to the C.P.R. and in due course Bennett wrote to the maverick editor telling him that if he continued to give these train wrecks such great prominence on the front page of every issue of the *Eye Opener*, the company would sue him and the *Eye Opener* for defamation. Edwards grudgingly said that in the future, he would not give so much space to the company's train wrecks. In the very next issue, there appeared on page one, over a large photograph of Richard Bedford Bennett, the caption: "ANOTHER C.P.R. WRECK!"

Pleadings that institute civil proceedings are often the source of humor. Legal jargon sometimes creates odd precedents that may be difficult for lay persons to understand or accept. Fewer lawyers today follow the old florid fcrms of pleadings, but the principal reason for continuing to use them is safety. Specific words and phrases take on a settled meaning after many years of judicial use. While innovative phraseology may stimulate fresh ideas, most solicitors believe it to be better that legal literature be safe than savory. Here is a typical example of the classic pleading in a statement of defense made on behalf of the owner of one of the motor vehicles involved in a roadway accident:

> The defendant says that if he was driving his car at the time and place alleged (which is not admitted but denied) and if he was in a collision with the plaintiff (which is not admitted but denied) the collision was caused solely by the negligence of the plaintiff.

It is an abbreviated variation of the classical pleading of the defendant who was sued by a plaintiff for damage done to a tea kettle that allegedly had been loaned by the plaintiff to the defendant and returned in a damaged condition:

> The defendant states that at no time whatsoever did he borrow a kettle from the plaintiff. If, however, the defendant

did borrow a kettle from the plaintiff, the kettle was in a damaged condition when the defendant received it from the plaintiff. In the alternative, if the defendant borrowed the kettle from the plaintiff (which is not admitted but denied) then the kettle was returned by the defendant to the plaintiff undamaged.

Words used by the man of law are often misused and misunderstood by clients and the general public. Charles Dickens, in *Pickwick Papers*, reports Mr. Weller as crying out, "Oh Sammy, Sammy, vy vorn't there an alleybi!" The misuse of the word *alibi* so annoyed the great Alexander Woollcott who wrote:

> Let me suggest that any man's vocabulary is a more precise and effective means of communication if he carefully reserves the word 'alibi' for its primal eldest meaning, instead of slipping into the sloppy practice of using it as another word for excuse. 'Alibi' is the Latin word for elsewhere and it was the lawyer chaps who first appropriated it for our convenience. If you can prove that when your Aunt Matilda's throat was being slit in Kenosha you yourself — though naturally under suspicion — were engrossed at the time in a game of six-pack bezique in Omaha, you will thereby establish an alibi. It is a handy term and all the color is washed out of it by those who use it for any form of self-exculpation, from a cold in one's head to an unfaithful alarm clock. In America this injurious practice has become so common that to rush now to the defense of the battered old word is probably enlistment in a lost cause.

But it remained for a boy in Gastown to explain it very simply to any interested lexicographer. "An alibi," he said, "is when you prove you wuz at a prayer meeting where you wasn't to show that you wasn't in somebody's cash register where you wuz."

In his practice at the bar, the man of law often has need of the skills and counsel of the man of medicine. He consults with him frequently and it has been my good fortune to have enjoyed the stimulating friendship of many members of the medical fraternity. There have been occasions when I have opposed a medical man, and times when I have been compelled to sue him. The lawyer will invariably make every reasonable effort to avoid litigation against a physician, appreciating as he does, many of the difficulties which are shared by the two professions. But that is not the only reason. The amicable settlement of all claims, especially those brought against professional persons ought to be sought and diligently pursued because of the ill effects of litigation, both physical and psychological, upon a plaintiff involved in a conflict that so intimately touches his health. Lawsuits of this nature develop into gruelling marathons. A plaintiff naturally dwells upon his ailments and the more he is concerned over them, the worse they become. *Litigationitis* is the aggravation of a patient's illness or injuries during the long preparation for trial. It manifests itself in real disability and genuine pain. These often continue until the lawsuit is tried and the fruits of victory are delivered, and then the pain, if not the disability, often subsides and disappears. However tempting it may be to suggest that such pains and debilities are feigned simply to support an ambiguous or bogus claim, I am convinced that the condition is real and the complaints have a verifiable basis in fact. Early settlements are therefore cheap settlements to a defendant. And to a plaintiff, since money is the only analgesic the law can offer the injured, however imperfect a form of compensation it may seem, the sooner it is accepted, the earlier will come the cure. Disability payments that are made over long periods of time, as under Workmen's Compensation statutes are always unsatisfactory because they accord no finality to a claim. Instead, each monthly payment serves only to remind the injured that he is crippled or disabled; that very thought goes to prolong or perpetuate the consciousness of his pain and his inadequacy.

The favorite story among insurance company counsel tells of a plaintiff who, having suffered injury in a motor car accident, claimed damages of one million dollars in an action against the negligent driver responsible for his troubles. Suspecting the injuries he suffered to be far less severe than the plaintiff represented them to be, the insurance company employed an investigator to follow him day and night, make careful notes of where he went, take photographs of what he did, and build a dossier to prove that his injuries were a sham and his claim a figment of the imagination, notwithstanding that he could travel only in a wheelchair and used crutches to stand.

In due course, the action came to trial, and despite the efforts of the insurance company to discredit the plaintiff, he succeeded in convincing the court to award him very substantial damages. As he was about to leave the courtroom, the investigator approached him and said: "You may think you have beaten us, but believe me, I'm going to keep on following you until I prove to the world that you're a fraud and a malingerer!"

"By all means, follow me," replied the plaintiff pleasantly. "I'll be glad to help you. I am about to go on a trip. Now tomorrow morning at 9:30 I plan to leave by Air Canada for Montreal; and on Tuesday I fly to Paris on Air France at noon. I shall be staying at the Georges Cinq Hotel until Saturday when I shall be driving to Lourdes. On Sunday morning at eight I expect to visit the sacred shrine; and if you are there, I promise you will witness the greatest God-damned miracle in all of history!"

"Go not for every grief to the physician, nor for every quarrel to the lawyer, nor for every thirst to the pot," is a proverb that is as wise as it is universal.[12] The story is told of a village doctor in an east European village many years ago who unfortunately thought more of his fee than of his patient. He was called to treat the sick wife of a poor tailor. After examining the woman, the physician turned to the husband and said, "This case will take a lot of my time and I can see that you will not be able to pay me for my services. I must therefore tell you that I cannot come to visit her again."

"Please, doctor, look after her. Save her life!" the anxious husband begged. "I promise to pay you, even though I shall have to pawn everything I own to get the money!"

"What if I don't cure her — will you pay my fee just the same?" asked the doctor.

"Whatever happens, whether you kill her or cure her, I promise to pay!" said the husband.

"Very well," said the doctor. "I shall look after her."

Treatment began, but within a few weeks the poor woman died. Shortly after her burial the doctor demanded 100 rubles as his fee. The unhappy husband informed him that he had no money to pay. The doctor insisted. After months of argument, as was the custom among the Jews in the small *schtetl* in which they lived, the doctor referred the matter to the local rabbi, a man respected for his wisdom and his sense of justice. The sage understood immediately what had happened.

"Tell me again," he asked the physician, "what was your contract with this man?"

"I was to get paid for treating his wife regardless of whether I cured her or killed her."

"I see," said the rabbi, stroking his long, soft beard. "Tell me, did you cure her?"

"No."

"Did you kill her?"

"I certainly did not!"

"Then," said the rabbi gently, "since you did not cure her, and you did not kill her, what right have you to the money?"

Oliver Wendell Holmes might have considered this old story when he observed that "the lawyers are the cleverest of men, the ministers are the most learned and the doctors are the most sensible."[13] It reminds us that the young lawyer may know all of the rules, but the old lawyer will know the exceptions.

As the years of practice lengthen, so also does the measure of the man of law's patience increase. He is not so prone immediately to take his client into court to litigate his every grievance and demand the court's redress. He learns that there may be other ways to resolve disputes — ways that are faster and less costly in money and time and in simple human wear-and-tear. Judges and even juries agree.

There is a story told of an all-Jewish jury that is trying a case. Its members deliberate for many hours. Finally, they return to the courtroom and the clerk says: "Ladies and Gentlemen of the Jury, have you reached a verdict?"

The foreman rises and says, "Well, my Lord, we have discussed the matter from all angles. Mr. Levy felt it was a shame the crime was committed and Mrs. Goldberg thought the accused was such a nice boy. Then, Mr. Finkelstein reminded us that . . ."

"Yes, yes," the judge interrupted. "But what is your verdict? Have you reached a verdict?"

"Our verdict," the foreman says, "is we shouldn't mix in."

Some clients are more appreciative than others for the services they have received from their lawyer. Clarence Darrow summed up the matter of legal fees in very few words. "How can I ever show my appreciation for all you have done for me?" a woman asked him after he had completed a highly successful trial.

"My dear lady," replied Darrow, "there has been only one answer to that question ever since the Phoenicians invented money."

Lawyers' fees traditionally have been the butt of grudging humor. Like most other members of the legal profession, I have had a client indignantly say, after I have quoted my fee to him for advice: "You're the first man who ever asked me to pay simply for letting me talk to him!"

"You are lucky," said I, "That I did not also charge for my talk to you."

I then told him that some writers demand more money for their writing than lawyers ever expect to receive. A group of Oxford University students once sent a letter to George Bernard Shaw:

Dear Mr. Shaw:
We have heard that you earn ten shillings for every word you write. Enclosed is ten shillings. Please send us one of your best words.
Yours sincerely, etc.

Shaw replied with one word: "Thanks."

We have seen that the lawyer has been criticized for his ambivalence in acting now for one party, now for another. "How is it possible," the lawyer is often asked, "for you today to argue the case of a wife seeking half her heartless husband's property, and tomorrow to represent a husband who resists the claim of his errant wife to any part of his estate?"

The answer is not so difficult when you remember that no two cases are the same. And why? Because no two people are alike. Even "identical twins" differ. If no two people can be the same, it is clear that the difference in their relationships vary even more. Every case raises different questions, and to each question there may be different answers, even though for all of them, the law remains the same.

It is then that the sophistication of the philosopher comes to the aid of the man of law. The wisdom of the rabbinate was highly regarded for centuries in Europe. Even in Nazi Germany it was a reality to be reckoned with. It is related that Goebbels, Hitler's notorious Minister of Propaganda, came to an elderly rabbi and said, "Jew! I have heard that you people employ a special form of reasoning that comes from the Talmud, upon which your ancient laws are based. I want you to teach it to me."

"Ah, Herr Goebbels," the old rabbi sighed. "I fear you are a little too old for that sort of thing."

"Nonsense! Why?"

"Well, when a Jewish boy wishes to study Talmud we first give him an examination. It consists of three questions. The young boys who answer the questions correctly are admitted to the study of Talmudic law; those who can't, are not."

"Excellent," said Goebbels. "Give me the exam!"

The old rabbi shrugged. "Very well. The first question is this: Two burglars climb down a chimney to steal from a house. When they get out of the chimney, one burglar is filthy, all covered with soot; the other is clean. Which one of them washes?"

Goebbels scoffed, "The dirty one, of course!"

"Wrong. The clean one."

"The clean one washes?" asked Goebbels in astonishment. "Why?"

"Because as soon as the two men emerge from the chimney, they look at each other, no? The dirty one, looking at the clean one, says to himself, 'Remarkable — to go down a chimney and come out clean.' But the clean one, looking at the dirty one, says to himself, 'We certainly got filthy coming down that chimney and I'll wash up at once.' So it is the clean one who washes, and the dirty one who does not."

"Ah," nodded Goebbels. "Very clever! Let's have the second question."

"The second question," sighed the rabbi, "is this: Two burglars climb down a chimney to steal. When they get down, and emerge from the chimney, one of them is filthy, all covered with soot; the other is clean. Which . . ."

"That's the same question!" exclaimed Goebbels.

"No, no, Herr Goebbels, excuse me. This is a different question."

"Very well. You won't fool me, Jew. The one who's clean washes!"

"Wrong," sighed the elder.

"But you just told me . . ."

"That was an entirely different question, Herr Goebbels. In this one, the dirty man washes — because, as before, the two men look at each other. The one who is clean looks at the dirty one and says, 'My! How dirty I must be!' But he looks at his hands and he sees that he is not dirty. His hands are clean. The dirty man, on the other hand, looks at the clean one and says, 'Can it be? To climb down a chimney and emerge so clean? Am I clean?' So he looks at his own hands and he sees that he is filthy; so he, the dirty one, washes, naturally."

Goebbels nodded. "Clever, Jew; very clever! Now, the third question?"

"Ah, the third question," said the rabbi, "is the most difficult of all. Two men climb down a chimney to steal from the house. When they get down and emerge from the chimney, one is clean, the other . . ."

"But that's the same question!"

"No, Herr Goebbels. The words may be the same, but the problem is an entirely new one."

"The dirty one washes!" exclaimed Goebbels.

"Wrong."

"The clean one?"

"Wrong."

"Then what is the answer?" Goebbels shouted.

"The answer," said the rabbi, "is that this is a silly examination. How can two men climb down the same chimney and one emerge dirty and the other clean? Anyone who can't see that will never be able to understand the law."

Neither will he ever understand the gentle humor of the model man of law. His obligations are onerous and often distasteful. Sometimes he finds he must do unpleasant things for disagreeable people who tell him after all is done and won that some other lawyer could doubtless have done it better at half the fee. The man of law then recognizes his kinship to W. S. Gilbert's police officer, and with him, will sadly sing:

> When constabulary duty's to be done
> The policeman's lot is not an 'appy one.[14]

Though the barrister may often seem grave, yet he must forever be an optimist and light-hearted enough to see the bright side of things, and smile and again sing along with W. S. Gilbert (himself a lawyer):

> All thieves who could my fees afford
> Relied on my orations,
> And many a burglar I've restored
> To his friends and his relations.[15]

What then, does this ingredient called "humor" mean to our model man of law? It is the pratfall that cracks the pretensions of the powerful and reminds everyone that, however high and exalted their chairs may be raised, all who are concerned with the law (and that includes judges, lawyers, clerks, reporters, litigants, witnesses, and police officers, and the journalists who adopt all of these as their own, yes, and those who legislate laws, and even those who bureaucratize them) all sit upon precisely the same human anatomy.

Because there forever will be at least two sides to every question, and usually many more, the man of law who espouses now one cause, now another, is by very definition now a traditionalist, now an anarchist, now a liberal, and now a conservative. While trained to conform to rules of conduct sanctioned by society, the lawyer at times seems to defy those rules. While sworn to uphold the law, in the defense of his client he may appear at times to condone violations of the law. While he is a citizen dedicated to the laws of the land and is a technician mindful of the principles of his craft, he is forever sensitive to the pain and anxieties of his client who, despite trouble, remains a fellow man and a kindred spirit. Condemned though his client may be, the man of law who is his counsel will watch the stars and know that:

> There sleeps in Shrewsbury jail tonight
> Or wakes, as may betide,
> A better lad, if things went right,
> Than most that sleep outside.[16]

A Deist at heart, the lawyer will often assume the character of the iconoclast. The ambivalence of his role endows him with the yogi's physical flexibility; his sensitive responses require the guru's calm reflection. He views the world with a childlike freshness but must come to take its measure with the lengthened tooth of age. He savors and enriches his craft with all of life's contradictions. When he has mastered his calling, he will be the first to observe that the emperor has no clothes. If he is courageous, he will be the first to tell the emperor that his tailor has bilked him. If he is resourceful, he will clothe his emperor in appropriate raiment. And if he is blessed with humor, he will survive his emperor's protean moods, enjoying the gifts of life as long as fortune allows, dodging the gallows as long as God pleases.

In success he will be a generous adversary; in failure he will remain a happy warrior. In the court which is his field of battle, he will manage to keep a cool head over a warm heart. His wit will be his sword, and humor his shield, and he will live the long and joyful life of a champion in the exalted empire of law and equity, of which no model can be fashioned, save in the hearts of the men who are bred to do equity and are wed to the law.

Notes

Why a Model?

1. William Shakespeare, *King Henry VI*, Part I, IV. ii. 86.
2. Daniel Webster, *Funeral Oration*, on Mr. Justice Story, September 12, 1845, appearing in M. Frances McNamara, *Famous Legal Quotations*, Aqueduct Books, Rochester, New York, 1967, p. 327.
3. Will and Ariel Durant, *The Lessons of History*, 1968, pp. 19-20.
4. Ibid., p. 20.
5. Ibid.
6. Miriam Siegler and Humphry Osmond, *Models of Madness, Models of Medicine*, MacMillan Publishing Co. Inc., 1974.
7. Most self-fulfilling prophecies are slow to detect, and their proof is often equivocal. A prophecy that was unhappily realized within the span of a short lifetime is reported by Robert M. Rennick in the *Bulletin of the American Name Society*, December 1972:

> In 1943 Joseph Mittel of Astoria, New York, named his newborn son Adolf Hitler. The father later assured reporters that it was no joke; nor did it involve a snap decision for the thirty-seven-year-old disabled woodworker had been thinking seriously of doing this for several months. "The real Adolf Hitler doesn't mean a thing," he insisted, "but I'm of German-Austrian descent, and that's one reason why I picked the name. I don't think the name would be a handicap because, after all, there are lots of people named after persons in the same category as Hitler, such as Napoleon, Caesar, and others. He'll grow up and be a good man despite the name."
>
> The name was duly registered with the Queens (New York) Department of Health on Feb. 3, and its oddity attracted press coverage and, of course, vigorous public disapproval. Mittel succumbed to the pressure of public indignation and, within a week, he renamed the child but only after a second meeting with reporters, on the evening of Feb. 9, to whom he expressed his surprise at the public response. He had no idea they would carry on so about the name; but since they were so anxious about his changing it, he invited the newspapers' readers to suggest another name for his child. He also pointed out that the child's name could not be changed except by a court order, but that was an expensive proposition. His financial resources were extremely limited, he said. He had been injured on the job some two years before and his sole means of support was the $14 workmen's compensation check

he received every week. If the public was so interested in the name he gave his child, he suggested that they contribute to his efforts to change it.

Change it he did, with or without their help, to Theodore Roosevelt, a name he had little reason to suspect would offend or antagonize anyone at that time.

What happened to Theodore Roosevelt Mittel? According to later reports, young Mittel may be said to have lived up to the example of his original protoname. At the age of nine he was arraigned in the Jamaica (New York) Children's Court for having pushed a six-year-old child off a pier. The body was found several days after the deed. When he was sixteen, he was arrested as the ringleader of a gang of teenage burglars. As he was being arrested, he pointed a Belgian automatic at the officer; another policeman had to disarm him. The youth also had a zip gun in his belt. He was charged with eighty-five burglaries and given a three-to-fifteen-year sentence in the Elmira Reformatory. In 1964, while on parole, he stole a truck from a Hertz rental lot and, after a one-mile pursuit, was captured when the vehicle crashed. Later that year he was indicted in the second degree, and was sentenced to Sing Sing for two-and-a-half-to-six-years."

8. Aldous Huxley quoted by Calvin R. Reber, Jr. "Africa — The Bruised Continent," *The Torch*, 38 (1965), 38.
9. Benjamin N. Cardozo, *Growth of the Law*, 1924, p. 89.
10. Lord MacMillan adopted as the title of his autobiography *A Man of Law's Tale* (MacMillan and Company, London, 1953), harking back to Chaucer's *Canterbury Tales*.

I. Sapience

1. "Of Studies," Francis Bacon's *Essays*.
2. George Santayana, *The Sense of Beauty* (Scribner's Sons, 1896; reprinted Dover Publications, Inc. 1955), p. 104.
3. Ibid.
4. Of the Faculty of Law, University of Toronto, in introducing me as the first speaker at the Symposium held at the University on "Contemporary Problems and the Law" in February, 1976, when the idea of a model man of law was first presented by me.
5. (1631) Dy. 118b (1688 ed.).
6. Benjamin Disraeli, referring to William Ewart Gladstone in a speech at Knightsbridge, July, 1878.
7. Oscar Wilde in a letter to Lord Alfred Douglas, *De Profundis*, January-March 1897.

8. This naturally flows from Parkinson's classic law that "work expands to fill the time available for its performance." But experience has now shown that it is not work that expands. It is jobs or slots for employees that are multiplied, not work.

    Parkinson has expressed two corollaries to his famous law:

    Corollary 1 — officials multiply subordinates, not work.

    Corollary 2 — officials make work for each other.

    For those, and numerous other laws, see Thomas L. Martin, Jr., *Malice in Blunderland*, McGraw-Hill Book Company, Toronto, 1973.

9. George Butterwick, an old friend and classmate, has undertaken the task of bringing out a new and enlarged edition of Power's *Practice*. I well recall the scholarly Kent Power who, from the window of his office in the Burroughs Law Publishing House that stood across the street of the old Calgary Court House, monitored the judgments that were written there, with the critical ear of a Jeremiah. Well-remembered also is Hedley Auld, Professor of Law and Assistant Dean to W. P. M. Kennedy during my post-graduate days at the University of Toronto Law School.

10. Micah 4:4-5.

11. Edmund Burke, "Facts."

12. Boswell's *Life of Samuel Johnson*, 19 September 1777.

13. Ibid., 26 September 1765.

II. Profession

1. Alfred, Lord Tennyson, "Ulysses," 1. 6.

2. Sir John Henry Newbolt, "The Island Race, *Vitai Lampada*."

3. Honest St. Ives was really St. IVO Helory. He was born in Brittany in 1254 and was sent to Paris at fourteen to study. He was made a judge of the ecclesiastical court of Rennes and then of Treguier, his home district, where he became known as "the poor man's advocate." His incorruptibility led to a Latin rhyme:

    Sanctus IVO erat Brito

    Advocatus, et non latro

    Res mirando populo

    (St. IVO was a Breton and a lawyer, but not dishonest — an astonishing thing in people's eyes! He died in 1303 at 49 and was made a saint in 1347.)

4. For a discussion of similar events in the trials following the October 1970 Quebec Crisis see Morris Shumiatcher, *Abuse of Power by a Political Minority*, Law Society of Upper Canada Lectures, 1979.

5. George Orwell, Appendix, "The Principles of Newspeak," *1984* (Signet ed.), p. 246.

6. Raymond A. Schroth, "Beyond Violence: Values for Change," *The George Washington University Magazine*, September, 1968, 8.

7. *Roncarelli v. Duplessis* (1956) Que. Q.B. 447; [1959] S.C.R. 121.
8. *The Queen v. Louis Riel No. 1* (1885), Terr. L.R. 20 (Q.B. Man.); *The Queen v. Louis Riel No. 2* (1885), Terr. L.R. 21 (Q.B. Man.).
9. *The Regina Leader,* 16 November, 1885.
10. On his death, Stalin was embalmed and laid to rest beside the revered Lenin in the famous glass mausoleum that stands in front of the Kremlin. After he was denounced by Kruschev, it became necessary to move his remains, and he was buried in an obscure place beside the Kremlin walls. A tourist visiting Moscow asked to be directed to the place in which he lay. His guide reluctantly led him to the grave. She said, "Now you see it as it is: a Marxist Plot!"
11. Aesop's fable of the swallow is a corollary. It is said that a swallow had built her nest under the eaves of a Court of Justice. Before her young ones could fly, a serpent, gliding out of his hole ate them all up. When the poor bird returned to her nest and found it empty, she began a pitiable wailing. A neighbor suggested, by way of comfort, that she was not the first bird who had lost her young. "True," she replied, "but it is not only my little ones that I mourn, but that I should have been wronged in that very place where the injured fly for justice."

III. Omnitude

1. *The Queen v. Schaumleffel,* Saskatchewan Court of Queen's Bench at Regina, Saskatchewan, 5 - 12 May 1959.
2. Quoted by Joseph Sedgwick, Q.C., in "Presentation of Evidence," *Law Society of Upper Canada Special Lectures,* 89 (1959), p. 90.
3. "How many things by season season'd are
To their right praise and true perfection!"
William Shakespeare, *The Merchant of Venice,* v. i. 107.
4. *Burnet v. Coronado Oil & Gas Co.* (1932) 285 U.S. 393, pp. 405, ff.
5. *Tooth v. Power* [1891] A.C. 284.
6. *Attorney-General of Canada v. Canada Temperance Federation* [1946] A.C. 193, p. 206.
7. *Can. Bar Rev.* 21 (1951) 1038, pp. 1069, ff.
8. Ibid., p. 1076.
9. [1966] i all E.R., ff.
10. Sir William S. Gilbert, *H. M. S. Pinafore, II.*
11. *Brewer's Dictionary of Phrase and Fable* (1817) Cent. Ed., 1970, p. 350.
12. Lord Moran's Diary.
13. Letter to Lord Burleigh, 1592.

IV. Ambivalence

1. *Gulliver's Travels:* "Houyhnhnms, Chap. 5.
2. A. J. P. Taylor, *English History 1914-1945.*

3. McMurtry, "The Future of Criminal Legal Aid in Ontario" *Law Society Gazette* 12 (1978) 317, p. 320.
4. *Regina* v. *Courvoisier* (1840) 173 E.R. 869. The case is described in Mark M. Orkin, *Legal Ethics*, 1959, pp. 113 *et. seq.*
5. Orkin, *Legal Ethics*, p. 172.
6. *Johnson* v. *Emerson* (1871) L.R. 6 Ex. 329, at p. 369.
7. Boswell, *Life of Samuel Johnson*, 1786.
8. Orkin, *Legal Ethics*, pp. 111-112.
9. William Shakespeare, *The Taming of the Shrew*, I. ii. 281-2.
10. *Regina* v. *O'Connell* (1844) 7 Ir. L.R. 261 at pp. 312-313, (in H.L., (1844) 11 Cl. & F. 155).

V. Expedition

1. John Webster, "Devil's Law Case", II, 1 (1619).
2. Lord Evershed, *Practical and Academic Characteristics of English Law*, (1956), p. 40.
3. Gilbert Burnet, *Life of Sir Mathew Hale*.
4. Alfred, Lord Tennyson, "Ulysses," I, 6.
5. *Paradise Lost*, p. 393.

VI. Artistry

1. Tennyson, "Sir Galahad."
2. William Shakespeare, *Othello*, III, iii, 323–5.
3. *Othello*, III, iii, 155–61.
4. Gilbert K. Chesterton, *Tremendous Trifles: The Twelve Men*.
5. *Smith* v. *Harris* [1939] All. E.R. 960, p. 967.
6. *The Dictionary of Biographical Quotation*, ed. Richard Kenin and Justin Wintle, Alfred A. Knopf, 1978, p. 221.
7. Ibid., p. 391.
8. Referred to by Honorable Sir Robert Megarry in "Temptations of the Bench," *Alberta Law Review*, 16 (1978), 406, p. 410.
9. Evergreen Edition, 1961, p. 198, originally published by Farrar, Straus and Cudaby, Inc., 1959.
10. Ibid., p. 309.

VII. Charisma

1. Edward Marjoribanks, *For the Defence: The Life of Sir Edward Marshall Hall*, The MacMillan Company, New York, 1929.
2. Edward Fitzgerald, *Rubaiyat of Omar Khayyam*, 2nd. ed., LXXVI.
3. John Selden, *Table-Talk: Power-State*.
4. *Wilkes* v. *Wood* (1763) 19 How. St. Tr. 1153, p. 1176.

VIII. Obligation

1. Oliver Wendell Holmes, "The Path of the Law", reprinted in *Jurisprudence and Action* (1953), p. 301.
2. Henry Fielding, *Joseph Andrews*, Bk. ii.
3. Wigmore, "The Judicial Function in Science of Legal Methods", 1917 XXVI, XXX 8 and 9.
4. (1951) 9 *Brief Case*, 4.
5. A. E. Housman, *A Shropshire Lad*, LXII.
6. F. Reed Dickerson, "How to Write a Law", *Notre Dame Lawyer*, 31 (1955), p. 25. See also Charles B. Nutting, "Newspeak, 1970," *American Bar Association Journal*, 56 (1970) 131.
7. *Murdoch v. Murdoch* [1974] 41 D.L.R. (3d) 367 (S.C.C.).
8. Sir Francis Bacon, "Essay on Innovation."
9. *LeRoy v. Starling Alderman de London et 16 Autres.*
10. John Dryden, *Preface to the Fables*, commenting upon the characters of Chaucer's *Canterbury Tales*.
11. Observation made about 1685 in New France. Quoted by Francis Parkman from an anonymous source in *The Old Regime in Canada*, 1874, and quoted in John Colombo, *Colombo's Canadian Quotations*, 1974, p. 318.
12. Samuel Johnson, Boswell, *Life of Johnson*, 1776.
13. Edmund Burke, "Speech on Conciliation with America," arch 22, 1775.

IX. Judgment

1. Upon learning that a lawyer whom he knew well had been "elevated", my friend, Gordon Kuski, exclaimed, "My goodness, I didn't know he died!"
2. Address to the Seminar for Journalists, Ottawa, 22 February 1978.
3. Benjamin N. Cardozo, *The Growth of the Law*, 1924, pp. 94-95.
4. Ibid., p. 96.
5. *Regina v. Drybones* (1967) 60 W.W.R. 321 (N.W.T.).
6. Address to the Seminar for Journalists, Ottawa, 22 February 1978.
7. *Cage v. Acton* (1699) 12 mod. 288, p. 294.
8. Boswell, *Life of Samuel Johnson*, 1776.
9. John Marshall, *The Virginia Constitutional Convention Debate*, 1829-30, p. 619.
10. *Micah* 6:8.
11. Sir John Fortescue, *De Laudibus Legum Angliae*, chap. 5.
12. The phrase "agony of decision" was used by Chief Justice Bora Laskin in his Address to the Seminar for Journalists, Ottawa, 22 February 1978.
13. *Prohibitions del Roy*, 12 rep. 63, p. 65.

14. *Deuteronomy* 16:18.
15. Sir Matthew Hale, *History of the Common Law*, 4th ed., XV.
16. *The Essays of Francis Bacon*, "Of Judicature", para. 2.
17. Ibid.
18. Sir John Fortescue, op. cit., chap. 51.
19. *De Ligibu* I, vi.
20. *Homilies and Recreation*, p. 218.
21. Blackstone, *Commentaries*, Bk. I, p. 69.

X. Humor

1. *Dale v. Toronto Railway Company* (1915) 23 O.L.R. 104, p. 108.
2. With apologies to William Wordsworth for liberties taken with his "Character of the Happy Warrior."
3. Reginald L. Hines, *Confessions of an Un-Common Attorney*, J. M. Dent and Sons, London, 1945, p. 96.
4. *Rex v. Nat Bell Liquors Ltd.* [1922] 2 A.C. 128.
5. (1882) 7 App. Cas. 829.
6. (1883-84) 9 A.C. 117.
7. [1896] A.C. 348.
8. [1902] A.C. 73.
9. A. E. Housman, *A Shropshire Lad*, LXII.
10. [1969] 2 W.L.R. 29.
11. Emery R. Buckner, Wellman's *Art of Cross-Examination*, chap. xii.
12. Herbert, *Jocula Prudenturn*, 1651.
13. O. W. Holmes, Sr., *Poet at the Breakfast Table*, chap. v.
14. W. S. Gilbert, *Pirates of Penzance*, Act II.
15. W. S. Gilbert, *Trial by Jury*.
16. A. E. Housman, *A Shropshire Lad*, IX.

Index

"Sir Frederick Pollock used to say that a man
who would publish a book without an index ought to be
banished ten miles beyond Hell where the Devil himself
could not go because of stinging nettles."

ROSCOE POUND, BOOK REVIEW,
(1951) 60 YALE L. J. 200